The Sense of Society

Other Books by Gordon Milne

George William Curtis and the Genteel Tradition
The American Political Novel

The Sense of Society

A History
of the American Novel
of Manners

Gordon Milne

Rutherford · Madison · Teaneck
Fairleigh Dickinson University Press
London: Associated University Presses

©1977 by Associated University Presses, Inc.

Associated University Presses, Inc.
Cranbury, New Jersey 08512

Associated University Presses
Magdalen House
136-148 Tooley Street
London SE1 2TT, England

Library of Congress Cataloging in Publication Data

Milne, Gordon.
The sense of society.

Bibliography: p.
Includes index.
1. American fiction — History and criticism.
2. Literature and society.   I. Title.
PS371.M56   813'.03   76-748
ISBN 0-8386-1927-4

PRINTED IN THE UNITED STATES OF AMERICA

This book is for my sister-in-law and brother

Mercedes S. Milne

Morton R. Milne

Contents

1

Introduction

ONE may safely say that we owe it all to Jane Austen. The novel of manners has never had a better practitioner than this skillful explorer of the world of the British landed gentry, and, if there were Fieldings and Burneys preceding her, the writers that followed took their cues primarily from Miss Austen, devoting themselves, in similar fashion, to the social dimension, to an examination of the class structure. The Victorians — and Continental novelists like Stendhal, Balzac, and Tolstoy as well — firmly established the genre in the nineteenth century, and its popularity has continued in our own times — indeed, probably always will continue. As Louis Kronenberger remarks:

> So long as there are old families or new millionaires, debutantes or dowagers, transatlantic liners and international marriages, boarding-house parlors and summer hotels — so long as there are social contrasts and social crises — the comedy of manners is sure to survive.[1]

Readers seem always to have been concerned about the hierarchy of class and to have enjoyed reading reports of the manners, special attitudes, gestures, and conventional responses that people make because they belong in a certain stratum of society. Miss Austen and her successors have happily furnished them with such accounts, offering entertaining pictures of English clerical circles, the French provincial scene, or the American antebellum way of life. Against such diverse backgrounds, the authors have developed favorite themes: the adjustment in standards caused by an environmental transplanting (from rural to urban, or from national to international); the effect wrought by time and circumstance upon a society (the Civil War's impact on the South); the problems besetting the social climber[2] (adjusting to new codes of behavior, coping with the intricacies of social deportment). At the root of the novelists' discussion is often to be found a conflict between individual self-fulfillment and social responsibility, the attempt on the part of a person to achieve fulfillment at the cost of the frowns of society. The independent action of the individual may lead to punishment or even expulsion from the circle to which he belongs, the "club" rejecting the "sensitive soul." Adherence to convention — called "social morality" by society — requires the correction of "ideals" that are regarded as fanatical or impractical and thus at odds with the necessary compromises and imperfections but essential rightness of the social order.[3] The not-quite-belonging figure whom the novelists of manners often select as a protagonist has a difficult time pursuing his intuitive code of conduct in the face of so much social "mediation."[4]

Such a conflict lends a note of seriousness to many a novel of manners. Yet the form usually retains an entertaining spirit, for, if occasionally possessing tragic overtones (as in *The Portrait of a Lady* or *The Late George Apley*), it more often chooses to emphasize the comedy in the situation to be developed, and the author's customary attitude of light irony does not encourage too somber a reaction.[5] Novels of manners are, in fact, closely akin, in their verve and sparkle, to the theater's "high comedy." Both the novel and the drama forms employ a carefully patterned structure; both offer a balanced, chiseled, polished style; and both are written in the vein of urbane, sophisticated humor. They evoke the same upper-class world as well, carefully describing its handsome drawing rooms, using appropriate imagery (e.g., mausoleum or formal garden figures) to suggest its flavor, and adroitly reproducing the brittle dialogue of its inhabitants. Their subject matter sometimes contains seeds of earnestness, to be sure, but the treatment of it is never ponderous.

Many critics have said that America has been slow to welcome the novel of manners. Blair Rouse declares that the form "has not enjoyed popularity in America."[6] Jonathan Baumbach calls its English model "not congenial with us."[7] A. N. Kaul speaks of the nineteenth century's merely sporadic concern "with social reality at the level of manners."[8] And Lionel Trilling finds that Americans offer a kind of resistance to looking closely at society and that their novelists seem incapable of reporting "social fact."[9]

Other critics cite reasons for our rejection of the genre, or, at least, our dilatoriness in accepting it. William J. Smith, observing only a "handful of practitioners" on this side of the Atlantic, argues that our aggressive democracy has made it seem tasteless, if not politically suspect, to notice differences in manners.

> Again, in our world of cyclonic social change, an emphasis on tradition — especially the notion that things were better in the good old days — seems to most Americans misplaced. To them an infatuation with the past betrays weakness and is essentially comic (what does it matter if your father and your grandfather went to Harvard? — the state university uses the same textbooks).[10]

Elizabeth Monroe adds:

> The fact of the matter is that anyone who elects to write about the
> "haut monde" in America has a bad time of it from the start. There
> has been no social tradition inclusive enough with us to be accepted
> as a matter of course in literature or in life. We are in too much of a
> hurry to get things done to bother with manners, customs, codes
> of any sort.[11]

Americans have been much more concerned with "social
presentation," however, than such negative remarks would
indicate.[12] If some have distrusted an "infatuation with the
past" and a sense of class distinction, a great many more have
been fascinated by such topics, and novelists of manners have
sprung up from the ranks of their countrymen to content
them. Fiction that can be fitted into the genre — sometimes
loosely, to be sure[13] — has appeared from the time that
James Fenimore Cooper first described the way of life of
the Westchester County squire. The Albany scenes in *Satanstoe* (1845), for example, illustrate Cooper's realization of the
importance of background as a conditioning factor, as the
American-British contrasts in that novel illustrate his awareness of manners-and-morals correlations.[14] A handful of
novelists chose to join Cooper in these new emphases, and,
later in the nineteenth century, a larger number followed
suit. The "formula" has continued to attract writers in the
twentieth century, and down to the present time there have
been those who, in varying degrees, have devoted their work
to a probing into the "manners, customs, codes" of a social
class.

One may point specifically to George Washington Cable's
account of the New Orleans Creole aristocracy, to Howells's
and James's depiction of the Boston Brahmins and/or expatriates, to Edith Wharton's New York Old Guard, or to Ellen
Glasgow's Richmond cavaliers as testimony that American
society did stand still, in certain regions, long enough for

manners to become readily identifiable. Wherever settled social conditions and firmly rooted conventions prevailed — in Charleston, Philadelphia, New York, or Boston — there the novels of manners were forthcoming, and there — and elsewhere — they were read. The American writer may not always have shown as much assurance in his treatment of society as his English counterpart,[15] but he has resorted to it almost as frequently as a framework for his comments on the human predicament, and has been almost equally aware of the insights to be gained from a careful distillation of social experience.[16]

This study combines a historical survey of the American novel of manners with concentrated attention on the major practitioners: James, Howells, Wharton, Glasgow, Marquand, and Auchincloss. The survey suggests what has already been cited — the sturdiness of the tradition in America. It also indicates the modifications of the genre over the course of time, emphasizing in particular the sporadic use of the "manners" ingredients on the part of a number of novelists who were primarily intent upon other aims, such as retailing a historical romance or stressing domestic realism and/or bourgeois comedy. It points out, too, the artistic shortcomings of some of the lesser exemplars, flaws in their narrative technique that militate against a really competent handling of the type, and it afford, hopefully, a sense of the role of manners in this country, especially in association with moral vision.

The study's more detailed examination of the major practitioners (backed up by others such as Fitzgerald, O'Hara, and Cozzens) offers proof, one trusts, of their distinct contribution to the genre — as well as proof of its value. James and his followers, wittily dissecting the follies of "high society," have amused many readers, and, in their penetrating analysis of the sensitive individual's battle against the socially derived and often shallow values that interfered with his personal ideals of conduct, they have stimulated and challenged these readers as well. Sustaining the proper note of social comedy throughout their novels, even as they examined a serious central issue, they have produced harmonious efforts and, in their blending of plot, structure, and characterization with suitable settings, style, and tone, have achieved aesthetic success. The elements of setting and style, elements of special importance in studies of manners, have been especially well managed by these major exemplars.

It goes without saying that complicated talents, like the talent of James, are not *fully* explained in terms of the novel-of-manners format. In the work of the possessors of these complicated talents, nonetheless, the format is central, revealed, for example, in the moral irony so constantly present in their view of the "social order." Their drawing-room milieu, if at first glance suggesting a limited sphere, can really encompass a good deal, from accounts of individual emotional impoverishment to statements of social protest made by a group. The testing of social appearances, involving as it does an exposure of hypocrisy and artifice, of the weaknesses of pride and vanity that are so often at odds with an ethical core, surely has universal application. The best and most consistent novelists of manners, from James to Auchincloss, reflect the universal and, in so doing, exemplify the worth of (not to be divorced from the enjoyment of) the genre.

NOTES TO CHAPTER 1

1. Louis Kronenberger, *The Thread of Laughter* (New York: Alfred A. Knopf, 1952), p. 289. Kronenberger's comment was made with regard to the drama rather than the novel, yet it seems quite applicable, there being a strong

bond between fiction's and the stage's treatment of the manners topic.

2. Amusingly described by Louis Kronenberger: "It is one of the more obviously paradoxical manifestations of society life that climbing can only be achieved through stooping, and that the best way to get through the door is to take up residence in front of it, as a doormat" (ibid., p. 291).

3. See "The Novel of Manners," a chapter in Richard Chase, *The American Novel and its Tradition*, (Garden City, N.Y.: Doubleday Anchor Book, 1957).

4. ". . . here enter all the prejudices, the traditions, the taboos, the aspirations, the absurdities, the snobberies of a group . . . partaking of a common background and accepting a similar view of life: through there will usually exist some outsider, some rebel, some nonconformist who, as the case may be, is ringing the doorbell or shattering the window panes; trying desperately to get out; bending the knee or thumbing his nose" (Kronenberger, *The Thread of Laughter*, p. 8).

5. According to one of its practitioners, Louis Auchincloss, "Pathos has a bigger place than tragedy in the study of manners" (Louis Auchincloss, *Reflections of a Jacobite* [Boston: Houghton Mifflin Co., 1961], p. 144).

6. Blair Rouse, *Ellen Glasgow* (New York: Twayne Publishers, Inc., 1962) p. 97.

7. Jonathan Baumbach, "The Economy of Love: The Novels of Bernard Malamud," *Kenyon Review* 25 (Summer 1963):438.

8. A. N. Kaul, *The American Vision* (New Haven, Conn., and London: Yale University Press, 1963), p. 64.

9. Quoted in Michael Millgate, *American Social Fiction: James to Cozzens* (New York: Barnes & Noble, Inc., 1964), pp. vii-viii.

10. William J. Smith, "J. P. Marquand, Esq., " *Commonweal* 69 (November 7, 1958), p. 148.

11. N. Elizabeth Monroe, "Ellen Glasgow," included in Harold C. Gardiner, ed., *Fifty Years of the American Novel* (New York and London: Charles Scribner's Sons, 1952), p. 51.

12. The debate about whether the novel of manners can be written in America — whether or not the American social experience is too meager to give substance to this type of fiction — has been, to say the least, extensive, contributions to the brouhaha having been made by such critics as Lionel Trilling, Richard Chase, John Aldridge, Delmore Schwartz, Arthur Mizener, Marius Bewley, and Allen Tate; see James W. Tuttleton, *The Novel of Manners in America* (Chapel Hill, N.C.: University of North Carolina Press, 1972), pp. 277-78. One should also see Laurence B. Holland, *The Expense of Vision: Essays on the Craft of Henry James* (Princeton, N.J.: Princeton University Press, 1964), pp. 61ff., and John J. Gross, *John P. Marquand* (New York: Twayne Publishers, Inc., 1963), pp. 165ff.

13. It might be useful to insert, as a cautionary measure, at this point James Tuttleton's precise definition of the genre: ". . . a novel in which the manners, social customs, folkways, conventions, traditions, and mores of a given social group at a given time and place play a dominant role in the lives of

fictional characters, exert control over their thought and behavior, and constitute a determinant upon the actions in which they are engaged, and in which these manners and customs are detailed realistically — with, in fact, a premium upon the exactness of their representation" (Tuttleton, *Novel of Manners in America*, p. 10).

14. Morton L. Ross has devoted a Ph.D. dissertation to the topic of Cooper's "rhetoric of manners," stressing his defense of the social utility of the landed gentry, gifted as they were with decorum, ease, grace and courtesy, the entire "strategy of social intercourse" (Morton Lee Ross, "The Rhetoric of Manners: The Art of James Fenimore Cooper's Social Criticism" [Ph.D. diss., State University of Iowa, 1964], pp. 6ff.).

15. Cf. the comments of Millgate, *American Social Fiction*, p. 196.

16. The conclusion of the critics Nona Balakian and Charles Simmons that the novel of manners is dying — "chiefly because the writer has ceased to believe that the social world can reveal the direction of man's soul" — (see Nona Balakian and Charles Simmons, eds., *The Creative Present: Notes on Contemporary American Fiction* [Garden City, N.Y.: Doubleday, 1963], p. XIV) is not borne out by the facts.

2

The Beginnings

*T*HE American novel of manners originates at the end of
the eighteenth century, at the time when the novel in
general began to take hold in America. H. H. Brackenridge's
Modern Chivalry (1792-1815) stands as a replica, in a very
rudimentary sense, of the work of his English contemporary,
Jane Austen. This many-volumed affair, a loose imitation of
Don Quixote in its detailing the adventures of its hero, Captain Farrago, and his servant Teague O'Regan, achieves its
importance primarily as a vigorous satire on the customs of
the America of Brackenridge's era. In his survey of both the
backwoods (of Pennsylvania) and the cities (Philadelphia and
Washington), Brackenridge comments frankly on a number of
aspects of American society.

His targets include matters of politics (whiskey settles
elections in the back countries, business interests, in the
cities), the medical profession (which is filled with quack
doctors), the law (which is filled with pedantic and/or

corrupt lawyers), and the social swing (bogtrotter Teague O'Regan, cuts a swath at a President's levee in Washington). About these matters Brackenridge writes in a style that is for the most part witty and entertaining, intermingles classical allusion and racy diction in an easy manner, and neatly maintains his lightly scoffing stance.

Modern Chivalry does not really qualify as a novel of manners, however, for, aside from its "social scene" focus and satiric method, it lacks the components of the form. Indeed, it barely qualifies as a novel. Brackenridge is really concerned with presenting a series of essays on an assortment of topics, and his picaresque adventure pattern only partially conceals the "essayizing" and does not convert the work into a sustained piece of fiction.

A forerunner Brackenridge may be, but it seems more accurate to call his successor, James Fenimore Cooper, the first genuine — or almost genuine — American novelist of manners. Cooper's reputation is based, to be sure, on his creation of the archetypal American romance, the Leatherstocking saga, but a number of his novels fall into the "social criticism" category and, as such, are close to the manners genre. One does well to remember that his first novel, *Precaution* (1820), was a story of English high society, and that later works like *Homeward Bound* (1838), *Home As Found* (1838), and the Littlepage Manuscript series stress a social thesis, the significant role of the landed gentry class. Even in the Leatherstocking tales one can observe Cooper defending the "patroon" aristocracy at the expense of a leveling democracy, assigning to them a place at the top of the social-and-political ladder as "wise" leaders. Much of his work, as a whole or in part, describes — one should really say "glamorizes" — their way of life.

His first effort, *Precaution*, served very much as a trial run for Cooper, not necessarily proving that he could write in the

Austen (or, more accurately, the Scott) manner, but simply that he could write fiction with some facility. The novel suffers from a number of flaws, such as a vagueness of setting, totally conventional characterization, and needlessly involved plotting. It does, however, single out some interesting issues of manners — applied this time to British society, but to be transferred later to the American social scene. The author talks, for one thing, about the aristocracy-plutocracy distinction. The newly rich Mr. Jarvis, moving into county society, is not readily accepted, for, though he possesses "good feelings," he lacks the "polish of high life," and he is handicapped, too, by his wife and daughters, whose manners are "too abrupt and unpleasant." The author also talks about the marriage market and the involvement in it of managing mothers, intriguing daughters, and fortune-hunting young men, and he chats, in passing, about less central concerns, like questions of precedence, the various "freedoms of high rank," and the "ease of fashionable life." Unfortunately, the picture of "fashionable life" that emerges is a stultifying one.

Cooper returns to comparable subjects — and continued praise of the upper class — a number of years later, especially in two novels, *Homeward Bound* and *Home As Found*, works which follow the usual Cooper adventure-with-love-story arrangement but also touch upon such "manners" themes as the international contrast and the gradations in American "society." *Homeward Bound*, displaying a range of English and American types, illustrates differences between the two nations, the former being more inclined toward chauvinism (whereas the American girl, Eve Effingham, is educated beyond the "reach of national foibles") and condescension (thinking, for example, that "money can do anything" when one is dealing with Americans) than their Yankee counterparts. Actually, the differences between Englishmen and Americans of the upper class are not marked, at least, when the latter have as much of the cosmopolitan quality as the Effinghams. On the lower levels, though, distinctions may be sharper, such as those between the Englishman Monday and his American "equal," Steadfast Dodge. Cooper really spends most of his time — that is, when not caught up in narrative passages of exciting action — attacking the demagogic Dodge, who is revealed as devious, intolerant, ignorant, and vulgar. He is not even a true "democrat," as one sees in observing his attentions to the assumed Sir George Templemore, the "aristocratical prize" whom he intended to exhibit to all his democratic friends. The ill-mannered, egotistical, and sneaky Dodge stands diametrically opposed to another American type, the honest, bluff seaman, Captain Truck, who is much admired by his aristocratic passengers, English *and* American, even if he "got into blue water the moment he approached the finesse of deportment." Dodge also contrasts, of course, with the Effinghams, whose intelligent and unprovincial views are endorsed by Cooper (even if he may find John Effingham *too* cynical about America).

Homeward Bound, while canvassing subjects worthy of attention, lacks artistry, one feels, in its presentation of them. The social criticism is not well integrated into the adventure sequence, the reader having to alternate, bumpily, between rather ponderous discussions of everything from sailing to society, and excessively detailed passages of action. The characterization bumps, too, following a black-or-white pattern, with Cooper vilifying Steadfast Dodge and gushing about Eve Effingham, and the style is circumlocution almost unrelieved — a method not well suited to the novel of manners.

Home As Found does not triumph artistically either, but it does provide some significant analysis of American society and also a spectrum of American types. Cooper has in mind, first, his aforementioned thesis that the landed aristocracy should occupy positions of power and control because they are educated and informed people and at the same time humble Christian gentlemen and ladies. If the Effinghams believe in political democracy and accept the rise to political prominence, because of his talent and shrewdness, of Aristabulus Bragg, they do not believe in social equality. Rather by chance Bragg finds himself at their "brilliant dinner table," and, when he does, he is all at sea.

Cooper has secondly in mind supporting the statement that he makes in the book's preface, that the governing social evil in America is provincialism. If his is a great country, yet it is "very far behind most polished nations in various essentials." Drawing his examples from New York society, he establishes a range from polished to unpolished people, from sophisticated to narrow. The former, of course, are equipped with "morality" and intelligence as well. Eve Effingham represents the ideal (though, in her role as a perfect being, she comes across to the reader as incredibly stiff and almost totally unconvincing). Back "home" after years of travel abroad, she heads "one of the most truly elegant and best ordered establishments" in America. Her cousin and house guest, Grace Van Cortlandt, ranks not far behind, for, though a stay-at-home and thus unworldly, she combines with her native "simplicity" a "perfect decorum and retenue of deportment" — "the exuberance of the new school of manners not having helped to impair the dignity of her character, or to weaken the charm of diffidence. Less finished in her manners than Eve, to be sure, but never unfeminine or unladylike." Others in this select circle include Mrs. Hawker, "a lady in every sense of the word; by position, education, manners, association, mind, fortune and birth," and Mrs. Houston, "feminine, well-mannered, rich, pretty, of a very positive social condition, and naturally kind-hearted and disposed to sociability." On the other hand, the social-climbing Mrs. Jarvis (a contrast to her unpretentious husband), Miss Ring, a "restless, beau-catching, worldly belle," and Mrs. Legend, the leader of a supposedly literary salon, do not belong in the top circle, and they exemplify what Eve Effingham has in mind when she criticizes New York society as just "unpleasant crowds," just "flirting, giggling, and childishness." It needs a "quiet retenue" and "good tone." The "country cousin" types like Bragg and Steadfast Dodge and the village gossip, Mrs. Abbott, are exluded as well.

For Cooper, then, New York remains "an encampment quite as much as a permanent and long-existing capital." Along with its narrowness of spirit, he deplores its stress upon materialism (New York is little more "than a strife in prodigality and parade") and upon chauvinism, an attitude embodied in the character of Mr. Wenham ("I believe an American has little to learn from any nation but his own"). The counterpart to this attitude, excessive Anglophilism (as seen in Mr. Howel, who finds "an English journal fifty years old . . . more interesting than one of ours wet from the press"), is, to be sure, equally shortsighted.

In sum, "home as found" proved distinctly disillusioning to Cooper — soured at the time of the writing of the novel by the Cooperstown Three Mile Point controversy in which he was embroiled. Even its "old families" have a shortcoming or two, like their excessive "Britishness," and everything, as Eve Effingham remarks, at best partakes of a mixed nature — "nothing vulgar yet little approached that high standard that her European education had taught her to esteem perfect."[1]

Though Cooper declared at one point in *Home As Found* that "our task in the way of describing town society will soon be ended," he found at least one more occasion for describing, and attacking, "town society." This came in *Autobiography of a Pocket Handkerchief* (1843), a slight work — amazingly slight for the long-winded Cooper — originally appearing in *Graham's Magazine* and later appearing in book

form. Uncharacteristic of the author in many ways, its con-
cision, its absence of adventure, its omission of a sentimental
love story, and its method of narration (a tale told by a
pocket handkerchief!), it does link itself with *Home As Found*
in its satire on New York society, especially in the city's
commercial aspects, and it takes its place in a long line of
similar satires extending from Washington Irving to Louis
Auchincloss.

In a tone more rollicking than usual, Cooper makes sport
of the plutocracy, as personified by the land speculator,
Henry Halfacre, and his family, chiefly his daughter Eudosia.
The latter attempts to throw a "golden bridge" across the
chasm dividing the aristocracy from the plutocracy by buying
an obviously very special handkerchief for a hundred dollars,
then displaying it ostentatiously at Mrs. Trotter's ball, as she
sets her cap for that "reputed six-figure fortune," Morgan
Morely. Despite being beautiful as well as basically good-
hearted, "Dosie" does not forge her way into society, for she
has been badly educated (q.v., her "very badly modulated
voice"), and she lacks knowledge of the "finesse of fine life."
Furthermore, her father fails in business, thus depriving her
of her lure as an "heiress."

The upper social spheres, such as those inhabited by the
Monsons, if far less gauche than the Halfacre world, are not
untouched by pecuniary emphases. The "true taste" and
"true morals" of people like the Monsons or the Shorehams
are at times endangered. Only Adrienne de la Rocheaimard,
a member of the French aristocracy even if currently reduced
to serving as a governess, avoids contamination, contrasting
sharply, as she does so, with American fortune hunters like
Tom Thurston.

Though the book contains jolly sequences, Cooper satirizes rather ponderously for the most part, thus turning the
Autobiography into broad farce, whereas it should have re-

tained the gay flavor of a jeu d'esprit. Cooper's clumsy stylistic propensities ("the retenue of a Manhattanese rout") add to the heaviness. The reader wants sparkling, not stilted, conversations, deft, not labored ("the great game of brag that most of the country had sat down to"), observations.

It is in the Littlepage trilogy — *Satanstoe* (1845), *The Chainbearer* (1845), and *The Redskins* (1846) — that Cooper most precisely hews to the manners line. The three novels are intended, in the first place, as a social history, a defense of the landed gentry as representing the ideal of the gentleman, who will promote the law and order that exemplify American democracy at its best. The Littlepages and the Mordaunts, colonial gentry of English ancestry (those of Dutch descent rank a little below), are at the forefront, seen as they found an estate in the then unsettled northern New York woods. Almost immediately, however, the Littlepage-Mordaunt security is threatened by leveling demagogues, as personified by the tribe of Newcomes and by Aaron Thousandacres, a believer in "unrestrained" democracy. The issue is brought to a head in the antirent wars, which serve as the background to *The Redskins*; in these the "levelers" refuse to pay rent to the landowners, insisting that every man should be allowed to possess whatever land he wants or needs. Cooper, throughout the series, has taken an opposing view. The Littlepage class exhibits a democratic spirit (e.g., Mordaunt Littlepage's recognition of the poor but perceptive chainbearer, Andries Coejemans, as a gentleman and his equal) but refuses to carry "democracy" to the free-for-all extreme. The landowners deserve, as Cooper sees it, their legitimately obtained possessions. Moreover, they deserve the highest position in the American social structure — owed to them, not on the basis of wealth and social grace, but as a reward for virtue and talent — and they will accept this position "with Christian humility and deep submission of the self to the moral laws of the universe." Cooper argues vehemently, as Donald Ringe points out, that "a social organization is after all but a reflection of the moral principles upon which it is based."[2]

In the course of the trilogy Cooper instructs the reader about a number of social issues: the role of the landed proprietor, cultural differences between England and America, American class distinctions, and so on. Freely mixing the social commentary with the adventure-love story plots, he outlines a "chronicle of manners" (the label he himself applies in his preface to *Satanstoe* — adding that "every such has a certain value"), one filled with reference to customs and habits in various social spheres.

Satanstoe, in particular, is given over to a portrayal of the way of life of New York's colonial aristocracy, providing, along with this, comparisons among the colonies (e.g., New York vs. New England) and among people of different racial strains (English vs. Dutch), and affording glimpses of other classes and of special types (the Negro, the Indian) as well. The opening sequences of the novel establish this sort of picture, as the narrator, Corny Littlepage, carefully "places" himself for the reader: "We happened to be in a part of Westchester in which were none of the very large estates." The Littlepages, one learns, belong to the "haute bourgeoisie," located between the aristocracy and the higher classes of yeomanry; they have a very adequate establishment at Satanstoe, not to mention the 40,000 acres in the North that will become the estate of "Ravensnest," and the male members of the family have served in the Assembly and the militia and are "well connected." Corny Littlepage has been brought up in a genteel and comfortable environment, first tutored by the Reverend Thomas Worden, rector of St. Jude's — and the American version of the English hunting parson type — then attending Nassau Hall. A sociable atmosphere prevails at Satanstoe, witnessed on the occasions of the visits of Colonel Van Valkenburgh, when hot flip facilitates the conversation, encouraging talk about cockfights and horse racing, and even about religion (when a man is really good, religion only does him harm, says the Colonel). Contrasts are made between the solid but stolid Dutch and the more graceful English-descended Americans, who are less averse to "education" and therefore more informed and polished.

The jolly country living is paralleled in New York City, as Corny Littlepage and Dirck Van Valkenburgh find out as they pay a visit to relatives there. Stopping en route at a country inn, they partake of a lavish dinner of ham, potatoes, boiled eggs, beefsteak, pickles, cole slaw, apple pie, and cider, hearty and appetizing fare, if less elaborate than the turtle soup and oysters they will have at urban banquets to come. In New York the provincials take note of town and country differences, of how, for example, Aunt Legge sups at half past eight, a little later "than my mother, as being more fashionable and genteel." Aunt Legge always dresses for dinner, too, even though she may dine on a cold dumpling. Dinner at the Mordaunts' is even more formal, involving many courses, a removal of the cloth, a series of toasts, and a separation of the ladies and the gentlemen, and we are made aware of "that peculiar air of metropolitan superiority" that strikes the "provincial ignorance" of Corny.

Cooper obviously enjoys describing "old New York," still a relatively small town, where people walk rather than ride, and where everyone participates in the "Pinkster," the "great Saturnalia" of the blacks, featuring sideshows and the drinking of "white wine" (buttermilk). Various social usages are noted: the servant-companion relationship among the upper classes, the vogue for "things French among us," the habit of addressing the British soldiers quartered in the city as "Mr." rather than by their titles ("such things never occurring in the better circles"), and the interest in the drama, spurred on by the garrison of British soldiers, who perform Addison's *Cato* and Farquhar's *The Beaux Stratagem*.

Cooper then turns his attention to the "inland" city of Albany, its inhabitants and their customs. A more relaxed and informal pattern prevails in Albany, partly because of the town's location in the "interior," says the author, and partly because most of the people are of Dutch rather than English descent and thus more free and easy, perfectly willing to condone a twenty-year-old "man" indulging in the sport of sledding on the town's hills, or robbing, as a prank, a family of its supper. Rector Worden one observes, looks down on the Albany Dutch "in a very natural, metropolitan sort of way," preferring the company of the English officers, a more sophisticated group. They — and the English Americans — would not be inclined to patronize the fortune teller Mother Doortje, as do the less worldly Dutch. If Jason Newcome proves an exception, he, it must be remembered, is a New Englander rather than a New Yorker, and indeed of the lower middle class, and, as such, one who "had not much notion of the fitness of things in matters of taste."

When the novel's scene shifts for a final time, to the remote northern settlements, a strong sense of "locale" is imparted to the reader again. As the group of principals depart from Albany for the backwoods, the girls assume veils of green (as protective coloring), and the men put on buckskin (with the exceptions of Jason Newcome and Mr. Worden, the latter keeping to his clerical garb). Now, too, the cast of characters includes surveyors, chainbearers, and Indian guides, and the manner of living begins to verge on the primitive. To be sure, the loghouse dwelling into which the principals settle has "five apartments," and is a forerunner of the one-day-to-be provincial Littlepage "estate" of Ravensnest.

The author's handling of setting does much to authenticate

the social background of *Satanstoe*. The pleasant pictures of the comfortable but not lavish country home of the Little-pages and of the more elegant town house of the Mordaunts suggest their class and role. A strong feeling of local color permeates the New York City scenes, with landmarks like Wall Street, Trinity Church, and the Battery appearing, and hilly Albany, dotted with neat Dutch edifices characterized by stoops and gables, is vividly drawn as well. The familiar Cooper "big nature" backdrops crop up, too, in the later stages of the book — for example the breaking up of the ice on the Hudson, and the forest clearings in the area of Lake George.

The book's social commentary contributes to the authen-tication process, particularly Cooper's discussion of American types, from the intelligent and firmly upright "English" Corny Littlepage, to the physically attractive but less bright "Dutch" Dirck Van Valkenburgh, to the narrow and greedy New Englander Jason Newcome, to the Negro Jaap, to the Indian Susquesus. Cooper also formulates a number of English-American contrasts, and it is worth noting that, though depicting the titled Englishman Bulstrode flatteringly, he bestows the hand of the American "heiress" Anneke Mordaunt on Littlepage rather than on Bulstrode. The latter, as Anneke says at one point, will function better at the head of his officers' mess than in the snug Dutch parlor of her cousin Mrs. Van der Hayden, where the "colony hospitality, colony good-will, colony plainness" are more suited to Corny Littlepage. Americans, according to Cooper, need not "ape" the British; their culture, even their language, is their own.

Though generally a charming book, *Satanstoe* suffers from a number of technical flaws. The author, as usual, structures his work loosely, mixing adventure with love story, genre painting with political debate, and, in this case, adding many a description of manners. Though his flair for storytelling makes itself evident in a number of gripping episodes, his tendency toward the prolix slows the book down as a whole. His "beau idéal" concept of characterization — Anneke Mordaunt and Mary Wallace are "lovely and delicate girls" even on an ice floe in a rampaging river — also seems a deterrent feature. Exceptions do exist, like the virile, fun-loving, but unstable Guert Ten Eyck or the sociable "Loping Dominie" Worden, but as a rule Cooper glamorizes his leading characters. Conversely, he paints his villains too darkly. Jason Newcome should not be *quite* so sneaky, materialistic, narrow, hypocritical, and lacking in taste. The Cooper stylistic habits of confused syntax, periphrasis, and stilted dialogue do not, needless to say, serve him well, either. If he writes less clumsily and with less "giftbook flossiness" in *Satanstoe* than elsewhere, he still does not often approximate the sparkling phrasing of later novelists of manners.

The remaining two novels in the Littlepage trilogy, *The Chainbearer* and *The Redskins,* reveal less concern with summoning up the way of life of the landed class and ignore, for the most part, details of dress, food and drink, deportment, and custom. Cooper continues to theorize, to be sure, about the function of the landed proprietor and indeed devotes himself increasingly to the antirent issue. In *The Chainbearer* much is said about the "gentleman," as about leveling democracy and majority rule, and there are passing comments on American-European distinctions. In regard to the latter, Cooper distributes praise and blame on both sides, attacking "Yankee" provinciality that can lead to mock-refinement (e.g., the Littlepage neighbors object to the name *Satanstoe* as undignified), but defending the naturalness of the American girl, as opposed to her artificial European counterpart.

He has more to say on this topic in *The Redskins* (mostly

because his protagonist, Hugh Littlepage, has traveled in Europe for a number of years and thus has a "vantage point"), tending, in this latter novel, to favor the Europeans. "New world" inhabitants should visit the "Old," says Cooper firmly, for travel acts as a decided corrective to narrow self-adulation. The traveler would recognize, he feels, that society in America "in its ordinary meaning" is not as well ordered, tasteful, well mannered, agreeable, instructive, and useful as that in almost any European country. The American watering places, for example, seem to Hugh Littlepage "very much inferior" to most of those abroad, and Americans would do well, he suggests, to adopt many of the trans-atlantic customs, especially those of the British. America, he admits, has at least one or two advantages, such as the absence of a peasant class, and even of the "mercenary" spirit (that is, "two men might be bought in any European country for one here").

The Chainbearer discusses on a number of occasions what Cooper means by the terms *lady* and *gentleman*. Dismissing birth and wealth ("the vulgar, almost invariably, in this country, reduce the standard of distinction to mere money") as proper claims,[3] he stresses the following characteristics: taste, manners, opinions that are based on intelligence and cultivation, a refusal to stoop to meanness, generosity, superiority to scandal, and a truthfulness that stems from self-respect. People like his protagonist, Mordaunt Littlepage, clearly encompass the list, as does the young lady, Ursula Malbone, whom Mordaunt marries. Though very poor, even reduced to helping her uncle as a surveyor, Ursula was born and educated as a lady. Education is central in Cooper's scheme of things ("the wife of an educated man," he notes, "should be an educated woman"), and, because of the lack of it, the chainbearer, Andries Coejemans, "is and is not a gentleman." Coejemans "*is*" because he possesses what is even more central, a belief in and ability to recognize principles. He contrasts sharply in this respect with someone like Aaron Thousandacres, for whom all sense of right was concentrated in selfishness. Wherever firm moral fiber appears — in the yeoman, in the servant, in the Indian — a "good specimen" of man will be found. Only among the "gentry," however, do *all* the characteristics of the gentleman appear, and thus it is that Mordaunt's father can state that "nothing contributes so much to the civilization of a country as to dot it with a gentry," the effect produced by "one gentleman's family in a neighborhood, in the way of manners, tastes, general intelligence and civilization at large," being of substantial proportions.

While echoing this thesis ("the aristocrat means, in the parlance of the country, no other than a man of gentlemanlike tastes, habits, opinions and associations"), *The Redskins* defines less and describes more, supplying more information than *The Chainbearer* about the practices and habits of the aristocracy. One hears of its cultural interests, like the theater (though it is "pretty much all farces"), of its church (Episcopalian — and with a canopy over the Littlepage pew), of its clothes (Hugh and his uncle keep "a supply of country attire at the 'Nest"; no man, Cooper has declared in *The Chainbearer*, assumes the "wardrobe of a gentleman without having certain pretensions to the character"), of its dinners (good habits at the table are "conventionalities that belong to the fundamental principles of civilized society"), and of its homes (e.g., Ravensnest, "a respectable New York country dwelling"). Such are the links that "connect cultivated society together" — and separate it from the "Heirs of New York merchants getting rid of their portion in riotous living," as also from the covetous antirenters, and from the "demagogues and editors." Cooper contentedly places on the top rung of the "social ladder" the "Patroon" contingent, those who are "equal" in "social position, connections, education and similarity of habits, thoughts, and, if you will, prejudices."

Since he employs the genre of manners only as a secondary focus[4] — after the adventure, after the love story, after the sociopolitical criticism — and since he lacks some of the necessary attributes of the novelist of manners, most notably, a smooth and suave style and a tone of reasonably detached irony, Cooper initiates the genre imperfectly. One can appreciate, however, his providing the impetus, a much stronger one than that which stemmed from Brackenridge.

Among his contemporaries, a few writers also attempted to kindle the spark — the New Englander, Catharine Maria Sedgwick, for one, and the two Southerners, John Pendleton Kennedy and John Esten Cooke. If making but partial and not very adequate contributions, still, they lent assistance in keeping the tradition alive.

Kennedy and Cooke, like so many other later Southern novelists, relied upon the historical romance as their formula, a type into which might be easily inserted, however, some manners embellishments, especially in the form of local-color touches. Kennedy's *Swallow Barn* (1832) illustrates this in its reproduction of life on a Virginia plantation, the Meriwether estate of Swallow Barn. Although pursuing two lines of plot, a litigation issue and a love affair, Kennedy seems more preoccupied with summoning up a vision of the feudal South, of graceful living in the hunting country. The vision certainly has its charms, yet these are gently minimized by the vein of satire that runs throughout the book. Kennedy mocks the chivalric ideal in his account of the courting of romantic Bel Tracy by down-to-earth Ned Hazard, and he lightly undercuts some Southern types and traditions, such as the landed gentleman model, Frank Meriwether; the "girlish" Prudence Meriwether who is so devoted to "good works"; Chub, the dogmatic schoolmaster; and the generally provincial

(Richmond is the center of the universe) and stultified Virginians. In its nimble mockery *Swallow Barn* anticipates, to a degree, the subsequent more severe indictment of nostalgic regionalism to be found in the work of Ellen Glasgow.

Cooke's *Virginia Comedians* (1854) also depends on an ancestral home for its background, this being Effingham Hall, a "stately edifice near Williamsburg." In the vicinity of the Hall events like governors' balls and fox hunts take place, and there are also festal days devoted to wrestling and running matches, ballad singing and fiddler contests, as well as formal picnics and regimental musters. The book's cast of characters includes conventional types, too, like the worldly clergyman and the class-conscious gentleman. *Less* conventional figures are present as well, actors and theater managers (Mr. Hallam of the *Virginia Company of Comedians*), and yeoman farmers, and the book contains some derogatory remarks about the "Influential classes," "aristocracy" and "feudalism," together with frequent defenses of the acting profession and of the unfairly maligned "poor playing girl." Despite the presence of some fresh types and of some refreshing commentary, however, *Virginia Comedians* does not really veer very far away from a standard tale of entertainment, filled with the customary elements of sentimental romance, low comedy, and suspense.

More in keeping with the manners format — perhaps because it was written thirty years later, and thus in the James-Howells era — is Cooke's *Fanchette* (1883). Shifting his locale slightly northward, to Washington and the Eastern Shore of Maryland, and eschewing a historical setting in favor of the contemporary period, Cooke turns his book into something less characteristically "southern" than *Virginia Comedians*. Issues of politics, journalism, the theater, religion, and economics now interest him, and these are discussed against

the background of a fairly cosmopolitan society. Some sense
of the Washington social scene is established — "Vanity Fair
in full blast" — with contrasts drawn between the old-rich
like the Delanceys and the new-rich like the Ordmores. The
former can produce "good company seated at a good dinner,"
whereas the latter stage less selective receptions, in a drawing
room that was "as magnificent as great wealth and questionable taste could make it." Those attending such dinners and
receptions may vary from journalists like Waring ("a flâneur
. . . but under the trifler is the honest gentleman"), to cultivated men of leisure like Armyn, to the "gentleman adventurer," Prince Seminoff, determined to marry a rich American
girl. Many members of the "best society" of Washington have
country houses in Maryland in the vicinity of the Chesapeake
Bay, Armyn owning "Montrose," an imposing dwelling with
"every mark of age," and the Delanceys inhabiting "Bayside,"
a "handsome country house" nearby. A "very social and
affectionate society" exists on the Eastern Shore, so Cooke
reports, the "best features of the old regime" lingering there
and making "life attractive."

Fanchette devotes itself for the most part to a suspenseful
plot involving the titular character, a young actress with a
mysterious background. After a rather inordinate amount of
intrigue, the book ends happily with Fanchette — who,
actress or no, is a "perfect lady" — being permitted to make a
proper marriage. Indeed, four weddings take place before the
close of the book. As this suggests, the element of romance is
uppermost in the novel, and the treatment of it, one has to
say, is conventional and uninspiring. The book is enlivened,
however, by the sprightliness of the heroine and by the
author's sense of humor, and the authorial reflections on
materialism (and its effect on politics in Washington in
particular) and on the drama command the interest of the
present-day reader.

The author most readily matched with Cooper as an incipient novelist of manners is Catharine Maria Sedgwick. Born into the upper class, she chose to describe it in her novels and indeed to defend it, provided that it exemplified an aristocracy of talent and virtue rather than one simply of birth or wealth. Though Miss Sedgwick could envision an approaching "American Utopia endowed with unlimited social grace,"[5] if such an aristocracy prevailed, she entertained serious doubts about the possibility, as her often tart thrusts at the higher social spheres in novels like *Clarence* (1830) and *Married or Single?*(1857) suggest.

Clarence is based on a town-and-country contrast, the rural gentry, Mr. Clarence and his daughter Gertrude, juxtaposed with New York City society, personified chiefly by Mrs. Layton. The former are well-read and well traveled individuals (in addition to being well supplied with money), who possess moderation and humility and thus act with delicacy in social situations. The latter, her graceful manners, spirited conversation, and engaging ways notwithstanding, is prone to self-indulgence and needless expenditure and to decided carelessness about principles. Miss Sedgwick says again and again that money corrupts (the "perils of a fortune") and presents numerous examples besides that of Mrs. Layton: the Browns, with their "nouveau riche immense parlor" and "costly, ill-assorted and cumbrous furniture"; Mrs. Stanley, "a rich, motherless, uneducated, unintellectual woman" and therefore "very pitiable"; Mr. Morley, obsequious to the affluent and fashionable and determined to marry among them; Major Daisy, a shallow social arbiter ("an Areopagite in the female fashionable world"); and Miss Patty Sprague, the "walking, talking chronicle of the floating events of the day," who is quick to associate with those on the way up, quick to forget those on the way down. Exceptions, apart from the Clarences, do exist, notably Mrs. Roscoe and her son Gerald, and the Marion family. The latter, one notes, have a Southern bucolic background; the rural gentry has the edge again.[6]

Miss Sedgwick fires away from the first page to the last: at the belles and dandies ("living personifications of their prototypes in the tailor's window, dignified, self-complacent morons"), the gossiping and too-dress-conscious matrons, the gambling and speculating husbands operating in their "bank-note world," the businesslike pursuit of pleasure and the avoidance of intellectual interests,[7] and the purely mercenary view of marriage. In the words of Mr. Clarence, the New York social scene is marked by vacuity, flippancy, superficial accomplishments, idle competitions, and useless and wasteful expenditure. Such, he adds, are the sins and follies of every commercial city, and, though he (and his creator) would not wish to "condemn en masse the class of fashionable society," he makes it clear that this "polite world" does not represent "the most elevated and virtuous class."

Clarence touches on other issues of manners, such as the role of women (the author declaring, for one thing, that talent is demanded in "housewifery" just as in other "departments of life"), the rites of hospitality, and the importance of setting (the air of luxury and refinement in Mrs. Layton's establishment is commended as going "beyond that usually produced by the union of fortune and fashion"). The book also contains a passage caricaturing the impercipient British traveler in America, one who draws inane and often faulty English-American parallels. Captain Edmund Stuart, the example in this instance, labels Benjamin West an English painter and even remarks that his name may not have reached America yet, "owing probably to the ignorance of the fine arts here."

Its well-directed satire aside, *Clarence* represents hard going for the present-day reader, for much of its author's energy is expended in unfolding a highly melodramatic and sentimental plot; the characters are carelessly motivated and/or dull; structural arrangements seem slipshod (letters are thrown in at random to convey necessary exposition); and the style is marred by epithets on the "crown matrimonial," "manly bosom" order.

In her later novel, *Married or Single?,* Miss Sedgwick spends most of her time discussing the question posed in her title, whether a married or a single life is preferable for a woman. After a sterling defense of the latter position, she allows her heroine to marry at the novel's end — once she has found the "right" man. Developing this discussion against a New York aristocracy background once again, Miss Sedgwick also satirizes once again, but more incidentally than she had in *Clarence.* So occupied is she in riding her thesis, that a woman's single life can be useful and dignified and is certainly preferable to a "bankrupt marriage," that she rarely delivers a satiric shaft.

When she does so, her targets recall those found in *Clarence* — the frivolous belle who thinks of feathers, lace, and fringe, but never of books; the Anglophile "lauding anything English";[8] and the arriviste Adeline Clapp, ignorant of conventions and with no proper instincts, the "fashionable" lady assiduously pursuing an empty social round, from morning reception to evening ball. As in *Clarence,* too, she utilizes foil characters, Grace Herbert contra Anne Carlton, corresponding to Gertrude Clarence contra Mrs. Layton. Anne Carlton epitomizes the socialite, pretty to look at and perfectly dressed, but flippant and shallow, materialistic and loosely principled. Grace, on the other hand, though too impetuous and more than a little worldly ("At twenty-two one can't turn hermit," she says, "and parties and receptions and their edifying accessories make up our social life, you know"), is intelligent, sensitive, and firmly principled.

Eventually she is rewarded for possessing these more positive traits; she escapes the clutches of the wealthy but corrupt man-about-town, Horace Copley, and attaches herself to the sturdy lawyer, Archibald Lisle, her equal in morals and — after his experiencing a European sojourn of a year or two — in manners as well. He has moved from his "narrow social sphere" into her world of "high breeding." Of course, Grace is still defending the single life even as she ventures upon marriage.

Married or Single? gives the reader a good deal of information about the "fashionable quarter" of New York, its materialism, coldness (e.g., Madam Copley), vanity and levity, and its easy morality. The benefits to be found — good dinners, tolerable operas, "practiced manners" — do not compensate. At one stage of the novel, Miss Sedgwick permits herself a severe tirade:

> A creature of Grace's rare gifts is about as well adapted to the fashionable world of New York as a first-rate ship would be to the artificial lake of a pleasure-ground. In other civilized countries, where a privileged class is sustained by rank, individuality of character is cultivated and developed in brilliant accomplishments that enamel society. But . . . who hopes to meet our poets, artists, historians at the "most brilliant party of the season"? Our society is characterized by monotony, infinite tediousness of mediocrity, a vulgar and childish struggle for insipid celebrities, celebrity for fine dress, palatial house, costly furniture and showy equipage.[P. 159]

Citing the recently published *Potiphar Papers,* Miss Sedgwick echoes the indictment of its author, George William Curtis, against New York society, with its parvenu emphasis on luxury at the expense of taste.

No more than *Clarence* is *Married or Single?* an artistic triumph, unfortunately. An exhausting two-volume affair, it piles intrigue upon intrigue, provides not one but two pathetic deaths of young ladies and one of a child as well, employs coincidence with abandon, idealizes its principal characters and caricatures others, and relies heavily on pompous dialogue. The presence of one or two interesting characters like Mrs. Tallis, an occasional witty remark ("persons of Grace's temperament are apt to mistake impulses for inspirations"), and the appropriately directed satiric attacks only partially redress the balance.

One has to conclude that the American novel of manners in the pre-Civil War era does not reach artistic heights. The polish and skill of a Thackeray, whom Miss Sedgwick speaks, in *Married or Single?*, of wishing to call to her aid, are generally lacking. Happily, they were soon to be supplied by James and Howells.

The question of artistry aside, the Coopers and Sedgwicks, Kennedys and Cookes, can still be praised for recognizing the value of social satire as novelistic material and for, in this and other ways, utilizing the genre of manners, thus keeping the tradition alive.[9]

NOTES TO CHAPTER 2

1. It is interesting to observe that, among America's imperfections, Cooper includes literature and music, the latter being "certainly the weakest side of American civilization."

2. Donald A. Ringe, *James Fenimore Cooper* (New York: Twayne Publishers, Inc., 1962), p. 121.

3. The reader would be inclined to argue that Cooper does not really dismiss the claim of "birth." One remembers that Ursula Malbone is a lady "by birth," as is Mary Warren, the heroine of *The Redskins*. Mary, like Ursula, is, though poor, rewarded with the hand of the protagonist, Hugh Littlepage, for she is educated as well as well born, refined as well as principled. Like many another Cooper heroine, she has everything!

4. *Autobiography of a Pocket Handkerchief* is the one exception.

5. Edward H. Foster, *Catharine Maria Sedgwick* (New York: Twayne Publishers, Inc., 1974), p. 99.

6. Vulgar little ladies like Mrs. Upton can be found in the country, however, and, as Mr. Clarence says, with wry amusement, to his daughter, six distinct social ranks exist in the village of Clarenceville.

7. Mrs. Layton, for example, attends lectures and the opera merely to be seen, and Gerald Roscoe's mind, "enriched with elegant acquisitions," is regarded as an embellishment but hardly a necessity. Miss Sedgwick anticipates later novelists of manners in her assignment of antiintellectualism to "society."

8. Unlike the Anglophile, Walter Herbert does not want his niece, Grace, to marry an Englishman, for she would be received on sufferance in England, whereas in America she is a "queen in her own right."

9. One observes the comment of Edward H. Foster that, "aside from various works by Cooper and Miss Sedgwick, very few good works of fiction were explicitly devoted to a study of manners in pre-Civil War America." He goes on to say that "there are women who industriously wrote domestic novels in which much attention was given to manners. . . . but few authors of distinction attempted this particular kind of fiction. Perhaps the very lack of a class, or at least a highly influential class, which based its principles upon a life of manners precluded the possible development of a tradition of novels of manners in the half-century before the Civil War" (Foster, *Catharine Maria Sedgwick*, p. 104.).

3

Henry James

*I*T would seem wise to assign to Henry James the title of, if not founder, certainly early master of the novel of manners. One who devoted so much of his fiction to the "mixture of manners" (preface to *Lady Barberina*, 1884), evident, for him, in the contrasting ways of life on the European and North American continents, and one who proved an expert in this, as in other types of fiction, he quite deserves the title.

Writing at the time of the "American conquest of Europe,"[1] the post-Civil War period when sightseers, students, and socialites flocked to England and the Continent, James chose to report on the "conquest," delighting in the divergences in social convention and degrees of social assimilation that became apparent as the invasion continued. Over the years he continued to study society's manners, peculiarities, codes, decencies, and shabbinesses.

He was bent on something more basic than social comparisons and contrasts, however. Believing that "we know a man imperfectly until we know his society . . . we but half know a society until we know its manners" ("Emerson," 1887), he chose to study manners in order to ascertain the essence of individuals and their civilizations. The "social heritage," he felt, revealed the country — for example, "the most perfect thing which the English have mastered . . . so that it has become a compendious illustration of their social genius and their manners is the well-appointed, well-administered, well-filled country house" ("An English New Year," 1879). Similarly, manners reveal the man, serving as the outward manifestation by which one sensed the quality of his mind and character. James believed, for example, that a New England puritan expressed his moral conscience through his ascetic manners. Manners must not be regarded as merely a "superficial gloss in the absence of depth of feeling,"[2] but, rather, as an exposure of man's moral fiber. The hollowness of Gilbert Osmond in *The Portrait of a Lady* is revealed, it might be said, through his lapses into pettish vulgarity.[3] The manners of the Marquis de Bellegarde in *The American* expose him as a cruel and egoistic person and by extension expose the French aristocracy as equally so (Proust's Duchesse de Guermantes serves the same function). James's view is crystallized in this statement:

> The idea of good breeding — without which intercourse fails to flower into fineness, without which human relations bear but crude and tasteless fruit — is one of the most precious conquests of civilization, the very core of our social heritage. ["The Question of Our Speech," 1905, p. 14]

So it is that the "reader who comes freshly to James must freshen up his feeling for the word 'manners,' "[4] being prepared to define it not merely as *fashion* or *gentility* or *form*, but in the more lofty terms that Emerson used and

James, in effect, borrowed — "good-nature or benevolence: manhood first, and then gentleness."[5] So it is that the reader must expect to find James looking upon social relationships as deeply significant, "as the primary source of even the most inward and personal of human experiences."[6]

For the most part, James found his example of good breeding and gentlemanliness among the members of the leisured, upper-class, "international set" and dealt with "social relationships" within this sphere. Certainly such a cosmopolitan yet closely bound world illustrated the "mystique of class" and brought out the best — *or* worst — of manners. Besides, James knew it well and could thus explore it in depth and with subtlety.[7]

Born into a family of wealth and learning, and one that moved in the proper circles, James was steeped from the first in a cultured, urbane atmosphere, the kind that his fiction so constantly exudes. He acquired, through association with cultivated people, through constant reading, through visits to the theater and to art galleries, an effective, if somewhat unconventional education, and many years of living in Europe developed in him a cosmopolitan spirit and encouraged a worldly sophistication.

When, in the mid-seventies, he began his years of European "exile," he had already established the pattern of his life, one devoted to literary and cultural pursuits and to a punctilious observance of society's rites. The writing routine and the dining out with lords and/or authors entertained and stimulated him and made his life, as far as he was concerned, thoroughly worthwhile. Able to function both as a "social animal" and as an "artist," James must be regarded as contented with his existence and at home in his milieu.

This milieu of the upper class — of weekends at those well-appointed country houses, of dinners at clubs in town, of browsing in art galleries and attendance at the theater,

of motor tours through the chateau country, of good conversation at tea — was utilized by James from the beginning
to the end of his writing career. In such a setting he could
canvas again and again the "international theme" so dear
to his heart, finding ever new ramifications to develop,
perpetually fascinated by the sense of dislocation engendered
in individuals as they endeavored to imbibe a foreign culture.

The "international novel" has been defined by Oscar
Cargill in terms that, one feels, James would have been
willing to accept:

> one in which a character, usually guided in his actions by the
> mores of one environment, is set down in another, where he
> must employ all his individual resources to meet successive
> situations, and where he must intelligently accommodate him-
> self to the new mores, or, in one way or another, be destroyed.[8]

James found this conflict in mores to be omnipresent and
would have agreed with Cargill that it thoroughly tested
the individual. His novels show, too, the individual's process
of "accommodation," a process ending in various ways —
the martyrdom of Mme. de Mauves, the "spoiling" of Roderick Hudson (admittedly, more through the weakness of
his character than through the "passes of a very old civilization"), the death of Daisy Miller.

Many of the early novels and novelettes — for example,
Mme. de Mauves (1873), *Roderick Hudson* (1875), *The
American* (1877), *Daisy Miller* (1878), *An International
Episode* (1878), and *The Europeans* (1878) — dwell upon
transatlantic differences, usually presenting, as James rather
melodramatically said of *Mme. de Mauves,* an "insidiously
beguiled and betrayed" American suffering at the hands
of persons pretending to represent the "highest possible
civilization and to be of an order in every way superior
to his own." In this first phase of his career, James almost

constantly asserted that the integrity and moral awareness of the "American innocent" fundamentally outweigh the sophistication and cultivation of Europe. At the same time, however, he cited weaknesses in the "native" position, thus remaining, in essence, objective in his exploration of the cross-the-seas contrast.

An International Episode provides a deft illustration. Bessie Alden, a socially entrenched if also fresh and innocent American girl, confronts, first at Newport, then in London, a titled Englishman, Lord Lambeth. Her charm and beauty so intrigue the nobleman that he seeks her hand in marriage. She feels forced to turn down his offer, however, because the English aristocracy (Lord Lambeth's mother and sister, if not the lord himself) do not recognize her premise that a young lady of good standing in the United States is in every way the equal of the "best people" in Europe. The crusty treatment accorded her sister, Mrs. Westgate, and her by the Duchess of Bayswater and Lady Pimlico affronts her sensibilities and causes her to reject Lord Lambeth.

Throughout the story the author draws comparisons between English and American social customs, showing the oddities of both, yet depicting American ways more sympathetically on the whole. If Mr. Westgate, like his fellow American males, is too exclusively devoted to business, still he reveals himself to be humorous and bright when he does appear on the edge of the social scene. His wife is also humorous and bright — and pretty besides. Though slightly *outré* by English standards (she speaks of herself as being eccentric, undisciplined, and outrageous), she really possesses many social graces, and, like her sister, regards herself as a match for the English aristocrats anyway. The less "initiated" Bessie Alden is equipped with a fine intellect and moral consciousness as well as beauty and charm, all of which adequately compensate for her slight lack of sophistication. One feels that Lord Lambeth would have been lucky to win her.

Lord Lambeth seems, at first glance, a very good choice, being handsome, charming, and good-natured — as well as titled and rich. A closer view, however, reveals that he is a tiny bit dense and a tiny bit snobbish; moreover, he lacks positiveness and a firm sense of responsibility. Bessie, sensitive to the life of the ancient aristocracies and admiring Lord Lambeth as in many ways a fine prototype, still is bothered by his failure to live up to his duties — his unconcern, for example, about serving in the House of Lords in his "hereditary legislator" role. One concludes that Bessie is just as well off without him.

The other Englishmen in the story do not fare too well at the author's hands either. Percy Beaumont, Lord Lambeth's traveling companion, is brighter than his friend but even more aware of class distinctions. Wrongly convinced (who wouldn't set her cap for a British title?) that Bessie is chasing Lord Lambeth, he tries hard to warn his friend off, apparently feeling that American blood might contaminate the pure British strain. Lord Lambeth's mother and sister would certainly share this feeling; uncouth Americans must be shunned. In attempting to upstage Bessie and Mrs. Westgate, the Duchess and her daughter do not succeed very well, however, and, in the process, their manners, which should be their chief claim to fame, are "not fine, not even good."

An International Episode scoffs, in fact, at many of the British peculiarities: their stiff demeanor, chauvinism, excessive sense of propriety, coldness (the "English people have grown great by dropping you when you cease to be useful"), insistence on hierarchical forms such as the proper procedure on going into dinner, and their scorn of literary and artistic celebrities.[9] Mrs. Westgate and Bessie — and James himself, one surmises — object to these characteristics, and primarily to the British lack of "pleasant manners," that is, of courtesy and kindness.[10] Americans may be bumptious and materialistic ("you could get everything in America nowadays by paying for it"), yet they are principled *and* kind.

As the narrative unfolds, the American and English locales are rather carefully differentiated from each other. One observes the general "brightness, newness, juvenility" of New York, raw perhaps, yet not without its attractions, even in mid-summer. Only the men of the "first families" remain behind in the city, to be sure, the women and children having taken the bustling and cheery if somewhat "garish" New York-to-Newport boat and domiciled themselves by the sea. In that fashionable watering place Newport, some of the summer inhabitants live in the hotels (characterized by airy corridors and gigantic verandas), but more of them live in their own "cottages" (also characterized by airy corridors and gigantic verandas). The emphasis in city and country falls on a relaxed, informal social intercourse. The London environment also possesses charm and interest — the Hyde Park promenade, the historic places like Hampton Court — but the atmosphere suggests a stiffer way of living. The English country house seems far more impenetrable than the Newport "cottage" — and indeed it is.

James makes his distinctions in *An International Episode* in a witty and diverting way. The two young British aristocrats, Lord Lambeth and Percy Beaumont, are lightly mocked as they languidly engage in an "animated discussion," or as they declare they must "learn to speak American." Lord Lambeth's somewhat limited vocabulary, running largely to "I say's" and the adjective "rum," is mimicked, too. Occasionally the thrusts go the other way — Mrs. Westgate, while sneering at British protocol, yet arranges for her sister to be presented at court. But usually James applies his rapier to the English: Mrs. Westgate, momentarily glad that the Duchess of Bayswater is looking at her distinguished appearance, feels her felicity mitigated almost instantly, for "having inspected her visitor's own costume, she said to herself, 'She won't know how well I am dressed!'" James's tone remains consistently ironic, as he exposes the British foibles.

The balance between "home" and "abroad" is somewhat distorted also in the novel *The American,* the best known and most sustained example from James's earlier work of the international contrast. Apparently more bothered by wicked French aristocrats than by fatuous British noblemen or slightly devious American expatriates, James attacks in this novel, more strongly than elsewhere, a "superstitious valuation of Europe."[11] Telling the story of the American businessman Christopher Newman, who seeks the hand of the French noblewoman Claire de Cintré, but who is prevented from achieving his goal largely through the machinations of her mother and brother, the Bellegardes, James praises his protagonist as one of "nature's noblemen" and derides the artificially noble French aristocracy as embodied in the Bellegarde family leaders. The subplot, concerning the intrigues of Noémie Nioche, a member of the petite bourgeoisie but aiming infinitely higher, parallels the main plot in its reflection of the French social code and in its accent on immorality.

In customary Jamesian fashion the story is unfolded slowly, with the central situation developed through a series of key scenes, for example, Newman's announcement of his intentions with regard to Claire, the Bellegarde acknowledgment (temporary) of their engagement, then the estranging interviews with the Bellegardes at Fleurières and in the Parc Monçeau. The climax is reached when Newman realizes the true nature of the faithless Marquise and her elder son but then decides to forego revenge (which might be achieved by his exposing their "murder," at an earlier time, of the Marquise's husband) for their having separated him from Claire. If aware that the revenge could prove unsuccessful — the chances are good that the Bellegarde circle of friends and relatives would continue its support, however infamous the Bellegarde actions — Newman acts nonetheless primarily out of a spirit of magnanimity.

To state the contrast baldly — as James does not — new world integrity is juxtaposed with old world corruption. Christopher New-man, long and lean and shrewd and yet an indomitably innocent Middle Westerner, confronts the Bellegardes, an ancient and worldly Parisian family. A self-made man, he has not had time to acquire a great deal of polish and insouciance, but he does possess a firm and upright character. The cultivated Parisians, on the other hand, lack honesty, cherish empty forms, and commit cruel actions.

James tempers the contrast, however, refusing to support the American "side" unreservedly. His "hero" Newman, it must be admitted, suffers lapses of taste — admiring copies of works of art more than the originals, gazing with "culpable serenity at inferior productions," liking the streetcars in Brussels as much as the Hôtel de Ville. There are a number of subjects, the narrator tells us, on which he has no ideas, his life having been circumscribed by the fact that he was busy making money, and he is guilty of gaucheries as well as gaps in his conversation. In short, he needs more "savoir vivre." On the other hand, he knows the "crooked from the straight at a glance," he is courteous and chivalrous, and he has the "instincts," if not all the "forms," of a "high old civilization."

No one could have clung more firmly to the forms of a high old civilization than the Marquise de Bellegarde and her son Urbain. But theirs was a harsh "monde," all but empty of value. The arranged marriages ruled out the possibility of love and were based entirely on mercenary considerations. A sterile sense of honor was to be found in Valentin de Belle-garde's dueling over a woman for whom he no longer cared and who wasn't worth his devotion anyway. Family was everything, but what had the 800-year-old Bellegarde line produced? A race that was "strange, cold-blooded, proud, absurd, impossible." Urbain de Bellegarde is hardly even "urbane"; his wife is an "elegant, painted, cracked phial," whose greatest ambition is to attend the risqué Beaux Arts ball; his mother is impressive in her imperiousness, but selfish, materialistic, indeed, even villainous.

If the cold and sinful old Marquise, her posturing son Urbain, and his frivolous wife reflect almost none of the grace of the French aristocracy, the other Bellegardes, Claire and her younger brother Valentin, brighten the picture and redress the balance to some extent. Claire, as Newman reports, gives the "sense of an elaborate education . . . ceremonies and processes of culture." She has breeding, intelligence, social grace, charm, an aristocratic bearing, uprightness, and spiritual dedication. Her portrait contains a shadow or two, however; she is, for one thing, so deferential to her mother as to appear almost sycophantic. This attitude can be explained on the grounds of her training, of course, yet it renders her a rather lifeless "heroine." Her brother Valentin epitomizes urbanity and charm; he looks well, he talks well, he shows himself to be at home in the world. Unfortunately, he also seems cynical (watching with amuse-ment the downward progress of Mme. Dandelard), indecisive, and weak — unable to overcome the lure of Noémie Nioche and unable to cope with the family rulers.

The minor French characters, the Nioches, in many ways parallel the Bellegardes, even though coming from another sector of Parisian society. Their sense of decorum (the father must escort his daughter home from the Louvre each day), their artificiality and pose, their lack of honor (we note how Newman's honesty embarrasses both the Nioche and Bellegarde groups), their proper appearance — all have their counterpart in the higher world of the Faubourg St. Germain.

The minor American characters, often mirroring the characteristics of Christopher Newman, help set the new world off against the old. To be sure, Messrs. Babcock and Tristram do not bring much credit to their native land, the former being far too serious, rigid, and suspicious as a traveler in Europe, and the latter being far too provincial an expatriate, one who never visits the Louvre, preferring to spend most of his waking hours at his poker-playing American club. Mrs. Tristram appears in a far more favorable light, appreciating Paris and Parisians, having learned to emulate their graces ("the harmonies of dress . . . she thoroughly understood"), and at the same time having retained her moral spark and patriotic fervor ("deep within me the eagle shrieks") — in contrast to her husband, who regards America as a "bad smell."

Both the European and the American characters in the novel are deployed against sufficiently realized backgrounds, the author utilizing settings in order to accentuate their differences. Christopher Newman's rooms, for example, gilded as they are from floor to ceiling and lavish in satin and elaborate ornaments, suggest both the openhandedness and the questionable taste of the owner, just as the Tristram apartment, filled with modern conveniences, indicates the American desire to be supremely comfortable. The Bellegarde "hôtel" contrastingly embodies proportion, refinement, and a measure of discomfort, the spacious rooms adorned with priceless antiques and with objects of art but not very well lighted or heated. Generally speaking, it gives the impression of gloom and decay, as does the Bellegarde home in the country, the chateau at Fleurières. This ancient estate, with its rusty bells, creaking portals, and cracked white slabs, has an even more depressing quality. The shut-in frozen aspect of the Bellegarde establishments underscores the Bellegarde character, as the garishly but warmly decorated apartment of Newman underscores his.

The American, written in James's early, less complicated manner, communicates clearly to the reader and at the same time offers numerous examples of the author's wit and of his ability to turn a phrase. The reader hears of Newman's "esthetic headache" when he faces all those pictures in the Louvre. The people of Claire's world he sees as all mounted on stilts a mile high and with pedigrees long in proportion. Mme. de Bellegarde's countenance, "with its formal gaze and its circumscribed smile, figured a document signed and sealed, a thing of parchment, ink and ruled lines." The imagery, suggestive of rigidity and precision, of contraction and withdrawal, aptly captures the Bellegarde world, a world, Newman thinks, so immutably decreed and so "closed." The coldness of Urbain de Bellegarde is seen in his "good wishes" that "seemed to flutter down on him [Newman] from the cold upper air with the soft, scattered movement of a shower of snowflakes," and the coldness of the entire "ancien régime" is expressed in Newman's feeling that everyone in the Bellegarde drawing room looked at him "with that fraudulent intensity of good society which puts out its bountiful hand but keeps the fingers closed over the coin."

In the last analysis, the new world very surely surpasses the old in *The American.* Newman wins out, in our eyes, over the Bellegardes, because his manners reveal the essence of his nature to be magnanimity, whereas theirs reveal selfish egoism at the core. James himself felt an imbalance in the contrast he had drawn − a too static representation of the French, he said. Yet, if American frankness decisively bests French poise in this instance, the book credits and debits *both* sides.

The earlier books of James set the pattern, then, for his dissection of the "haut monde." The subjects — opposing sets of manners,[12] the problems of the across-the-seas marriage,[13] and the conflict between natural and artificial "nobility" — are posed, and the technique is established. One observes the weapons in his literary arsenal: the neat structure and the consistent point of view, the believable characterization (the graceful but morally chilly grand-seigneur Europeans versus the angularly provincial yet upright and spontaneous Yankees), the realistic atmosphere (a world of resort hotels, comfortable apartments of "soigné" expatriates, splendid sights, and the social routine of teas, receptions, and promenades), and the suitable style (with its Austenish tang in the easy conversation — the direct and laconic New Englanders contrasting with the more verbally complicated and figurative Europeans — and satiric aphorisms — "nothing exceeds like the license occasionally taken by the imagination of very rigid people"). It is particularly by means of his graphic painting of social types, his precise notations of setting, and his facile style that James lends conviction to his treatment of the topic of internationalism.

The stream of fiction flowing from James's pen in the 1880s and subsequent decades gives abundant evidence of his continued preoccupation with the international contrast. The "middle" and "late phase" works again set up distinctions between European aplomb and American seriousness, between landed gentry and arriviste types, between the socially adroit and the socially anxious. In these works, however, he goes well beyond the social surface and offers a more significant analysis of the manners-morals problems lying beneath the surface. Such an analysis involves not only the historian of manners, but the psychologist, the civilized mind, and the profound moralist as well — all the qualities that give to James his well-deserved reputation.

That "rich study of men, manners and morals on two continents,"[14] *The Portrait of a Lady* (1881), is a case in point. Examining the cosmopolitan theme with consummate skill and penetration, James lends new depth to his study of the "American young girl abroad." His transatlantic vision, heretofore seen primarily in terms of comedy or pathos, now becomes tinged with the tragic, as New World "romanticism" founders upon the hard realities of the Old World, as the protagonist's "free spirit" and "vital energy" are fettered by the European sense of form.

The plight of the heroine is outlined through the marriage issue. Isabel Archer rejects as suitors Lord Warburton, who would be too safe and easy, Caspar Goodwood, who would subject her to a dull environment, and Ralph Touchett, who is too ill, as well as being more nearly a brother than a lover. She accepts Gilbert Osmond, who, ironically enough, in the end limits her freedom the most. A deceitful and egotistic dilettante, he has "collected" her as a "portrait" of a superior "lady" and is prepared, if possible, to kill her spirit, to grind her in the mill of convention. Isabel, her innocence destroyed when she realizes what her deliberate choice has brought her, faces a not-very-happy existence, but at least she has learned to know herself.

The growth of awareness of the heroine is carried out against an international background, with the individuals who people that background contributing to the "growth." James focuses here, as always, on character in developing his American-European legend. One of those who "educates" Isabel is Mrs. Touchett. Her influence proves largely negative, however, for she does not offer an example of contented expatriation. Mrs. Touchett has left America behind and pokes fun at American types, like Henrietta Stackpole and Isabel's sisters and brother-in-law. Yet she shows little respect for the people in whose countries she now lives. the British and the Italians. If equipped with intelligence and worldliness, she has lost her American freshness and has become too involved in social forms and punctiliousness. As James says, when she objects to Isabel's traveling to London alone, "like many ladies of her country who have lived a long time in Europe, she had completely lost her native tact on such points, and in her reaction, not in itself deplorable, against the liberty allowed to young persons beyond the seas, had fallen into gratuitous and exaggerated scruples."Mrs. Touchett often seems to make the worst of both worlds.

Her husband, on the other hand, has adapted much more skillfully to an environmental transplanting and lives happily in his gracious English home, while retaining his Vermont forthrightness and solidity. Their son Ralph likewise displays a civilized sweetness, which the social atmosphere of Europe would seem to have encouraged. His taste and perception are strong, his sympathies developed, his spirit humane.

The other American expatriates in the novel fare less satisfactorily than the Touchett men and are indeed a rather "wretched set of people." Ned Rosier, the collector of "bibelots," must be dismissed as attractive but weak, and the same might be said about the girl he loves, Pansy Osmond. Brought up entirely in Europe, Pansy is a "made" personality (with a "finish not wholly artless"), winsome, likable, but without spirit. Her aunt, the Countess Gemini, can barely be given even a qualified endorsement, her surface glitter failing to mask her amoral and frivolous nature.

The more major characters, Mme. Merle and her onetime lover Gilbert Osmond, represent the moral corruption that often lies hidden under an appearance of taste and social elegance. The former, a flexible, useful, ripe, "final" expatriate, but too perfectly the social animal, appeals to Isabel greatly at first (though not to the more worldly Ralph Touchett, who sees her as "too complete"), but the shady side of her character is gradually exposed — her materialistic concerns (when Isabel inherits a fortune, Mme. Merle's reaction — "clever creature" — gives her away), her failure to keep promises, her "different morality." Isabel comes to sense in her "values gone wrong, or, as they said at the shops, marked down." Since she is left with nothing at the end of the novel, the reader does feel a touch of pity. None is extended, though, to her partner in deceit, Gilbert Osmond. Devious from the first, he has pursued Isabel solely for her money and as an ornament to his drawing room. Describable as a sterile egoist, one whose greatest success comes, he feels, in "not attempting," he leads a selfish, negative existence. Ironically, he does not deserve the man-without-social-identity label that Isabel would apply to him, his life being a matter of forms and ritualized attitudes. "I am convention itself," he tells Isabel, but, alas, she doesn't take him at his word. Even his "adorable taste" may be called into question, thus leaving him with nothing other than a presentably social manner to recommend him. A fabricated surface does not hide his essential vacuity.

Those characters who retain their native flavor on the whole appear to better advantage in *The Portrait of a Lady*. Lord Warburton, is slightly dull, yet stands as the prototype of the English nobleman at his best, impressive in appearance, considerate of others, concerned about his responsibilities. The much more lively Henrietta Stackpole, an American journalist, may be too extremely "American" (James himself felt her to be "over-treated"), too brash and pushy and suspicious (Isabel, Henrietta warns, must not marry one of those "fell Europeans"), but she is not so set an individual that she can't learn, and indeed her manners improve and her personality grows less idiosyncratic as the novel progresses. The other reasonably prominent American character, Caspar Goodwood, does not similarly modify his nature, but his "type" has merits — those of energy, manliness, and shrewdness. To be sure, he lacks imagination and a broad viewpoint, knowing all about business but less about love and far less about European museums, galleries, parks, and cathedrals.

Throughout the novel the focus remains on the heroine, of course, that "particularly engaging young woman" setting out to "conquer" Europe. Given her intelligence and sensitivity, Isabel Archer is destined to react positively to the high civilization before her, and her experience of Europe is not invalidated even if it includes a disastrous marriage. Isabel was almost certain to make mistakes, for, along with her spirit, charm, and finish (at least, as compared with Daisy Miller), she exhibits too romantic a nature and too large a share of self-importance (when she is called exceptional, she demurs, but really thinks there is considerable truth in the appellation) as well. But she learns about herself from her mistake, as she learns exteriorly from observation of Continental culture, and when one adds this increased perception to her always firm moral code (she "thinks much of promises"), he finds the sum to be a thoroughly attractive and sympathetic young woman. Her plight in being allied to an idle, even villainous, expatriate thus moves him the more.

The Portrait of a Lady "places" its characters precisely in their world, that of the old countries, a continuing spectacle of "society." The various dwellings described in the novel assist in conveying an impression of the social sphere, for example, Gardencourt, the gracious and open house of the Touchetts, set down in very pleasant countryside. The nearby home of Lord Warburton is similarly attractive, though far more baronial — almost as a "castle in a legend" — nobly proportioned and elaborately festooned with antiques and tapestries. Gilbert Osmond's Florentine villa is strewn with antiques and tapestries, too, but — even if not so cluttered as Ned Rosier's bibelots-dotted apartment — it gives off an almost too precious effect. Such a domicile seems to suggest stagnation as well as refinement.[15]

James thus delineates, in *The Portrait,* both the charm and the threat of European high manners, both the glamor and the seediness of the Continental scene. In exposing the characters who populate this scene, he remains more dispassionate, one feels, than in his earlier work, for, despite his obvious affection for his American heroine, he this time avoids the note of stridency, which one may detect in *The American,* in drawing his Old World-New World contrast.

For a time in mid-career James turned away from the international theme, but, even when he did, he did not forsake the question of manners. In all his work, it has been said, "life is primarily a social matter,"[16] and, since manners meant for James the crystallization of *social* experience, in which moral and aesthetic values met, he really could not escape the topic; it was all in all.

His three climactic novels, *The Wings of the Dove* (1902), *The Ambassadors* (1903), and *The Golden Bowl* (1904), decisively illustrate his continued focus on the manners-morals interconnections in social life. At the same time they return the reader to the international format. The "tragi-comedy of manners" is once again to be played out on the European stage, with Americans as key figures. As before, differences among the principal characters stem from their differing social backgrounds, and the strength of the surface, the importance of preserving good manners, is not to be forgotten. Life is perpetually seen by James as an adventure in the social world, and thus the importance of traditions (good if they represent the free expression of spirit), conventions, and stable social relationships cannot be minimized.

In these three novels, however, cultural differences between the New and Old Worlds clearly become secondary to moral problems. James's later protagonists all wrestle with such problems. It is worth noting, too, that, in their struggles, they take more fully into account the complexity of society — recognizing, for example, evil as an ineradicable condition of life anywhere — and do not remain, not even Milly Theale, in so "dislocated" a state after their European experience as had the earlier heroes and heroines.

At first glance *The Wings of the Dove* seems to follow a previously employed Jamesian formula, the American girl who ventures abroad with high hopes, only to have them blighted by a dismal reality. The beautiful and wealthy, but mysteriously ill, Milly Theale travels in Europe, accompanied by a companion — Susan Shepherd Stringham from Burlington, Vermont and Boston. Mrs. Stringham, a refined Henrietta Stackpole, having been educated abroad and therefore considering herself worldly and knowledgeable (five years in the "embalmed Europe" of her "younger time" had firmly convinced her that she was a "woman of the world"), is prepared to introduce Milly to the charms of Europe. In England they encounter a polished but shabby crowd, the entourage of wealthy Mrs. Lowder (the "terribly hard English gang," Howells called them). The group includes such as Kate Croy, Merton Densher, Lord Mark, and Lady Aldershaw, the latter rather representative in being "not fresh, for not young, but she was vivid and much bejewelled for the midsummer daylight; and she was all in the palest pinks and blues." Thus surrounded by "every English accessory," Milly is thoroughly intrigued. Though by no means unintelligent, she is essentially innocent, and therefore remains for a long time unaware of the various deceits and selfishnesses that lie beneath the "perfect manners" of her new companions. When she at length realizes their machinations (chiefly, the

Kate-Densher scheme to secure her fortune), she suffers disillusionment so severe that she loses her will to live. This, combined with her physical malady, brings about her death. Her bequeathing her money to one who has deceived her, Merton Densher, demonstrates, however, the goodness that has survived her disillusionment. Milly the "dove" has "stretched out her wings and they cover us," as Kate Croy reports, her influence lingering and notably affecting Densher, who will, in effect, reject the inheritance, thus endorsing the American valuation of spirit.

If American idealism wins out again over European "corruptness" — best described, in this instance, as English empiricism — yet the issue is not quite so clear-cut as it has been in earlier fictions. The Americans, for one thing, have their limitations (Susan Stringham's "civilization" is a "sometime thing"), and, conversely, the British have their distinctions. James admires Kate Croy's intelligence and "talent for living," as he also admires Densher's exquisite taste and his ultimate humaneness. He even credits Mrs. Lowder and Lord Mark with good intentions, and he appreciates the "air," the "pitch," the "tone," demonstrated by all. Social codes, as manifested in "proper" marriages, James seems to feel, cannot be ignored; in making her will, Milly Theale overlooks the social intrigue that has caused her death — evil is an ineluctable condition — and recognizes the inevitability of "practicality," always vying to some degree with moral righteousness.

The Wings of the Dove, like the earlier tales, makes much of backgrounds in order to give density to the social picture. The novel opens in the Chirk Street flat of Kate Croy's impoverished father, a place of shabby sofas, sallow prints, a small lamp in colored glass, and a knitted white centerpiece wanting in freshness. Comparable in dinginess is the home of Kate's sister Marian Condrip, who has made an unfortunate marriage and has consequently sunk to a vulgar little dwelling in Chelsea. No wonder that Kate lingers, as a companion to her aunt, Mrs. Lowder, in the "tall, rich, heavy house at Lancaster Gate." If decidedly philistine (Densher finds the gilt and glass, satin and plush, rosewood, marble, and malachite "gregariously ugly"), Lancaster Gate represents solid wealth and ranks immeasurably higher on the social scale than the Croy ménages. Higher still one takes to be the country estate of Matcham, a great historic house that has, "as the center of an almost extravagantly grand Watteau-composition, a tone as of old gold kept 'down' by the quality of the air, summer full-flushed, but attuned to the general perfect taste," and equally grand is the Palazzo Leporelli, the Venetian palace rented by Milly, a place of high, florid rooms and palatial chambers with painted "subjects" in the splendid ceilings. Such a romantic setting provides a perfect "home" for Milly — just as for Kate, who "saw how material things spoke to her," massive Lancaster Gate seems the only natural habitat.

Through character vignettes, too, James creates his social sphere. We progress from Lionel Croy, all pink and silver as to skin and hair, straitness and starch as to figure and dress, "so particularly the English gentleman" in appearance, but so poor and so deceitful that he has been dropped by his clubs and indeed by all the "world." Equally the gentleman — "a longish, leanish, fairish young Englishman" — is Merton Densher, but his position in the "world" remains, because of his want of means, precarious. Thoroughly assured, on the other hand, are such figures as Lord Mark, "seasoned and saturated," and the accomplished physician Sir Luke Strett, "large and settled," looking half like a general and half like a bishop. The feminine contingent reflects variety, too, including such as Marian Condrip, a "ragged relic," and, in contrast, her prosperous aunt, Mrs. Lowder, "all brilliant gloss, perpetual satin, twinkling bugles and flashing gems," one who is "vulgar with freshness, almost with beauty." In between stands Mrs. Lowder's other niece, Kate Croy, handsome, intelligent, and, above all, "made for great social uses," one who always lived up, but especially at festal hours, to the "value" Mrs. Lowder attached to her. Milly Theale, the novel's protagonist, serves as Kate's foil, equally lovely, equally bright, equally charming, but, despite her "big house, her big fortune, her big freedom," quite unworldly and quite upright, the American "princess" but also the "dove."

Throughout the novel the sense of the social order is maintained, in part by James's use of phrases such as "social situation," "social man," "social atlas," in part by his reproduction of the patterns of the Continental environment. The design includes a Bohemian fringe (parties given at art galleries and including Spanish dancers, American reciters, Hungarian fiddlers), forlorn individuals like Kate Croy's mother, who repeatedly retreated to Dresden, to Florence, to Biarritz, in a "weak and expensive attempt at economy," and accomplished servants such as the majordomo Eugenio, whom Milly hires in Venice, as suave and tactful as a "residuary legatee." The atmosphere displays a high gloss, a "concert pitch" of smartness and urbanity, of culture as exhibited in conversations strewn with references to Bronzino, Maeterlinck, and Veronese, of "county aristocracy" refinement.

The Wings, written in James's "late" manner, is weighted and complex in its style, but this style, in its employment of dextrous turns, vivid imagery, and symbolic suggestions, carries a flavor appropriate to its material. Sometimes succinctly (Marian Condrip's marriage as a "kind of spiritless turning of the other cheek to fortune"), sometimes elaborately (the nineteen-line sentences), James unfolds his tale.

The similes abound: Mrs. Lowder steers a course in which she calls at subjects as if they were islets in an archipelago, then resumes, with a splash of her screw, her cruise among the islands; the Bishop of Murrum has a voice like an old-fashioned wind instrument; the Venetian air was like a clap of hands, and the scattered pinks, yellows, blues, sea-greens, were like a hanging-out of vivid stuffs. So, too, do the foreign phrases and the symbolic hints. Of particular interest in the latter connection is the juxtaposition of Kate, the "panther," who dresses impeccably but with considerable ornamentation, with Milly the "dove," who wears black ("so little superstitiously in the fashion") or white, set off only with rows of pearls. Social glamor and decay oppose simple taste and freshness, as the unencumbered spirit learns from the European social machine yet remains uncontaminated by it.

In *The Ambassadors* James momentarily forsakes his young-lady protagonist in favor of a man, and an older one at that, but the process of "education" is similar. Lewis Strether, in pursuance of the author's plot scheme, is dispatched to Paris by matriarchal Mrs. Newsome on a mission to rescue her son Chad from the clutches of a designing French woman and to return him to safe and sound and "moral" Woollett, Massachusetts. However, in the atmosphere of amoral but charming Paris, Strether expands, loses his provinciality, reorients from Woollett and an essentially deadening tradition, and discovers how much an American may profit from association with European culture. Not that he, finally, discards the moral absolutism of Woollett in favor of the amoral secularism of Paris. Rather, he learns that one can be free *and* virtuous, thus having the best of both worlds and avoiding the worst, the immorality and rigidity. The important thing is to "live," and test ethical dimensions, and to learn that moral sufficiency should perhaps override moral seriousness.

In order to place before the reader the merits and defects of the two systems, Woollett's abstemious puritanism and Paris's casual laxity, James contrasts American and European ways throughout the book, utilizing, as he has before, character juxtapositions (the "subtly civilized" Maria Gostrey vs. the suspicious traveler Waymarsh, the French "jeune fille," Marie de Vionnet, vs. the American, Sarah Pocock), setting,[17] and a high style, marked by an appropriate image patterning and by an epigrammatic cast. The assessment of man as a social being, the unfolding in all its implications of the impact of Europe upon Lewis Strether, is a very artful performance.

The third in James's "major phase" trio, *The Golden Bowl*, clearly qualifies as a "cosmopolitan" novel. It is also, according to Leon Edel, James's "supreme novel of manners."[18] Certainly social forms loom large in the book, and its thesis seems to be that they can, in the last analysis, work for good ends. If society presents sinister aspects, it also includes commendable ones; both its good and bad must be recognized and accepted, and the social ideal of harmony promoted.

The Golden Bowl relates the activities of a quartet of major characters, Maggie Verver, Prince Amerigo, Charlotte Stant, and Adam Verver, though focusing on the first of these — the young-American-girl motif again. This time the girl clearly grows up, Maggie Verver emerging from her all-but-fatal attachment for her father and winning back her husband, Prince Amerigo, from Charlotte. This is too bluntly put, of course, the shifting relationships among the four principals being explored with typical Jamesian subtlety — the author's primary purpose being to stress Maggie's accommodating to evil, learning to love people for their good and bad together.

The international contrast is drawn once more, expatriate Charlotte Stant and the Italian nobleman standing off against

Maggie and her father, and, as usual, the European side is long on taste, the American, on principle. The Prince states it figuratively: "Your moral sense works by steam. . . . ours is slow and steep and unlighted, with so many of the steps missing . . . not a 'lightning elevator.' " One sees in Charlotte Stant intelligence, poise, a sense of ensemble — her clothes "were simply the most charming and interesting that any woman had ever put on" — also ruthlessness and flexible morals. One sees in Prince Amerigo amenity, gracefulness, social finish — also ambiguity and flexible morals. On the other hand, Mr. Verver is, to quote his son-in-law, the "best man I've ever seen" magnanimous and idealistic. He is not without his social shortcomings, however, tending, as a successful businessman, to judge so much by material standards that his powers of discrimination are somewhat muted. His homes seem opulent, too opulent (in Portland Place he "had pitched a tent suggesting that of Alexander furnished with the spoils of Darius"); even his celebrated art collection appears to have been assembled as much with the market value of the objects in mind as with their artistic merit. His daughter Maggie, equally generous and romantic, is at the same time more filled with social presence than her father. Yet she by no means measures up in "world-quality" to Charlotte and Amerigo. Somewhat uneasy as a hostess, rather timorous about her clothes, she appears to such as the socially aware Colonel Assingham as "very nice, but . . . more than anything else, the young woman who has a million a year."

Surrounding the principals, James places other characters who firmly belong to the upper-class milieu he is once again manufacturing for us. His "ficelle" in this novel, Fanny Assingham, is a wonderfully adroit American expatriate. "New York had been, recordedly, her birthplace and 'Europe' punctually her discipline." She serves as the "doyenne" of her transplanted tribe, the quite large group of American girls who have made foreign marriages. Others on the "big London stage" include such as Lady Castledean, mistress of Matcham and owner of "the biggest diamonds on the yellowest hair, the longest lashes on the prettiest, falsest eyes, the oldest lace on the most violet velvet, the rightest manner on the wrongest assumptions."

These people attend, in town, "large, bright, dull, murmurous, mild-eyed, middle-aged dinners," and make leisurely country visits at Matcham or Fawns, occasionally resorting, for variety, to places such as Brighton when the season is, "in local parlance, 'on'" — a town of big, windy hotels and swarming with "types." Always the business of social representation goes blithely on, and one is aware of the Almanach de Gotha, the best shops, the best hotels, the best servants — all the accoutrements of this polished world.

Again the style accompanying the picture seems harmonious. The sentences flow elaborately but precisely on (Mr. Verver's "easy way with his millions had taxed to such small purpose, in the arrangements, the principle of reciprocity"), filled with interrupting phrases, with foreign terms, with deftly placed adverbs and adjectives. The images emerge from the scene naturally,[19] as in this instance: "There was a long moment, absolutely, during which her impression rose and rose, even as that of the typical charmed gazer, in the still museum, before the named and dated object, the pride of the catalogue, that time has polished and consecrated." They often have symbolic value as well, as the keeping to the fore of the Verver wealth by means of gold and gilded images. The phrasing, when not figurative, is often sharply epigrammatic, the Jamesian vocabulary sparkling. Inversions and ellipses are often employed, providing the halting cadence that conversation (and very much of the book is dialogue — a characteristic of the novel-of-manners format) normally has.

While making the familiar American-European distinction in this the last of his precisely cosmopolitan novels, James no longer goes so far as to suggest that the New World must reform the Old. He seems to feel that the human situation itself produces the intense moral evil in the world, that America as well as Europe is couched in moral error, that American as well as European characters are flawed. One must hope for the eventual perpetuation of good in both worlds, for the coinciding of the social and moral ideals. Moral corruption may be hidden under the decor of art and social form, says James finally, but the decor also reveals the moral significance of style, beauty, and order. James envisaged his international dramas — at least, his later ones — in basically impartial terms.

NOTES TO CHAPTER 3

1. Christof Wegelin, "The Rise of the International Novel," *PMLA* 77 (June 1962): 30. Wegelin cites R. B. Mowat, *Americans in England* (Cambridge, Mass.: Houghton Mifflin Co., 1935, as his source.

2. Walter F. Wright, *The Madness of Art: A Study of Henry James* (Lincoln, Neb.: University of Nebraska Press, 1962), p. 10.

3. See ibid., p. 11. Wright says, "Gilbert Osmond and Madame Merle . . . have been cited as examples of persons with excellent manners and wretched morals. Actually, all that James credited to each was a limited discernment in esthetics and a wish to conform in conventional standards. Osmond's manners are, in reality, execrable."

4. Wright Morris, *The Territory Ahead* (New York: Harcourt, Brace & Co., 1958), p. 195.

5. R. W. Emerson, "Manners," included in *Essays*, second series (Boston and New York: Houghton, Mifflin & Co., 1856), p. 120.

6. A. N. Kaul, *The American Vision* (New Haven and London: Yale University Press, 1963), p.65.

7. The critics and readers who have complained of the narrowness of this world (cf. "James had to represent life from the narrowest base that any major novelist has ever had, with only one toe on the ground," [J. B. Priestley, *Literature and Western Man* (New York: Harper & Bros., 1960), p. 361]) should remember that James firmly believed in writing of what one knew, in deliberately tethering one's self in his own backyard.

8. Oscar Cargill, *The Novels of Henry James* (New York: The Macmillan Company, 1961), pp. 46-47.

9. James echoes here a note sounded earlier by Catharine Maria Sedgwick, the tendency on the part of the aristocratic set to relegate the artistic group to a social limbo.

10. Leon Edel cites the Jamesian comment, "An aristocracy is bad manners organized," an observation stemming from his having discovered certain members of the British upper classes to be guilty of rudeness and arrogance (Leon Edel, ed., *Henry James: A Collection of Critical Essays* [Englewood Cliffs, N.J.: Prentice-Hall, Inc., 1963], p. 176).

11. Some years before the publication of the novel James had written of the need for fighting against such a valuation. See Christof Wegelin, *The Image of Europe in Henry James* (Dallas, Tex.: Southern Methodist University Press, 1958), p. 3.

12. An interestingly offbeat example is the story "The Siege of London" (1883), in which an American divorcee from the Far West overcomes the seemingly insuperable handicap of this background to find a place in London society simply on the grounds of her accomplishments as an "American humorist."

13. The American quest for coronets and the coronets' quest for dollars, says Christof Wegelin. See Wegelin, "The Rise of the International Novel," p. 30.

14. Leon Edel, *Henry James,* University of Minnesota Pamphlets on American Writers, no. 4 (Minneapolis, Minn.: University of Minnesota Press, 1960), p. 7.

15. Blanche Gelfant reminds us of how, to James — as to Edith Wharton — "a house projects an individual's social class and personal taste as well as his moral sensibility" (Blanche H. Gelfant, "Beyond Nihilism: The Fiction of George P. Elliott," *The Hollins Critic* 5 [December 1968]: 8).

16. Wright, *The Madness of Art,* p. 244.

17. If the constricting environment of the small Massachusetts town of Woollett is but passingly suggested, its opposite, sophisticated, lively, urbane Paris, is most fully described, the city serving as a pervasive presence in the novel.

18. Edel, *Henry James,* p. 32.

19. Most Jamesian fiction contains imagery peculiarly appropriate to the "tweed-and-waterproof" upper classes he is describing. *The Tragic Muse* (1890), for example, is filled with references to garden-parties, private theatricals, tennis-lawns, and the like. In this respect, as in so many others, James serves as a model for his successors.

4

William Dean Howells

*H*ENRY James's good friend and confrere, William Dean
Howells, might well be said to share with him the
appellation "early master of the novel of manners."[1] Insistence on social distinction and on the preservation of the
"forms" provides the note of social comedy that runs throughout so much of Howell's fiction, just as it does — somewhat
less friskily — throughout that of James. Even the theme of
the international contrast, so familiar to the reader from the
latter's work, can be found in Howells at an equally early
date.

Both writers were anticipated, as seen above, by a number
of other authors in the utilization of social themes (e.g.,
Cooper's contrasting the Littlepage landowners with the
"getting-on" Jason Newcomes), but certainly the popular-
izing of the genre was accomplished by James and Howells,
and the contributions of both have been far more notable
than those of their predecessors. Their concentration on the

"parlor-game" has been more intense, their accounts of social advancement or regression more incisive, their styles infinitely more accomplished as they have surveyed the social scene.

Differences in emphasis may, to be sure, be discerned in their approaches to the topic. James lingered far longer on the international scene than did Howells, who chose this as his foreground only occasionally. Again, although each author functions as a "Demonstrator of the American Girl," James prefers to juxtapose his young lady from Schenectady with the European nobleman or American expatriate, whereas Howells will contrast the provincial young lady from Eriecreek with the Boston socialite. Howells, more suspicious than James of the injustices and depravities of, for him, still faintly feudalistic Europe, attaches a rather strong note of "alienation" to the living-abroad experience and usually confines his discussions of the rites of "civilization" to home grounds.

It was natural for Howells to stress to a greater degree than James the "young man from the provinces" theme, since he himself was a small-town boy from Ohio. Having been brought up in rural, almost frontierlike, surroundings and in an easy, democratic society, he possessed memories of a childhood far different from that of James with his cosmopolitan, upperclass background. Howells never forgot his early environment and was inclined to measure and remeasure it against the urban, less democratic world he later came to know. More than one of his characters hailed from "Des Vaches, Indiana" and served as a Christopher Newman-like protagonist in this or that fiction, standing for the homely virtues, for the "simplest and purest and kindest" life that is "the highest civilization."[2]

Howells left the Middle West behind him when he was still in his early twenties. His first stop of any permanence thereafter, Venice, represented a giant step. In this perpetually fascinating city he resided for four years, serving as the

American consul there. These "Venetian days" equipped him, early in the game, with an "international" point of view, permitting him to observe contrasting cultures, and then to make literary capital of these observations. Travel books such as *Venetian Life* (1866)[3] and Venetian-set novels of manners *A Foregone Conclusion* (1874), *The Lady of the Aroostook* (1879), and *A Fearful Responsibility* (1881) convey the charm of an older, more sophisticated civilization while at the same time not forgetting to note the freshness of the younger culture on the other side of the Atlantic.

His tour of duty as a consul completed in 1865, Howells returned to America. Plunging directly into the magazine world, he first occupied himself with the editorship of the *Atlantic Monthly* in Boston, then, fifteen years later, with the editorship of *Harper's Monthly* in New York. In Boston he was quickly accepted, despite the fact that he was a "foreigner" from the hinterlands of Ohio. The city's Brahmins welcomed him into the fold — Longfellow issuing the cherished invitation to a Dante Evening at Craigie House — and he thereafter moved in proper circles, the "academics," in New England at least, having their place in the social sun. Again Howells made literary profit of the experience, drawing, in such novels as *A Chance Acquaintance* (1873) and *The Rise of Silas Lapham* (1885), a contrast between the aristocratic Bostonian and the individual from fresh-water, up-country regions.

After his move to New York, though increasingly involved in such concerns as spreading the doctrines of literary realism and defending socialist politics, Howells continued to deal, in his fiction, with problems of manners and conflicting social patterns, as such works as *Indian Summer* (1886), *April Hopes* (1888), *Their Silver Wedding Journey* (1899), *The Kentons* (1902), and *The Vacation of the Kelwyns* (1920) testify. Much of the stock-in-trade of the novelist of manners

— focus on a segment of society, the excessive reliance on dialogue and "good talk," the employment of a precise and witty style,[4] the exact depiction of background — found its way into his writing from the beginning to the end of his literary career.

Several of Howells's early novels explore the problem of social relationships and reflect the author's amused recognition of the presence of social distinctions in a society that does not like to admit their presence. American women are epitomized, Howells suggests, in Isabel March of *Their Wedding Journey* (1871), who is "in principle democratic enough" but "a bitter aristocrat at heart." American men, represented by Isabel's husband Basil, may be less sentimental, yet they too sense, if not always approve of, class barriers. Basil March readily recognizes the difference between the "man of sudden gains" and the "smoother rich man of inherited wealth," granting the latter's more elevated status. He also recognizes, however, the latter's shortcomings:

> There was something pleasanter in the face of the hereditary aristocrat, but not so strong, nor, altogether, so admirable; particularly if you reflected that he really represented nothing in the world, no great culture, no political influence, no civic aspiration, not even a pecuniary force, nothing but a social set, an alien club-life, a tradition of dining. [Pp. 68-69]

Their Wedding Journey is sprinkled with such reflections on class, together with comments on varying modes of living (the New Yorker differing from the Bostonian, and both from the Canadian), with deft sketches of character and amusing bits of conversation. It all adds up to a pastiche rather than a novel — as Howells disarmingly admits at the beginning[5] — but is of interest in its gentle satire on human foibles ("And having begun, they did not stop till they had taken their friends to pieces. Dismayed, then, they hastily reconstructed them . . . ") and in its introduction of the Marches, a charming couple — Mr. and Mrs. Howells thinly disguised, one senses — who frequently crop up in the author's later fiction.[6]

A Chance Acquaintance functions very much as a sequel to *Their Wedding Journey*. Though the Marches retire from the center of the stage, their place is taken by a couple remarkably similar, Colonel and Mrs. Richard Ellison, and the journey framework, mostly within the environs of Quebec, is sustained. The novel is devoted, too, to continued commentary about the modes of social intercourse and to witty badinage about variant social usages.

Actually, attention in the novel focuses not on the Colonel and his wife, but on their young relative Kitty Ellison and her "chance acquaintance" Miles Arbuton, the ill-fated love affair between whom provides the book with its "story." The affair goes awry — realist Howells will not necessarily allow a happy ending — because of the marked discrepancy in the background of the hero and heroine. Kitty, an attractive, Daisy Millerish girl, is immediately drawn to the handsome, if stiff, Mr. Arbuton, as is he to her, but each feels oppressed or bewildered by the other's antecedents. About the little town in upper New York State from which Kitty comes, Arbuton can only vaguely surmise. "Milwaukee [the home of the "westerner" Ellisons] was bad enough, though he understood that it was largely peopled from New England and had a great German element, which might account for the fact that there people were not quite barbaric. But this Eriecreek, New York State!" Ruefully, Mr. Arbuton brought "his fancy to bear upon Eriecreek and wholly failed to conceive of it." Kitty naturally resents so narrow a point of view and is disturbed by his "exclusiveness," by his, for example, snubbing her acquaintances the Marches because they live in Boston's South End rather than on Beacon Hill. She is bothered not only by his seeming "alien" to her, but also by his seeming to stand for ideas of which she must express disapproval. So snobbish is he that he talks about the lower classes and tradesmen and the best people and good families "as I supposed nobody in *this* country *ever* did." "He seems," she says, reflecting on his inflexibility, "to have lived in a world where everything is regulated by some rigid law that it would be death to break. . . . seems to judge people according to their origin and locality and calling and to believe that all refinement must come from just such training and circumstances as his own."

The egalitarian Kitty objects to such narrowness,[7] yet she finds redeeming qualities in Arbuton and, almost in spite of herself, accepts his affection and his proposal of marriage. They grow "better strangers," she whimsically says, yet they are irresistibly attracted to each other. Their engagement is broken almost as soon as it is entered into, however, for Arbuton, in a key incident, does not introduce Kitty to two Boston ladies whom they meet while sightseeing. She sensibly recognizes that she could not be happy with a husband who would thus keep her snubbed and frightened after he had lifted her from her "lowly sphere." Besides, she wants nothing to do with Arbuton's Boston. It does not correspond with her family's ideal image of Boston as the sacred city of antislavery heroes and martyrs, nor with the easy, sympathetic Boston of Mr. and Mrs. March.

This new Boston with which Mr. Arbuton inspired her was a Boston of mysterious prejudices and lofty reservations; a Boston of high and difficult tastes, that found its social ideal in the Old World, and that shrank from contact with the reality of this; a Boston as alien as Europe to her simple experiences. . . . A Boston that would rather perish by fire and sword than be suspected of vulgarity; a critical, fastidious and reluctant Boston, dissatisfied with the rest of the hemisphere, and gelidly self-satisfied in so far as it was not in the least the Boston of her fond preconceptions. [Pp. 152-53]

Howells will not, in subsequent novels, indict the Boston aristocrat as severely as he does in *A Chance Acquaintance*, and even in this novel a lightness of tone is maintained. One hardly feels that Kitty Ellison's life will be permanently blighted by her rejection of Arbuton — no dying of Roman fever contracted by an ill-timed visit to the Coliseum for her, as for Daisy Miller, rebounding from Winterbourne's confusion, but probably a successful marriage to a person less "formed" than Arbuton. Meanwhile, Howells has had a good time commmenting on the complacently rigid Bostonian, and on the foibles of mankind generally ("who can deny that the cut, color, texture, stylish set of dresses has not had everything to do with the rapture of love's young dream?").

In his next novel, *A Foregone Conclusion*, Howells makes a tentative exploration of a new locale, the European environment, and continues the exploration in *The Lady of the Aroostook* and *A Fearful Responsibility*. Substituting Venetian palazzi for Quebec boarding houses and masked balls for picnics on the plains of Abraham, he offers a more "foreign" setting, and one that he obviously found charming. The novels also introduce new types of individuals, such as the American expatriate, the European gentleman, and the American-jeune-fille-abroad. If these characters remain, in some instances, decidedly pallid, and if the novels as a whole contain only a modest measure of the customary Howells wit, the books do produce some interesting contrasts between Continental and American mores.

The international theme is most fully developed in *The Lady of the Aroostook*, this despite the fact that only the last quarter of the novel has a European locale. The larger portion of the story takes place aboard ship and contrasts opposing Amcrican types rather than Americans versus Europeans. In both instances the issue is one of conflicting social customs.

The heroine of the novel, Lydia Blood, comes, like Kitty Ellison, from a small village (South Bradfield, Massachusetts) and is consequently untutored in the ways of the world, if at the same time possessed of native intelligence, innate good taste, and firm values. The latter qualities will always stand her in good stead, of course, but cannot altogether compensate for her "country cousin" upbringing, and thus Lydia will have her ups and downs when she ventures into the "great world."

Lydia has first the ordeal of the voyage across the Atlantic to survive, an ordeal since she happens to be the only woman on board ship, and since she, as such, is subjected to much speculative comment on the part of her fellow passengers, notably two attractive but almost too sophisticated young Bostonians. Despite a natural freedom of manner that startles them, she wins their respect, and, in fact, the love of one.

She is further tested during her stay in Venice when confronted by Europeanized Americans like Mrs. Erwin, as well as by worldly-wise Venetians, all very different from the inhabitants of South Bradfield. If she makes mistakes through her innocence (e.g., going about the city alone, or speaking too frankly), yet her homespun virtues support her and in the end achieve for her the admiration of the "smart set" around her. Profiting, too, from the new experiences into which she is plunged, she widens her horizons, shifts from the country girl of narrow views to the more polished — but still upright — young lady, and is thus better equipped for marriage with the city-bred James Staniford — who, of course, has meanwhile learned from her.

In telling Lydia Blood's story, Howells concentrates on delineating the effects of a removal from one society to another, first positing rural-urban distinctions, then the larger American-European contrasts. The former barrier, that between town and country, is broken down here, as it was not in *A Chance Acquaintance*. If James Staniford, possessing a slightly warped sense of convention and more than enough snobbery, at first does not appreciate Lydia's spontaneity and innocence, he comes to his senses quite quickly, forgets his surface propriety, and seeks her hand in marriage, humbly ignoring his superior background. Win her he does, but it is worth noting that they plan to settle in California, not in Boston.

The international barrier can be less easily surmounted than the regional one. Expatriated Englishmen like Mr. Rose-Black and Lady Fenleigh, and natives like Colonel Pazzelli and Miss Landini, seem worlds removed from Miss Lydia Blood in both principles and habits. Most sharply counter-pointed against Lydia is her hostess Mrs. Erwin, herself an American, but corroded, the author makes us feel, from many years of living abroad. Concentrating on "good form" to the exclusion of a moral sense, and having grown deliberately anti-American, Mrs. Erwin hardly seems an ideal mentor. Lydia quietly avoids her precepts, refusing to conform to the Venetian pattern (which permits women to have lovers, young ladies to swear), and preferring the example of Mrs. Erwin's husband, who has retained his "sweet and fine courtesy" and "American sturdiness."

Howells tips the scales in favor of his heroine and her moral standpoint, but, really, not until after he has endeavored to weigh both sides carefully. Lydia's narrowness, for example, her "meteorological patriotism" that makes her prefer the New England to the Italian sky — is scored against her, and, conversely, the charm of Venice, its palaces, its art galleries, its canals, and the grace of some of its inhabitants are highly praised. With something of the Jamesian detachment and with similar wit and urbanity, if not quite a corresponding subtlety, Howells makes his statement about conflicting social situations and about the "education" of the American girl.

In a work that followed close upon *The Lady of the Aroostook, The Rise of Silas Lapham*, Howells created an equally engaging novel — and one that is more clearly indicative of his writing skill. Precise in structure, graphic in its rendering of "place," consistent in tone, and thorough in its delineation of the emergence of a plutocracy in late-nineteenth-century America, with a concomitant modification of the social order, the book undoubtedly deserves its reputation as Howells's best.

Though theoretically devoted to describing the financial fall but moral rise of its protagonist, businessman Lapham, to being, then, a "business" novel, the work contains an important subplot focusing on the manners issue.[8] Repeating the "intramural" contrast between city and country dealt with in *A Chance Acquaintance* and, in part, in *The Lady of the Aroostook*, the novel carefully describes the way of life of the Boston aristocracy, as represented by the Bromfield Coreys, and the quite dissimilar way of life of the Boston plutocracy (newly arrived from Vermont), as represented by the Silas Laphams. The latter experience, initially, a social rise, but this is eventually followed by a social fall, reflected in their return to Vermont at the book's end. The marriage of Penelope Lapham to Tom Corey is not altogether an antidote to this retreat to the farm and consequent blunting of social aspiration; the young Coreys will live in Mexico rather than in Boston.

At the opening of the novel the author makes it clear that the Laphams, despite their recently acquired wealth, have made no social progress in Boston. They live in the South End — from which "society" has long since fled in haste — and they confine their activities to the family circle. With such a locale and with such a routine, they are, at this point, perfectly content. But a fortuitous meeting with members of the Corey family in Canada (and a friendship of sorts, owing to the rendering of a service to the Coreys by Mrs. Lapham) stirs a latent social ambition in Mrs. Lapham, and shortly after their return to Boston she declares to her husband that, if their daughters are to marry in Boston, "we ought to get them into society."

Such an advancement is not impossible. As Old Guardsman Bromfield Corey cynically declares, the suddenly rich are on a level with any of us now; money buys position at once. Corey exaggerates, however. The plutocracy cannot so readily establish itself — and certainly not in Boston. There the aristocracy is entrenched, with generations of taste and refinement and breeding behind it. As Bromfield Corey also says, society is different from good sense and ideas. The Laphams possess these, but these are not enough.

The difference between the two families is crystallized in the book's famous dinner party scene, where the Lapham lack of "civilization" becomes painfully apparent. In the first place, Mrs. Corey has carefully made up her invitation list to include such as Charles Bellingham, a Corey relative and very genteel, but at the same time a man who has "been around" and thus can be trusted to get along with all sorts of "different" people. Meanwhile, the Laphams have been consulting the "etiquette man" with diligence, uncertain about this or that point of protocol. Even so, Silas makes the mistake of wearing gloves — and saffron-tinted ones, in which his hands look like "canvassed hams." These he sheds quickly before any awkwardness results, but Mrs. Lapham cannot so deftly cover up *her* mistake, a failure to notify her hostess in advance that Penelope will not appear at the dinner. She is "at her bluntest, as country people are when embarrassed," in explaining her daughter's absence. Then Silas, unused to wine, gets drunk, talks unceasingly and boastfully ("pours mineral paint" all over Mr. Corey), and generally makes a fool of himself.

Throughout the novel the contrasts between the Coreys and the Laphams are constantly drawn — for example, the grace and beauty and eminently tasteful decor of the Corey home on Beacon Hill versus the unattractive, bric-a-brac-strewn house of the Laphams in the South End[9] — and it is impossible to imagine a thoroughly harmonious relationship between them. Though the Coreys are prepared to accept Penelope Lapham as a daughter-in-law, they can hardly be said to relish the prospect, Mr. Corey dreading the thought of family dinners and Mrs. Lapham's "strictly domestic range of conversation" or Mr. Lapham's equally limited business monologues. Luckily, the Lapham reversal of fortune (and their consequent return to the country) and the departure of the newlyweds for Mexico eliminate the necessity for intimacy. The social gulf, then, is not bridged.

In the character drawing, notably that of Silas Lapham and Bromfield Corey, one sees most vividly the discrepancy between plutocrat and aristocrat, and the impossibility of a smooth union between them. Howells — while, in perfect fairness, showing the virtues and shortcomings of both types — makes them seem, whether on their best or worst behavior, basically irreconcilable one to the other.

Go-getting businessman Silas Lapham has much to recommend him. He is shrewd, thoughtful, affectionate, and essentially upright. At the same time his life, in its single-minded application to the paint business, has not permitted him any time for "gentlemaning." He therefore talks ungrammatically, lacks an aesthetic sense, as evidenced by his willingness to put mineral paint on the scenic rocks around the landscape, distrusts culture (he tells Bromfield Corey that his son's going through college won't hurt him; he'll slough that off), and suspects the elegance of the Bromfield Corey type. Tom Corey sees him as a vulgar, uncouth, gross, stupidly arrogant self-made man. Yet, significantly, Tom Corey retains his faith in and affection for Silas, recognizing the moral firmness and attractive sturdiness underneath the limitations. Tom might have noted, too, that Silas had acquired some social polish — for example, appreciating the good taste of the architect who designs his new house, during his "stay" in Boston — and was no doubt the better for it.

Bromfield Corey, a blend of the Brahmin and proper Bostonian, stands in juxtaposition. He is cultivated, urbane, witty, cosmopolitan, worldly-wise (it is just as easy, says he, to fall in love with a rich girl as a poor one), and smart enough, too, to know the shortcomings of the Boston breed to which he belongs, "a faded tradition." These shortcomings include excessive snobbery, coldness and detachment — their never being much surprised, nor much concerned, about anything. Corey can even show a "delicate, impersonal appreciation" of his son's most unfortunate predicament, that of having Irene Lapham, as well as both the Corey and Lapham families, think he is in love with her rather than with her sister Penelope. Bromfield Corey shrugs away the heartbreak involved and "cuts his orange in the Neapolitan manner." In the long run, Howells suggests to us, Corey's "sterile elegance" does not measure up to Lapham's "stalwart achievement."

Other characters in the novel reinforce the contrast. Mrs. Lapham, a simple country woman, surveys the world from a limited horizon. Mrs. Corey, chilled by her "ancestral halls," is a block of "Wenham ice," pure and rectangular, and lacking in savor; her daughters, too, never look "quite warm enough." The Lapham girls do not thus lack vitality, but they demonstrate the weaknesses of a limited education and a restricted environment. Penelope will make Tom Corey a better wife than her beautiful but dumb sister would, since she is witty and perceptive, but the marriage, Howells forecasts, may have its slightly rough moments. Tom Corey will not always unaerstand his wife, whose background is so very different from his own.[10]

Though Howells is concerned about the moral problem that lies at the root of his story, the shabbiness of business ethics, he devotes so much attention to the social picture and maintains a tone so consistently spiced with mockery that one is more inclined to read *The Rise of Silas Lapham* as a comedy of manners than as an ethical treatise. Part of the book's charm lies in the author's graceful style and in the gentle satire that he bestows on the problems of status, Boston smugness, and parvenu crudity. Shrewd observations are made by Howells on his characters: Bostonians "don't really care what business a man is in, so it is large enough and he doesn't advertise offensively; but we think it fine to affect reluctance." Well-turned phrases abound — "she based her statement upon Nanny's sarcastic demand; and perhaps seeing it topple a little, she rose hastily, to get away from its fall." The symbols are appropriate — the new house as social aspiration, its burning as a purgation. Revelatory actions lend humor as well as define social discrepancy, for example, Colonel Lapham's endeavoring to puzzle out Mrs. Corey's fashionably illegible handwriting, or Mr. Corey's tilting away from the ugly Emancipation Group statuary in the Lapham drawing room. And the dialogue, especially when Penelope Lapham or Bromfield Corey are on the scene, contains an appealing sparkle (the former's chaff to her sister about love letters in the form of puffs for a cattle ranch, the latter's rueful soliloquy about the awful prospect of being married under a horseshoe in tuberoses, which would be the Lapham "style").

The Rise of Silas Lapham presents in considerable detail, then, the class alignment observable, if not in America as a whole, at least in Boston. This tight-knit society rarely breaks ranks to admit an outsider, especially one with a Vermont twang and interests limited to business or to horses. If approving of money as much as the next person, it never talks about things material, and until the plutocracy learns this subterfuge — as well as learns to acquire the Corey elegance — it will not mingle successfully nor for long with the aristocracy. Howells admits that the price the "risen" family may pay for "civilization" may be too high: snobbery is cruel, the world of Papanti's dancing class and Harvard-class spreads and visiting cousins at Bar Harbor is narrow, the force of convention is sometimes oppressive, and family affection dissolves in the smart urban environment. Yet "civilization" also means grace and amiability and knowledgeability (the Empire style is not, as Silas Lapham would have it, the "ongpeer"), and the village American might be the better for the addition of some Boston culture.

Howells's subsequent novels continue the commentary on man's behavior in ordered social situations and furnish further contrasts in manners and mores in the rustic community — where there is "propinquity," if not "society" — and in the urban environment, whether this be Boston or Venice, New York or Florence.[11] Howells ranges from front porch to Roman villa, canvassing his favorite subjects of courtship and marriage, the family, the careers of professional men, and the impact of travel, always with an eye to the social texture. He seems in the process, the most civilized of writers, sharply observing, sensitively recording "vanity fair."

His best comedy of manners appeared in his most productive decade, the 1880s. The Jamesian *Indian Summer* (1886) offers a charming picture of Americans abroad and at the same time represents a decided advance in subtlety and thoughtfulness over the earlier Venetian novels, and an advance in craftsmanship as well. Because it temperately explores the international theme, and because it is gifted with a unity of time, place and mood, well-drawn characters, and a felicitous style, the book reaches a high level of artistry, comparable to that of *Silas Lapham*.

In telling the story of Theodore Colville, the newspaper editor from Des Vaches, Indiana, now vacationing — and perhaps finding a new life for himself — in Florence, Howells is preoccupied with contrasting America and Italy, Des Vaches and Florence, even the Wabash and the Arno. If concentrating on his theme of the unsatisfactoriness of love between different generations and of the folly of needless self-sacrifice, he suggests how the Continental background has affected the love predicament, the Americans, moving amidst different Florentine conventions, being more confused and unsure of themselves than they would have been at home. Their plight is intensified by the foreign setting, the novel thus indicating the problems that arise in the wake of transplantation.

Howells mingles praise with censure as he examines both the American and the European scene. The former lacks refinement and culture — an architect is the last thing anyone wanted in Des Vaches; the jail and the courthouse, after all, had been built. "Society" doesn't exist, at least not in the Middle West. After the courting period and marriage, people are too busy working. On the other hand, Americans display sturdy moral fibre, which is much to their credit. Moreover, nothing in Europe can measure up to the sweet freedom and genuine innocence of the American girl. Howells was as entranced as James by this phenomenon.

Howells's protagonist Colville feels properly patriotic about his native land, yet recognizes its drawbacks, those of a small Indiana town anyway, and, as he ventures abroad to study architecture, he anticipates a more rewarding existence. Certainly he seems to turn into a happy expatriate as the result of his stay in Florence, and when he marries Mrs. Bowen (herself an expatriate) at the end of the novel, one feels that they will probably remain abroad, despite their half-hearted talk about going home.

The attractions of Europe for Colville include the evidences of taste and cultivation, of which his own country is in short supply. He is delighted with the treasures of art in the churches and galleries, with the scenic splendor of the history-marked landscape, with the adroitly conducted social round of teas, "at homes," balls, dinners, and fêtes. Tea from "the Russian samovar which replaces in some Florentine houses the teapot of Occidental civilization" and Madame Ucelli's receptions (where the tea-urn is replaced by rum punch, and where "we have officers when there is dancing") strike him as pleasantly novel. The exotic quality of the surroundings entices him as well, the "operatic spectacle" that is Florence, a mingling of simple trattorias, sunny squares, and elaborate gardens like the Boboli, of officers, dandies, and beggars. He admires, too, the graceful manners of the natives, the "sweet plenitude of politeness" of the hotel porter, for example, who manages to be a marvel of aplomb even in shirt sleeves and with only one suspender.

It must be admitted that not everything about "Florentinity" pleases him. He is bothered, in particular, by the evidences of imperfect expatriation that he observes among his American compatriots. If the retired minister Mr. Waters, now "thawing out" his many New England winters, has adapted delightfully, the lives of others appear more empty, their pleasures more brittle.

The greater part accepted the Florentine drawing-room as their landlord had imagined it for them, with furniture and curtains in yellow satin, a cheap ingrain carpet thinly covering the stone floor. . . .all were bound together by a common language and a common social tradition; they all had a Day . . . had one another to fine . . . evening parties, with dancing, and without dancing. . . . They seemed to see very little of Italian society, and to be shut out from practical knowledge of the local life by the terms upon which they had themselves insisted. [P. 93]

The expatriate band of artists, with whom Colville occasionally mingles, has amalgamated to a greater degree, yet even this group seems faintly uneasy in the still alien atmosphere.

Colville is also somewhat dissatisfied with the superficiality of the Florentine social world, and with its binding conventions as well. The latter cause difficulties that a little frankness might have alleviated. The European worldliness, so apparent in the freedom of the masquerade ball or in the sophisticated talk in the salon of Madame Ucelli, disturbs him, too, and he finds many of the compromises and imperfections in the social order both unattractive and unnecessary. It is quite clear that, although he will "retire" contentedly to cultivated Florence, he will yet retain a stout Americanism — the "honor," as he says, "of the country which we all have at heart." Like Mr. Waters, he hopes to have the best of both worlds.

The characters in *Indian Summer* are largely drawn from one class, an upper-middle expatriate grouping. With the exception of the bouncy artists, the Inglehart boys, they are prosperous Americans or English, mostly with a Continental overlay. Although Mr. Waters remains his own self, the others show varying degrees of Europeanization, an influence in part harmful, in part beneficial. Imogene Graham, the ingenue, is undergoing a molding process in her visit to Europe, where the "social exercise" will remove the abrupt and undextrous in her, replacing them with finesse, while at the same time, it is hoped, not robbing her of her moral innocence. The older Mrs. Bowen, in her late thirties, is already formed, of course, and has emerged from her expatriate experience as an accomphished woman of the world ("receiving" — in brown silk of subdued splendor, and with hands and fan and handkerchief tastefully composed before her), and one with principles, too. However, her "education" has encouraged in her a few undesirable attributes, for example, the brittleness of "the woman of fashion" and the habit of paying undue attention to conventionalities. Her Europeanized sense of etiquette and desire to conform complicate the love triangle, for one thing, causing her to flout common sense and thus to delay the happy resolution of the triangle. The third principal, Colville, is a realistically drawn "hero" — middle-aged and with a figure that "had swayed beyong the strict bounds of symmetry" — pleasant and witty and morally aware, but just a bit bewildered by Florentine ways of living, and not as quick as he would have been at home to see that Mrs. Bowen rather than Miss Graham is his proper destiny.[12] Dazzled by the "veglione" and the "conversazione," he loses his balance for a time, allowing himself to trail, rheumatic and sleepy, after Miss Graham, even to make a fool of himself dancing — or trying to — the lancers in Madame Ucelli's drawing room. Eventually he recovers his senses, however, and wisely settles for Mrs. Bowen's comfortable fireside, with only a very occasional foray into society.

The genially satiric tone of the novel seems very much in keeping both with its antisentimental theme that people should exercise common sense even in love affairs and with the comedy of manners format that is employed to convey this theme. Howells — in person or through his alter ego Colville — indulges in frequent drollery and persiflage and scatters throughout the book delightfully ironic observations: "He practised these economies of material in conversation quite recklessly, and often made the same incident or suggestion do duty round a whole company" . . . "The librarian knew the interlocutor's English but not the meaning of it" . . . "The Hotel d'Atene dinner made an imposing show on

the carte du jour, but tended to peter out in actuality" . . .
"There are artists and artists. This painter was one who had a
distinct social importance."

The author's "asides," and his narrative passages, character
descriptions, and conversation sequences as well, are couched
in witty language. Snobbish English ladies are quickly defined
as "faintly acknowledging, provisionally ignoring." Colville's
romance with Imogene goes "hitchingly," the mistake of the
engagement whirling away into mazes of error. He tries to
"hang his pillowed head for shame," as he goes to places in
the character of a young man but is not readily accepted in
that character. Much more comfortable is the saintly yet
sprightly old Mr. Waters, who is even able to "speak of the
mind and soul as if they were the gossip of the neighborhood."

Whether in dialogue or narrative Howells composes his
phrases neatly — "moral mayonnaise," the "new friend who
was not yet his acquaintance," "their conversation was
perfunctory; they showed one another they had no pleasure
in it" — and the dry style (Isis and Osiris, "little one-horse
deities — not very much") appropriately complements the
book's ironic tone. It all adds up to a harmony of parts,
as well as a clever illustration of the author's Balzacian view
of man as conditioned by his social frame. Here the scrupulous but sometimes maladroit American is associated with
the protocol-ridden, polished but perhaps too blasé European,
expatriate or native, a person from another frame. The amusement that results from their intercourse, always somewhat
perplexing in its evidence of conflicting customs, provides
a pleasant study of human nature.

In subsequent novels Howells frequently yields to his
propensity for contrasting ways of living, Europe-American,
West-East, North-South, Boston-New York, city-village,
aristocracy-plutocracy. *April Hopes*, for example, presents
the first of these, dealing with the Pasmer family, who have

lived long abroad — "upon the edges and surfaces of things, as Americans must in Europe everywhere" — but have now returned to America. In thus setting the international contrast against an American background, Howells interestingly varies his *Indian Summer* arrangement. The ex-expatriate Pasmers, he points out, encounter some difficulty in adjusting to life in their native land, having forgotten about its high moral tone, about the preeminent position of the young, about the provinciality evident at least in Boston (Washington, in contrast, demonstrates an absence of "provincial anxiety" and thus seems to the Pasmers more pleasant, "a lighter and friendlier London").

More precisely a novel of manners, one feels, and neater in craftsmanship, even if, like so many Howells novels, it trails away toward the end, is *The Kentons*. It is described by Clara and Rudolf Kirk in complimentary terms:

> In *The Kentons* people from Ohio, New York, and Europe come together, misunderstand one another and quarrel or smile their way to the end of a novel as absorbing as any Howells was able to write in the full flush of the novel writing of the eighties.[13]

The work does, as the Kirks suggest, engross the reader as it outlines the mishaps and contretemps befalling the Kenton family, once removed from the serene village of Tuskingum, Ohio, to the more turbulent worlds to the eastward, worlds for which they are not fully prepared.

The Kentons are first seen in their own environment, Howells drawing an affectionately nostalgic picture of rural Tuskingum. In accordance with the town's easy camaraderie, the young fellows observe a practice long since disused in the centers of fashion, that of making morning calls on the girls; they make evening calls as well, though these are "scarcely more authorized by the great world." Life is simple and uncluttered by conventions in Tuskingum, and people like the Kentons, despite their ignorance of social customs like chaperonage, are "sweet" and "good," as the young New York minister Breckon describes them. To be sure, the village includes the bounder Bittridge, sneaking his way into the affections of the older Kenton daughter and darkening the scene, but he is to meet the unenviable fate of a horsewhipping, and always to seem an "outsider."

When the Kentons pay an extended visit to New York City, as they do to remove Ellen from the attentions of Bittridge, they ensconce themselves, somewhat uneasily, in an old-fashioned downtown hotel. Though trying to feel at home in the big-city environment and to absorb its "atmosphere of culture," they never regain their Tuskingum serenity — partly, of course, because the Bittridge business is still in the process of being settled, but partly because the West, as Ellen frankly says, is different (she admits to its being "not interesting") from the East and can never mesh perfectly with it.

The Kentons move on to Europe, encountering aboard ship some worldly — to them, anyway — types like Mr. Breckon, a fashionable minister, the society girl Miss Rasmith, and the Englishman Mr. Pogis. Neither "side" fully understands the other, but there is friendship between them. Pogis, for example, though utterly bewildered by Lottie Kenton's outrageous flirting, is fascinated by it, and, more important, recognizes the innocence underlying it. Breckon, though somewhat troubled by the Kentons' uncertain manners — for example, Mrs. Kenton's allowing her daughters a free rein — perceives their worth, especially as it manifests itself in warm family affection.

The final scenes of the novel, taking place in Holland, illustrate the continued lack of savoir faire of the Kentons, reflected in Lottie's misreading of most of their fellow travelers as "Cook's tourists" — the label belongs, of course, at home — and reflected, more seriously, in the ill-starred attempt of young Boyne to address the youthful Queen of Holland. His action, based on a misunderstanding of European protocol, leads to temporary imprisonment. All ends happily, however. Not that the Kentons turn into sophisticated expatriates, but rather that Ellen and Breckon plight their troth and prepare to settle down in New York, to which Ellen, as much the most intelligent and least Tuskingumed of the Kentons, will presumably make a successful adjustment. Meanwhile, the others in the family will scurry contentedly back to Ohio, where life is "purest," a state that is to Judge Kenton's mind the "highest civilization."

Very late in his career Howells produced a "social novel" that is certainly one of his best, *The Vacation of the Kelwyns.* "An Idyl of the Middle Eighteen-Seventies," as the subtitle has it, the "Idyl" is tempered by a gritty sense of reality, and its gentle reminiscence quality, by clear-sighted reflections on human nature. Before he has finished his tale, Howells raises questions involving class, manners, work, property, education, and religion, resolving most of them in a half-humorous, half-ironic way.

The story describes the summer vacation of Professor and Mrs. Kelwyn and their two boys, a vacation spent at a farmhouse in the New Hampshire hill country. Visiting them are a cousin, Parthenope Brook, and also an itinerant schoolteacher, Elihu Emerance, and attending to their wants — theoretically — are a farmer and his wife, Mr. and Mrs. Kite. Howells, with subtlety, delineates the social cleavage between the Kelwyns, professional people and of the upper middle class, and the Kites, working people and of the lower middle class. The struggle of the Kelwyns, especially Mrs. Kelwyn, to preserve their status in the face of the Kites' proudly asserted independence is amusingly recounted, the Kelwyns fighting manfully to improve the services rendered — to persuade surly Kite to hitch the professor's horse for him, or to modify Mrs. Kite's incredibly bad cooking technique — while keeping a proper distance. They are not notably successful, being stymied by the farmer's rude assurance and by his wife's bland lady-of-the-house manner. Eventually they relax to a degree, recognizing the intricate blend of the real and the ideal in the world, specifically the fact that human involvement inevitably impinges on social distinctions and blurs them.[14] The developing love affair between Miss Brook (of a respectable Boston family) and Emerance (of not so respectable a family) supports this recognition. Parthenope's idealism will be tempered by Elihu's pragmatism. He is, she admits, her intellectual superior as well as basically more kind, and thus more than "good enough" for her.

The picture that is drawn in the novel of social types — seen against a vivid background of rural New England in decay — impresses one with a sense of its accuracy. Initially Howells suggests the academic milieu, a social sphere all its own in that one's position is prominent, but the financial resources with which to support it are limited. As Howells puts it, the Kelwyns were able to maintain themselves on a scale of refined frugality, which was the rule in the university town, able to indulge, now and then, a guarded hospitality. By virute of his profession and of his intellectual capacity, Professor Kelwyn qualifies as a "gentleman," if not as a gentleman by birth. Howells explains:

> In America society does not insist that one shall be a gentleman by birth; that is generally impossible; but it insists that he shall be intelligent and refined, and have the right sort of social instincts; and then it yields him an acceptance which ignores any embarrassing facts in his origin, and asks nothing but that he shall ignore them too. [P. 3]

Mrs. Kelwyn, sharp in her "social insistences and moral

opinions,"[15] acts as her husband's "gentlewomanly" counterpart, and linked with them is Parthenope Brook, who belongs, on the social scale, just below the proper Bostonian level.

Emerance occupies a lower niche — "in derivation and education he was entirely middle-class" — but may perhaps be described as socially mobile, at least, sufficiently so as to make an alliance with Parthenope Brook seem not implausible. Surely he displays the good manners that come from a good heart, as Mrs. Kelwyn points out, even if he "hasn't the least notion of society as we know it," and "in these picnicking and camping times," as Mrs. Kelwyn also says, the "young people throw off a good many social trammels" anyway.

Between the Kelwyns and the Kites a gulf will always remain, the differences in education, breeding, and background being huge indeed. The latter, as rather shiftless farm folk uninterested in books, in current affairs, or in nature, or even in decent cookery, appear to be worlds removed from the professor and his wife. Howells comments on the barrier early in the novel: perhaps it is really the inferiors that despise the superiors, and it is that which embitters the classes against one another. The barrier is not removed by the novel's end, nor is the embitterment; yet, as stated above, the distinction between Kelwyns and Kites becomes slightly less sharp even so, for each family has arrived at a measure of respect for the other, the Kelwyns granting the sturdy independence of the Kites, and the latter recognizing kindness and humanity as well as intelligence in the Kelwyns. Both couples seem more relaxed about superiority-inferiority complexes.

The novel's setting takes on importance because of the city-bred - country-bred contrast and is well defined by the author. The action takes place in a slightly decaying rural area, dotted with run-down farms and rather worn-out land and stagnating settlements. The decay is emphasized by the presence of a Shaker community that is dying out, as the younger members leave for the city and the rule of celibacy takes its toll. A quiet life it is, only briefly enlivened by the appearance of itinerants such as the huge Negro tramp, or the Canuck with his trained bear, or the gypsy van, or the Italian organ-grinders, the latter so much more graceful than the uncouth "Yankee country-folks" whom they strive to entertain.[16] If the rural scene has its idyllic aspects, it seems deadening in the long run. The lively *Atlantic Monthly* school of culture in Boston and the Cambridge university circle have more to recommend them, pretentious and straitened though they may sometimes be.

The book, proceeding at a leisurely pace and being mostly given over to a series of conversational exchanges, often conveys the wit of the author and delights the reader in so doing. The character descriptions — of slightly pedantic Mr. Kelwyn, of hard-shelled farmer Kite ("as if he were hewn out of hickory, with the shagbark left on in places"), of Mrs. Kite, who has a "sort of blameless middlingness" — seem apt, as does the localism-strewn dialogue. The figurative language is properly vivid (a storm is a vast globe of bluish fire, with little crimson flakes like pieces of burning paper), and the gently ironic tone ("the Kites shut themselves in with the comfort of their opinions"), entertaining, as it reveals to us a writer engaged in lightheartedly exposing the weaknesses of mankind, apparent at any social level.

Many another Howells novel, even when it is primarily concerned with other topics, touches on the issue of manners. *Annie Kilburn* (1889), for example, makes use of the international contrast, setting the "showy affection" of Italians alongside the "cold kindness" of New Englanders, and draws rural-urban parallels, the "natives" standing apart from the summer visitors like Mr. Northwick, the manufacturer who owns a "fancy farm." The novel is, however, chiefly devoted to exploring an economic thesis, the cause of socialism. *A Hazard of New Fortunes* (1890), though also primarily economic, has its manners aspects, too; these are especially apparent in the Dryfoos family subplot, an illustration of the abrasions suffered by the newly rich as they endeavor to gain social mobility. And *A Modern Instance* (1882), if precluded from being regarded as a "pure" novel of manners by its extremely sober analysis of the divorce question, which constitutes its theme, still "fringes" the form, as Howells talks about social sets and levels of social acceptability, the importance of tradition, and the special world of those who can afford the spring season in Europe. This novel, too, in the character of Ben Halleck, offers a good example of what "civilization" meant to Howells. Halleck, as a model of Chaucerian "gentilesse" — not by virtue of his first-family-of-Boston heritage, but rather because of his considerateness, tact, taste, and decency — personifies the truly civilized individual, the one who might bring, Howells thought, "enlightenment" to society. The reader may not wholly agree, to be sure, since he is apt to find Halleck too colorless and vacillating a character to play so lofty a role.

While chronicling the world of property, money, travel, and professions, Howells, then, looked for something deeper, searching for the moral dimension beneath the social veneer. The social indices and regulations masked but could not hide the moral problems (e.g., the corrupting power of sudden wealth). Thus, Howells was able to attach weight to the subject of "manners," which may well have been for him "only morals in bloom"[17] In his many discourses on the matter, however, he did not forget to couch his discussion in diverting terms, thus lending a distinct note of charm to his fiction of social information.

NOTES TO CHAPTER 4

1. According to Alfred Kazin, Howells is the "inventor" of the novel of manners in America. See Alfred Kazin, "Howells the Bostonian," *Clio* 3 (February 1974): 226.

2. William Dean Howells, *The Kentons* (New York: Harper and Brothers, 1902), p. 144. Stress upon the "simplest life" did not preclude pretensions to culture and refinement, however, and "society" had a part to play even in Tuskingum, Ohio.

3. It is worth observing that novelists of manners usually traveled widely and made extensive use of their travel experiences. James, Howells, and, to a lesser degree, Mrs. Wharton have produced outstanding travel books, which offer absorbing studies of foreign cultures, while also containing occasional reflections on the authors' own civilizations.

4. Alfred Kazin speaks of "the remarkable poise of his style" as being Howells's "great gift" (Kazin, "Howells the Bostonian" p. 232).

5. "I shall do nothing but to talk of some ordinary traits of American life as these appeared to them, to speak a little of well-known and easily accessible places, to present now a bit of landscape and now a sketch of character" (p. 2).

6. Several characters appear in more than one of Howells's novels, as they do also in those of Mrs. Wharton. One consequence of this is a sharpened sense of the social setting and of its continuity.

7. For her, as for Howells, one feels, "social allegiance" and "custom" and "convention" must be put aside if they conflict with what constitutes true gentlemanliness, honesty and courtesy and "heart."

8. The subplot is thoroughly interwoven into the main plot and indeed dominates the first twenty of the twenty-seven chapters (see Kermit Vanderbilt, *The Achievement of William Dean Howells* [Princeton, N. J.: Princeton University Press, 1968], p. 134).

9. Howells shares with other novelists of manners a fondness for architecture, indulging here in precise descriptions of the Corey and Lapham abodes, and also in a detailed account of the new house that the latter family, as a part of their "social rise," build "on the water side of Beacon Street."

10. It is difficult to be quite so sanguine as Kermit Vanderbilt about this wedding of "streamlined Brahminism and de-provincialized agrarian America." One can hope, yes, that the combining of the moral and intellectual values of the one with the energy and vision of the other will prove a successful blend (see Vanderbilt, *Achievement of William Dean Howells*, p. 137).

11. Howells was obviously convinced that social conditions in America had been sufficiently settled to permit the establishment of stable class lines and thus to render observable contrasting classes and contrasting manners. Equally convinced would be his successors in the field of manners — at least, those

operating in such "cultural pockets" as New England, Old New York, or the Southern Tidewater — and they, too, would subject the privileged and less privileged circles to a satiric scrutiny, finding comedy in the contrasts between them.

12. William Gibson, though calling Colville a proto-Prufrock, declares that he is a paragon of common sense compared to the women of the novel (see William M. Gibson, *William Dean Howells,* University of Minnesota Pamphlets on American Writers, no. 63 [Minneapolis, Minn.: University of Minnesota Press, 1967], p. 23).

13. Clara M. Kirk and Rudolf Kirk, eds., *William Dean Howells, Representative Selections,* American Writers Series (New York: American Book Company, 1950), p. xciii.

Henry James also praised the book, as "that perfectly classic illustration of your spirit and form," in a letter to Howells of February 19, 1912 (see Percy Lubbock, selector and ed., *The Letters of Henry James* [London: MacMillan and Co., Ltd., 1920], 2:233).

14. Howells is thus, perhaps, producing a variation of one of his favorite themes, that of complicity.

15. Richard Chase, *The American Novel and Its Tradition* (Garden City, N.Y.: Doubleday Anchor Book, 1957), p. 178.

16. The fact that the bear-leader, the Negro, the gypsies, and the Italians all move outside of the restrictions of local customs and conventions and seem more vital and free thereby lends an added dimension to the "social-ladder" discussion.

17. Stow Persons uses this phrase in his book *The Decline of American Gentility,* in a discussion of the difference between "fine" manners (based on simplicity, truthfulness, consideration of others) and "fashionable" ones (based on convention and form) (see Stow Persons, *The Decline of American Gentility* [New York and London: Columbia University Press, 1973], p. 37).

5

Turn-of-the-Century Figures

A number of authors, in their fashion, continued the novel-of-manners tradition as the nineteenth century waned and the twentieth loomed ahead. Showing some kinship with James and Howells, writers like George Washington Cable and F. Hopkinson Smith, Arlo Bates and Robert Grant, Anne Douglas Sedgwick and Booth Tarkington also dealt with the social order, developing such themes as the influence of the past, the counterpointing of Europe and America, or the impact on American civilization of the "smell of money," and relating these themes to upper-class types placed in urban settings. The group were lesser artists, to be sure, less polished in style, less adept at characterization, and often less controlled in their structural patterning.

To be truthful, they were also far less devoted to issues of manners than either James or Howells. Their books often diverged into other channels — perhaps that of the conventional romance, or regional humor, or even a sermon on economics — and they seemed bent primarily on telling an involved story, a sentimental, often melodramatic, tale. If there lay a social problem behind the plot (frequently, divorce, a "topic of the times"), this, at best, led the writers to an approximation of the usual "manners" focus on indivi-dual-fulfillment-in-the-social-arena. Other ingredients of the type were missing as well. In fact, the novelists modified the genre so drastically that they really barely belong in the tradition.

George Washington Cable is a case in point. He did, of course, in a work like *The Grandissimes* (1880), examine a distinctive society, the various classes, castes, and races that make up the colorful melting pot of New Orleans, and he chose to treat one of the classic situations of the novel of manners that it revealed — the dissolution of one class, the Creole aristocracy, and its replacement by another, the bourgeois "Americains."[1] The exotic Creole way of life, of quadroon balls, duels, voodoo worship, and ancient family rivalries, was vanishing before the onslaught of the non-caste-conscious, business-minded, prosaic middle-class American. Cable pictured with care the changing sand in the social hourglass and thoroughly capitalized on the exotic New Orleans background.

In later novels like *Dr. Sevier* (1885) and *John March, Southerner* (1894), however, Cable by and large ignores the peculiar social structure of New Orleans and its environs, barely touching on the black-white relationship or on the position of the Creoles. Intent on the problem of commer-cialism in *Dr. Sevier,* as also in *John March, Southerner* (within the framework of the Reconstruction period, in this instance), Cable preaches about greed and larceny among the rich, as about the evil institutions of the Charity Hospital and Parish Prison, which confront the poor, but he does not do so in terms of class barriers or social climbing. Moreover, he peoples his books with stock types from sentimental romances or local-color stories and goes on endlessly about their entanglements. An occasional redeeming touch (e.g., the well-realized stiffness of the character of Dr. Sevier) does not mitigate to any great degree the pedestrian telling of a pedestrian narrative.

It would seem that Southern writers like Cable could have utilized the novel of manners format more effectively than many of their contemporaries from other areas of the country. For these novelists had, one feels, an ideal subject — a close-knit, homogeneous society, placed against the plantation background, a dashing group of people in a colorful setting. Indeed, they did reproduce, like John Esten Cooke and John Pendleton Kennedy before them, the elaborate scale of life of the Southern gentry, the hunt breakfasts and ceremonial dinners, the house parties and balls, the warm spirit of Southern hospitality in general. They also dotted their plantation scene with "local" (and, alas, stereotyped) people, for example, the courtly planter, chivalrous and courageous but also intolerant and intemperate; the dainty and beautiful mistress of the plantation, gracious but also somewhat faded; their handsome children, the young cavalier and the Southern belle; and, serving the family, in an idealized relationship, the blacks, the plantation "uncle," the mammy, the jolly cook, the frisky youngsters who companion — up to a certain age — the planter's children. Despite the shadows here and there of antislavery agitation and miscegenation, the picture, as presented, is generally idyllic, a golden age of gentility in the stately antebellum mansions, adorned with family portraits and heirlooms, and harboring a caste-bound and tradition-bound but fascinating class. Unfortunately, the sentimentality of the majority of these accounts of pre-Civil War Southern life vitiates them as novels of manners since it robs them of a necessary irony and balanced perspective. Their romantic backward glance conveys too fulsome an epitaph for a vanished civilization.[2]

The novels of F. Hopkinson Smith illustrate this pattern, his *Kennedy Square* (1911), for example, containing such ingredients as a staple setting (the gracious mansions on Kennedy Square), a staple cast of characters (Kate Seymour the belle, Harry Rutter the dashing hero, Miss Lavinia Clendenning, the indomitable spinster, Todd the devoted servant, and the protagonist, St. George Wilmot Temple, "the perfect embodiment of all that was best in his class and station, and of all that his blood had bequeathed him"), and a staple series of events ("ducking trips down the bay," duels and balls, and occasional evenings of "Readings" of Irving, Thackeray and Poe). The action focuses on the impoverishment of St. George Temple, owing to the uncertain economic conditions prevailing in the post-Civil War South, with the Kate Seymour-Harry Rutter love affair as an interwoven subplot. All ends happily, of course, the "Temple Mansion" and the fortunes of its owner restored, and the lovers united. As this suggests, *Kennedy Square* remains, in essence, a gushy and standardized romance, though Smith inserts, to be sure, some acute touches of characterization and some humorous passages that offset the book's saccharine flavor. He also conveys in a believable fashion the charm of the Temple world, with its lavish hospitality, kindly conversation, and keen concern for honor.

Smith's earlier *Colonel Carter of Cartersville* (1892) also treats the impoverished Southern gentry and outlines a comparable action, the restoration of Carter Hall and of the fortunes of the Colonel, thanks to the discovery of valuable coal deposits on his land. The novel has considerably more appeal than *Kennedy Square*, however, for it is couched throughout in comic terms and makes pleasant sport of the Colonel and his world.

The Colonel is initially observed living in straitened circumstances in New York. He still manages to enjoy a comfortable existence, however, dining well in an inviting dining room, with a fire laid, and with his faithful slave Chad to serve the terrapin, the Madeira, and the claret (from a cut-glass decanter resting on a silver coaster). It must be noted that he is living on credit at the grocer's and with financial support from his Aunt Nancy, and that he pursues his impracticable business schemes from an office given to him rent free by a friend, but it must also be noted that the Colonel quite innocently charms his "supporters" — the free use of stamps and clerks in the firm of his friend was "to him only evidence of a lordly sort of hospitality which endeared the real proprietor of the office all the more to him, because it recalled the lavish display of the golden days of Carter Hall." His sunny personality ("open, bright and with a great draft of enthusiasm always rushing up a chimney of difficulties") carries him serenely along until the great stroke of luck involved in the finding of the coal deposits[3] restores him to prosperity. The reader shares the Colonel's delight in his return to Carter Hall, where he can refurbish the house and grounds and return to the routine of gracious living.

Smith makes of the Colonel a figure of fun (his card, "Colonel George Fairfax Carter of Carter Hall, Cartersville, Virginia," omits "U.S.A." because this would add nothing to his identity or dignity), but he is sturdy and endearing at the same time. The Southern "types" surrounding him are, with one exception, equally generous, honorable, and appealing. The exception, Major Yancey, a down-at-the-heels trickster, diverges from their "quality folks" pattern and even seems to anticipate a Faulknerian Snopes.

Smith, one feels, writes more nearly in the manners vein than Cable, for he has a sharper eye for idiosyncracies of class, and he maintains a suitable tone, one of light comedy.

If he does not contribute nearly as much to the tradition as a subsequent Southern writer, Ellen Glasgow, who was equipped with more subtlety, irony, and ethical solidity, he does, because of his wit and his pellucid sense of the Southern "scene," pave the way.

Other novelists of the period interested themselves in sectional mores as well, the Eastern seaboard and the Middle West coming in for attention along with the South. Two who chose the former locale were the Bostonians Arlo Bates and Robert Grant, whose work, in its just slightly jaundiced view of the proper Bostonian and his environs, establishes a link between William Dean Howells and John P. Marquand.

Bates may also be associated with John Cheever and John Leggett — at least, in one respect, their propensity for drawing parallels between Boston and New York. Like them he favors the former locale (Howells and Marquand were less decided!). In *The Puritans* (1898), while deploring Boston's "spiritual and intellectual gymnastics" and the puritanical strain that encourages "decorous conventionality," a "savor of lineage amounting almost to godliness in dark, self-contained parlors," and too much "moral stamina and asceticism," he nonetheless stoutly recommends "old Boston blood and traditions," finding them preferable to those in indifferent and bad-mannered New York.

Bates's *The Philistines* (1889) examines issues of manners much more thoroughly than *The Puritans,* discussing relevant topics such as the impact of Puritanism on Boston society, marriage for money, the "mariage de convénance" (e.g., the Staggchase alliance, the husband and wife providing "good backgrounds" for each other), the parvenu versus the patrician, and the place of the artist in society.[4] Pointing out at the novel's outset that Boston society is a "complex and enigmatical thing," Bates explores its "wavering and uncertain lines" — "governed by no fixed standards, whether of wealth, birth or culture, but at times apparently leaning a little toward each of these three great factors of American social standing." Mrs. Amanda Sampson, for example, has been ostracized, even though of excellent family, for she "has no capabilities of respectability in her composition," and her relatives cannot "keep her within the bounds of propriety." On the other hand, Miss Merrivale, though known to have the "incurable disease of social ambition," still manages to obtain a "recognized and very comfortable footing." Society's rulers demonstrate shaky opinions about taste and refinement, and especially about morals ("society can't be squeamish," says one, "on questions of morals").

Bates speculates about these issues in a knowledgeable way, and at the same time in lively terms. His book has a lightly satiric edge that is both appropriate and entertaining. Characters like the portraitist Fenton (who blunted his talent in his desire for the "complacency of a portly bank account"), or the dashing social adventurer Mrs. Sampson (to whom society was a ladder, "and being so, to climb it was but to follow the use for which it was designed"), or the self-made man Alfred Irons (whose public air of stiffness and immaculate propriety fails to conceal his "vulgar, ill-bred self") are mocked, and institutions as well — the Browning Club, whose central principle is that a Browning poem is a "prize enigma," and the "select sewing circle," that "peculiar institution by means of which exclusive Boston society keeps tally of the standing of all its young women." Bates reports on this world in a witty, often epigrammatic manner, and, like his confrere Grant, often in sociological terminology ("social misdemeanors," "social condition," "social position"), thus lending both verve and authority to his account.

In such a work as *The Chippendales* (1903), Robert Grant also dealt with the Boston social world. A little more severe than Bates, he "exposed" the Brahmin circle as narrow and provincial, confined to respectable (i.e., stocks and bonds) businesses, respectable (i.e., Episcopalian) religion, and respectable family ("all simon-pure Bostonians know their genealogies by heart"). Pinpointing with accuracy its habitat, the august houses on Beacon Hill and the substantial summer places at Pride's Crossing, and outlining with care its plethora of customs, Grant faithfully reproduced the Brahmin sphere. One watches the Chippendales and their fellows attending Puritan Balls and Friday Dancing Classes, philanthropically buying old masters for the Art Museum, financing the building of women's dormitories, and socializing with the Harvard professors. Grant took particular note of their chief distinguishing characteristics, commercial honesty and a New England conscience, the latter sometimes allied with Philistinism.

Mildly threatened by the nouveaux riches, the Boston aristocracy, Grant indicated, though having surrendered to the Irish in the political field, still remained quite firmly in the saddle, content with its provinciality, its exclusiveness, and its stabilized and rather dull social routine. Making fun of their foibles — Mrs. Avery's abode on Dartmouth Street is just beyond the pale of fashion, yet within breathing distance of an aesthetic atmosphere — Grant wrote amusingly about the Apley type. Choosing to instruct (his employment of such phrases as "social albino," "urban and suburban social sets," "social usages," and the "socially trained mind" suggests a sociological concern), as well as to entertain, he, in both moods, neatly "caught" the New England tone.

Though Grant moved away from the Boston area in other books, he was still concerned with the social sphere, and with "society" as a factor in character motivation. In *Unleavened Bread* (1900) he unfolds the "career" of his protagonist, Selma White, against three backdrops, the "rising Midwestern city" of Benham, New York City, and Washington. In every case Selma, though theoretically an advocate of feminism and, as such, "above" an interest in the social whirl, is exceedingly anxious to achieve social position. This she never does, even when, in her third marriage, she becomes the wife of a United States Congressman-then-Governor-then Senator. The select members of Benham society, those living on the River Drive, still show no desire to make her acquaintance. Selma fails to understand the message of her sometime friend, Flossy Williams: "a true lady . . . represents modesty and sweetness and self-control, and gentle thoughts and feelings. . . . she is evolved by gradual processes from generation to generation, not ready made." One feels that Selma will continue to overdress for presidential receptions and will continue to misconstrue the "simple, unaffected refinement" of her former sister-in-law, Pauline Littleton.

Grant is primarily bent on exposing, in *Unleavened Bread,* the "New Woman" manquée.[5] Throughout the book Selma sees herself as destined to play important roles, neglecting the fact that she lacks training and education to serve in any of the roles in which she fancies herself — Women's Institute lecturer, stage tragedienne, college president, hospital trustee. She is still fancying herself at the book's end, however, facing the future as a senator's wife, with a "seraph look, as though she were penetrating the future even into Paradise." Blind to her shortcomings, particularly her lack of moral fiber, she serves as a devastating example of self-deception.

As in *The Chippendales,* Grant fills his book with social terms — "social jargon," "social grace," "social influence," "social success," "social reception," "social demonstration," "social perception" — and he has a good deal to say about such matters as the interior decoration of homes (Selma, as a girl from the country, had been used to "formalism in house-hold garniture — to a best room little used and precise with the rigor of wax flowers and black horsehair," and she never does acquire the taste possessed by her second husband, a genteel architect) and the rites of social climbing (taking a box at the theater, giving "select dinners," avoiding the nouveaux riches in their rich garments and excessive jewelry). In sum, Grant offers a firm defense of the "most dignified and august" aristocratic set, stating his view through Wilbur Littleton, who, in reply to his wife's charge (hypocritically made) that to have social distinctions is un-American, declares

> where fortunes have been made so rapidly, and we have no formal aristocracy, money undoubtedly plays a conspicuous part in giving access to what is known as society. But it is only an entering wedge. Money supplies the means to cultivate manners and the right way of looking at things, and good society represents the best manners and, on the whole, the best way of looking at things.[p. 152]

In other Grant novels, for example *The Undercurrent* (1904), "good society" also provides the background, and social problems such as incompatibility in marriage and revolts against the "mandates of society" are discussed. However, the author slackens his emphasis on these problems in favor of spinning a complicated tale, one in which the element of intrigue clearly outweighs the theme. Since he also does not progress beyond stock characters and situations in developing his intrigue, the novel falls short of serving as a thoughtful disquisition on manners. Here, and in part elsewhere, Grant turns away from the "tradition," seemingly content to satisfy a "women's magazine" audience.

His contemporary, Anne Douglas Sedgwick, likewise, one suspects, had such an audience in mind in writing her books, and relied, for the most part, on a routinely "popular" format. At the same time, her novels often show insight into manners situations. Married to an Englishman and living abroad, Mrs. Sedgwick, not surprisingly, replaced the regional approach utilized by writers such as Cable, Smith, Bates, and

Grant with an international one, and chose, like James, to set most of her fiction in foreign climes, or perhaps to present a combination of locales, most often a London-New York one. Such is her axis in works like *A Fountain Sealed* (1907), *Tante* (1912), and *Adrienne Toner* (1922). A variant is found in *The Little French Girl* (1924), which combines English country-house settings with Paris and a coastal resort in Brittany.

This latter novel distinguishes between French and English temperaments and ways of arranging life, for example, the precise running of the Verrier household versus the casual disorder of its English counterpart, the Bradley home, or the French defense of the arranged marriage, a custom less readily accepted in England. Within the novel there are intra-England contrasts as well, Cresswell Abbey and the aristocratic Hambles differing from Heathside and the middle-class Bradleys. Throughout the work, Mrs. Sedgwick comments on "Society" — and sometimes tartly. "Society" will, for instance, exclude a woman who has had lovers if they are known about, but will accept her if they are not. "It's very harsh; it's very hypocritical . . . but it is the only way in which a civilized society can protect itself."

The other novels present upper-crust Americans, often expatriates and usually "placed" in England. The graceful Mrs. Upton of *A Fountain Sealed* lives much more contentedly in her small house in Surrey, surrounded by Watteau and Chardin engravings, lacquer cabinets, and vases of Chinese porcelain, than in the stiff and pretentious house of her deceased husband's family in New York. Gregory Jardine of *Tante* occupies a civilized but not deliberately "cultivated" flat in London. The perhaps representative English home is that of the Chadwicks in *Adrienne Toner*, shabby but comfortable, and indeed charming in its Cotswold country setting.

The characters, all belonging to a Jamesian kind of world,

include such figures as the typical English gentleman, Sir Basil Thremdon, with his air of "delightfully civilized rurality,"[6] the polished but "cheerfully impervious" Britishers in *Tante,* the untraditional (because neither rich nor beautiful nor noticeably well dressed) "London American," Mrs. Aldesey, and the "interesting, original and charming American girl," Adrienne Toner.

Much is said in the novels about the dispensing of tea in lofty drawing rooms, attending concerts at old St. James Hall, hunting in the Coldbrooks country, and traveling on the Continent, and the reader is aware of the importance of *manners*, as, for example, Mrs. Upton, in *A Fountain Sealed*, quells a scene caused by the thoughtlessly chauvinistic Mr. and Mrs. Potts — "They were drawn helplessly into her shuttle and woven into the gracefully gliding pattern of social convention in spite of themselves. In fact, she preserved appearances with such success that everyone, to each one's surprise, was able to make an excellent dinner."

Still and all, sociomoral problems and even the manners trappings tend to slide into the background in Mrs. Sedgwick's fiction. She seems much more concerned with unfolding love triangles of various sorts (Mme. Okraska-Karen-Gregory in *Tante*, Mrs. Upton-Sir Basil-Imogen in *A Fountain Sealed*) and stretching out the web of relationships at tedious length. The books often begin well, with an amusing setting of the scene (see *Adrienne Toner*), but they rather quickly degenerate to the level of soap opera. An occasional interesting character sketch, a judicious handling of point of view, or a thoughtful authorial observation about social and moral contiguities compensate the reader only in small measure.

The equally facile Booth Tarkington, if perhaps more consciously a social critic than Mrs. Sedgwick, also uses the manners genre both casually and at best intermittently. In *The Plutocrat* (1927), for example, while choosing an international contrast thesis, he seems bent simply on producing an entertaining farce, filled with very broad satire on an assortment of people who can only be described as caricatures. Cardboard figures are such "types" as the woman of the world, Madame Momoro, the artist, Lawrence Ogle, the stuffy Englishman, Sir William Broadfeather, and the provincial, Mrs. Tinker (whose voice was "appropriate for reading the Secretary's Report to the Ladies' Entertainment Committee of a Church Fund Drive in the Midlands"). The latter's husband, the "plutocrat" of the title and the focus of the novel, is a caricature, too, the loud, free-spending, uncouth, ill-mannered American businessman. It must be admitted, however, that Tinker wins the reader's respect by the end of the novel, for, his boorishness aside, he exhibits an endearing largeness of spirit and an affable simplicity. Tarkington sees the type as "not Carthaginian nor barbaric Goth," but an empire-building "new Roman," practically progressive and humanely generous, more praiseworthy, in fact, than the intellectually snobbish aesthete Ogle. Even Ogle, who first calls Tinker "our most terrible type," comes to recognize his "barbaric stateliness" and to admire him.

The Plutocrat, an amusing sequence or two notwithstanding, does not have a very strong appeal, exhibiting as it does an elementary kind of plotting, a vagueness of setting, a but partial exploration of its theme (the money-power conjunction), and the aforesaid stereotypical characterization.

Tarkington seems more firmly anchored when he confines himself to his "midland country" of Indiana. Many of his books depict the Indianapolis of his time, or a few years earlier, and take as a theme the class categories displayed in the region, and the effect upon them of the increasing industrialization that marked the turn of the century. His trilogy Growth, comprised of The Turmoil, The Magnificent Ambersons, and The Midlander, embodies this thesis. If industrialism introduces disorder and change in society, it will eventually, so Tarkington concludes, foster progress, as an "enlightened" plutocracy grows out of the old aristocracy.

The Magnificent Ambersons (1918) first outlines the fall of the aristocrats, symbolized by the declining fortunes, financial and social, of the Amberson family, no longer the dominant figures in their midland town. Their replacement by booster-like arrivistes, symbolized by the Morgans, does not immediately seem an advancement. The new, "Morgan Place" merely repeats the old "Amberson Mansion," despite its suburban rather than urban locale, and the "great new people" often closely resemble the old. The majority of the citizenry present a pedestrian image, and their mushrooming city lacks the appeal of the quieter town out of which it grew. Gone are the serene times of all-day picnics, serenades, and New Year's Day open houses. On the other hand, a stagnant quality has been removed as well, and, when George Minafer, an Amberson grandson, has to buckle down to work, it is suggested that the aristocracy will be revitalized. His marriage, too, to Lucy Morgan — just as charming as Isabel Amberson was — will provide a happy amalgam of the best of both classes.

The Midlander (1924) chronicles further change, as the "big-walled solidity" of National Avenue in the "comfortable nineties" turns from residential to commercial, until the last of the Victorian mansions disappears.[7] Smoke — a symbol for Tarkington, as also for Ellen Glasgow — drives out the old families as the midland town turns into an industrial city. Again, however, Tarkington anticipates renewed vigor coming from a union of aristocracy and plutocracy, as seen in the marriage of fastidious but capable Harlan Oliphant and solid Martha Shelby (far more sensitive than her "self-made" father, who buys a Corot but never bothers to look at it). Thus he proves less willing than Edith Wharton to deplore the "custom of the country," and places more faith in "the newer materialism."

Social concerns crop up in other Tarkington novels, very incidentally in the idyllic and comic *Gentle Julia* (1929), which, in Penrod-and-Sam fashion, talks of love and gossip and children's pranks along the "best residence street" in the town, and more centrally in *Alice Adams* (1921), which treats the attempt of the titular character to rise above her family's poverty and achieve standing with the best people in town. Money makes the mare go, it would seem, but it has corrosive effects, especially on the Adams family. Tarkington is chiefly occupied in showing Alice's futile attempts to establish herself — by tall tales about her background, by keeping up with the fashions, by various social pretenses. His sympathetic but honest account wins the reader over to Alice's side, and one wishes that, her pretensions notwithstanding, she might take her place in the Palmer world and obtain her attractive suitor. Inevitably, though, such is not to be; the "frozen-faced gang" rule her "off the track," and she ends up at Frincke's Business College, settling for a career as a secretary.

On the whole, Tarkington, like Cable and Grant and Sedgwick, underplays the study of manners aspect of his fiction, offering instead a farce, or a children's story, or a character study, or — and this is the most proximate — social criticism. He is thus rather tenuously linked with the genre,[8] and it remained for contemporaries like Wharton, Glasgow, and Fitzgerald really to nurture the form.

NOTES TO CHAPTER 5

1. Richard Chase, *The American Novel and Its Tradition* (Garden City, N.Y.: Doubleday Anchor Book, 1957), p. 169.

2. Francis P. Gaines, in his classic little book, *The Southern Plantation* (New York: Columbia University Press, 1924), gives a thoroughly informative picture of this society, explaining, among other things, the persistent appeal of the aristo-leisure class culture. Americans, he says, have an innate love for feudalism; we may vaunt our democracy, but our imaginative interests appreciate social gradations, and our romantic hunger is satisfied by the allegory of aristocracy.

3. The deposits are actually located on his aunt's land, but this was "to him simply one of those trifling errors which sometimes occur in the partition of vast landed estates." Fortunately for him, Aunt Nancy does not disabuse him, perhaps because she is that "greatest of all blessings, a true Southern lady."

4. Bates talks at some length about this James-and-Wharton theme, usually through his protagonist, a fashionable portrait painter. It becomes apparent that if, not surprisingly, the "City Hall" attitude toward art is a philistine one, the attitude of the city's cultural leaders is frivolous. The awarding of a sculpture commission becomes, finally, a political decision, not one based on merit.

5. The "New Woman" topic received much attention in the novels of this era, and sometimes within the novel-of-manners format (see also Bates's *The Philistines*).

6. The middle-class English scholar, Miss Bocock, cheerfully accepts Sir Basil as "big, and we aren't," and in a very different class from herself. Quite unperturbed about this distinction, she does not fawn upon Sir Basil and gets along very comfortably with him. After all, she is "the intellectual equal of anybody in England." In contrast, the consciously "democratic" American girl, Imogen Upton, is bothered by these differences of class, or seems to be. Later, when she marries Sir Basil, she becomes very snobbish and, in the worst sense, most "devotedly English."

7. Houses for Tarkington, as so often for novelists of manners, serve effectively to express status.

8. Other writers of the period who make use of the genre include Howard Sturgis, a specialist in international backgrounds, and Constance Fenimore Woolson, who also contrasted Old World and New (though mostly in her short stories) and pointed out "good society's" strong impact on the individual.

6

Edith Wharton

*F*OLLOWING the lead of James and Howells much more closely than Cable or Smith, Bates or Grant, Sedgwick or Tarkington, Edith Wharton may more rightfully be said to inherit the manners tradition.[1] She saw in the topic — which she canvassed in novel after novel — not merely comic interplay but significant questions of values. Sharing the James-Howells view of manners as "morals in bloom,"[2] she treated them, in her fiction, with serious concern.

In reality, Mrs. Wharton took several leaves out of the James-Howells book. She, too, set her tales in the world of smart drawing rooms, a world that she knew at first hand, and one that she viewed through an inside-outside lens, appropriately combining identification with perspective. She, too, dealt with themes such as the attempt of moneyed invaders to scale the social ramparts and showed sympathy for the socially misplaced artist types. In these, and in still other respects (e.g., her use of sophisticated image patterns), she acts as a link between James and Howells and their successors, illustrating, in the process, the remarkable unanimity of purpose and technique that binds the novelists of manners.

Because she was a woman of ripe culture and keen intelligence, Mrs. Wharton proved a natural devotee of the form. In offering, or offering up, the mores of New York City's "Four Hundred" of the late nineteenth century, she was, after all, simply writing autobiographically.[3] For this was her background, or, to be chronologically more proper, that of her parents. Mrs. Wharton knew "Old New York" thoroughly, its culture compounded of purity and snobbery, its financial incorruptibility, its impeccable taste, its social amenability — good qualities essentially, but counterbalanced by its sense of "superiority," its dread of change, its overinsistence on good manners, and its placing "decency" before courage. A mixed bag of virtues and vices, so Mrs. Wharton concluded, as she set out to analyze her social environment.

A dominant theme in many of her novels and stories is that of the fate of this particular social group of which she was a part — the retreat of little old New York of the 1870s, the Knickerbocker aristocracy, marching backward when faced with the invasion of the plutocracy, the Astors and Vanderbilts, "the men who have risen," in the 1880s and 1890s. Mrs. Wharton knew well that the latter dynasty was to succeed, indeed, had succeeded, as symbolized in many cases by marriages uniting aristocrat and merchant. Her interest lay in contrasting the two social groups. Though her dislike of the arriviste — the Looty Arlingtons, the Indiana Frusks, the Undine Spraggs, even the Julius Beauforts, all those people from Pruneville, Nebraska — is more than apparent, and though her sympathy is drawn to the aristocrats proudly affirming their caste, she views the struggle between the two societies with detachment, not allowing her sympathies to warp her judgment. So, in *The Age of Inno-*

cence (1920), the "first families" are shown wavering before the onslaught (the weeds pushing up between the ordered rows of social vegetables) of tasteless materialism, but deserving to be upset because their ostrichlike attitudes and dread of scandal indicate a declining culture. Similarly, in *The Buccaneers* (1938), Mrs. Wharton's last — and uncompleted — novel, the merchant class is conquering even the last stronghold of the aristocracy, England, a process that the author by no means wholly regrets, since the fresh charm of "the buccaneers," the invading American girls, counteracts the stodgy narrowness of the old society.

To explore this "old order changeth" theme, Mrs. Wharton makes full use of the novel of manners format. Her best-known novel, *The Age of Innocence,* may serve, initially, as our prototype, since it distinctly illustrates many characteristics of the genre. In the first place, the novel, from beginning to end, gives us a strong sense of contrasting social groups, the aristocrats and the plutocrats. The reader is told on the opening page that the Academy of Music is cherished by the "conservatives" for being small and inconvenient, and thus keeping out the "new people" whom New York was beginning to dread and yet be drawn to. The Old Guard endeavor to maintain their defenses — the van der Luydens defending Ellen Olenska in order to lend support to the Mingotts — but they begin to have their pet "common people," for instance, Mrs. Struthers, the shoe-polish widow, who is snubbed at the beginning of the story but accepted by the end. Thus, says Mrs. Wharton, New York managed its transitions, conspiring to ignore them until they were well over.[4]

Endless examples, some positive, some negative, are proffered of the manners of the ruling — if threatened — class. Its members are wholeheartedly governed by "the thing," for example, the convention of arriving late at the opera. Such conventions, the reader is told, play as important a part in social circles as did the inscrutable totem terrors that had ruled the destinies of the forefathers of this society thousands of years ago. Life is molded by the conventions and the forms, with considerable deference paid to the arbiters of these, such as Lawrence Lefferts. Even the novel's hero, Newland Archer, however aware of some of the shams of his society, often yields to the pattern — "few things seemed to Archer more awful than an offence against 'Taste,' that far-off divinity of whom 'Form' was mere visible representative and vice-regent." Form consists of practicing "beautiful behavior," of avoiding scandal (not everyone does behave well, but it doesn't matter if the scandal is covered up and the surface of society remains unruffled), of creating an atmosphere of "faint implications and pale delicacies," of preserving family solidarity. The most apt demonstration of the importance of form is discerned in the scrupulous carrying out of various social rites: the exchange of betrothal visits (packed in the family landau they rolled from one tribal doorstep to another); the formal dinner routine (the Archer ladies retiring to the drawing room after dinner to stitch, while the men smoke; the 'rites' of Letterblair's dinner); the nineteenth-century New York wedding ceremony (one that seemed to belong to the dawn of history, clothed as it was in faded sables and yellowing ermines and the smell of camphor); the final dinner to Ellen Olenska (in the old New York code, the tribal rally around a kinswoman about to be eliminated from the tribe).[5]

Harmless foibles some of the forms, to be sure, but other qualities on display among the "Four Hundred" seemed more disturbing to Mrs. Wharton. She was bothered by this society's narrow attitude toward divorce, in particular, its endorsement of the double standard, and to a lesser degree by its excessive worship of "the mode." The mode also gave no place to the development of a taste for art and beauty.

New York, as the Marchioness Manson reports, has no conception of pictures, priceless furniture, music, and brilliant conversation. Most deplorable of all were its hypocrisy and basic lack of moral fiber — except in financial matters — which tolerated far too much, provided the forms were preserved and the surface decorum maintained.

This, then, was the way of life among the slightly seedy New York aristocrats, the Mingotts, Wellands, Archers, van der Luydens, and Dagonets. Sheltered and stuffy and full of pretense, they all lived in a kind of hieroglyphic world, where the real thing was never said or done or even thought, but only represented by a set of arbitrary signs. They were, said Newland Archer, patterns on the wall, smug and myopic to boot.

Perhaps it was just as well — Mrs. Wharton almost suggests — that the plutocracy should edge in among them.

In her discussion of the fluidity of the social order, Mrs. Wharton mentions another group, the artists,[6] who might, she reports, very possibly be absorbed into "old New York." Even if these "scattered fragments of humanity had never shown any desire to be amalgamated with the social structure," such a jointure could be mutually helpful. It would at least enlarge the Jones-Newbold-Rhinelander-Roosevelt world, minimizing its near-sightedness and, in particular, counteracting its antiintellectual attitude. A mingling might enlarge the artistic world as well, gentling its Bohemian quality to which Mrs. Wharton strongly objected.[7] Some day, says Mrs. Wharton, not too hopefully, a stage of manners may be reached where the two groups would naturally merge.

The Age of Innocence is given enormous sparkle by the tone of light irony maintained throughout the work. The narrator tempers her sympathy for her subject, the established rich, with a tart quality. Recoiling as she does from "society's" matriarchal aspect, its shrinking from responsibility, its dread of innovation, and its confining innocence and distrust of the creative intelligence, while at the same time approving of its *douceur de vivre,* she presents a frank, often satiric, occasionally nostalgic picture.

The setting of *The Age of Innocence* is vividly and quite extensively treated, as is apt to be the case in a novel of manners, in which the reader must see the people against the background that conditions them. Mrs. Wharton, herself very sensitive about both exterior and interior decoration,[8] lovingly describes the houses in which her principals dwell. The list of dwellings includes Mrs. Manson Mingott's cream-colored affair, courageously built far above the fashionable 34th Street region; the Beaufort town house, with its ball-room seen through a vista of enfiladed drawing rooms as the crowning feature; and the almost equally elaborate Beaufort country house at Newport. The Welland houses, in town and country, are less sympathetically described, Newland Archer objecting, if May Welland does not, to the purple satin and yellow tufting of the drawing room and the wilderness of purple satin and malachite known as the back drawing room. The solid but not very tasteful sumptuousness of this New York establishment offends Archer, as does the similar atmosphere in the Welland place at Newport, an atmosphere so dense, so charged with minute observances and exactions, that it always stole into his system like a narcotic. The houses of the Old Guard so often suggest a deadening, conventional environment, one contrasting with the charming, free air given off by the wonderfully tasteful living room of Mme. Olenska. Mrs. Wharton, of course, always votes for taste over fashion and convention, for the perfect old Dutch manor house on the van der Luyden estate rather than the pretentious mock-Italian villa that is the main house, but she etches in the too lavish habitat like the Newport "cottage" or gilded opera house as faithfully as the simpler structures she prefers. In every case she conveys a precise sense of the uppercrust milieu and of a distinct way of life.

The people in this "world" step briskly before the reader, sharply delineated by Mrs. Wharton's often acid pen. In *The Age of Innocence* the hero's mother, Mrs. Archer, and her daughter Janey — tall, pale, slightly round-shouldered and long-nosed, most genteel and proper, and more than a little malicious — begin the parade. Then come the van der Luydens, with their look of frozen gentleness, social leaders contrasting somewhat with the equally prominent and respected Mrs. Mingott, who can afford to cut many of the conventions and avoid the primness of the van der Luydens. Her relatives the Wellands return the reader to the conventional, as does Sillerton Jackson, the authority on family, A rare exotic is the bedizened Marchioness Manson, she of the hair that had tried to turn white and only succeeded in fading, and of the miscellaneous heap of overshoes, shawls, and tippets.

The characters in the love triangle that forms the novel's chief point of interest are naturally treated at greater length than those who constitute the social background and are more complexly rendered. May Welland appears as representative of the young women in society. A Diana-like girl (she even wins an archery contest), she is handsome but shallow, having, as Mrs. Wharton expresses it, "the vacant serenity of the young marble athlete." Though not devoid of feeling, she lacks imagination — and intellect, too. Traveling for May merely provides an enlarged opportunity for walking. Her loveliness is an encouragement to admiration, but her conversation is a chill to repartee. Her dreamy silences do not indicate thought, Newland Archer discovers, and she is, he concludes, bland and superficial. However, Archer underestimates her a little, not realizing that her innocence masks some penetration, not only her recognition of the Ellen-Newland affair but also her awareness of how to break it

up (by pushing up her wedding date, and, later, by antici-
pating a pregnancy). The "tinge of hardness" in her fresh,
frank voice should not be overlooked, and, though she
cannot be called a bad wife or mother, at the same time she
stands for the hypocrisy of her type and for its rigidity.
May is always "a part of the tribe and incapable of growth;"
moreover, she is not incapable of some of the nastiness
lying behind the "age of innocence."

Newland Archer, like many another Wharton "hero,"
possesses education, intellect, and feeling, but lacks force or
courage, and, if a sympathetic protagonist, is certainly not
a strong one. He suffers from considerable vanity and from a
follow-the-crowd spirit, which, if it permits him to see that
those in the social swim are inferior people, yet does not
encourage him to strike out for himself. While recognizing
that the "green mold of the perfunctory" tends to spread
over him, and while finding that the "taste of the usual" is
like cinders in his mouth — in other words, while aware of
the futility of his way of life — Archer continues to accept
the dictates of his peers and to remain in his rut. Intelligent
and honorable though he is, and able though he may be to
perceive the disloyalty, cruelty, and indifference of old
New York, he lacks the strength to escape from "the invisible
deity of Good Form," with all that it involves. He sees himself as the dwindling figure of a man to whom nothing was
ever to happen — a Jamesian type, surely — and by and
large the right things do not happen to him.

The third member of the triangle, Ellen Olenska, receives
the largest measure of Mrs. Wharton's approval, even if, as
a woman separated from her husband, she is not so favorably
regarded by her social circle. A natural, cultivated, witty, and
charming person, she appeals to the reader as well. If slightly
unconventional, she is so only because she has lived in
"bigger places" than New York, places where the codes of

conduct are less inflexible. As a simple, kindly, and honest individual, she seems destined to fare badly among the snobbish and pretentious New Yorkers, even if her questionable past had not given them a "clear right" to eye her askance.

Mrs. Wharton's theme in *The Age of Innocence* is derived from an examination of the interrelationship among Countess Olenska, May Welland, and Newland Archer. In the novel she expounds, as she had before and would several times again, upon the cruelty of social convention and the tyranny of the "in" group. The social arbiters militate against the individual, forcing him to give up his happiness for the duty that they dictate, causing him to yield his ideals, which they regard as impractical in the social order. Here, Ellen Olenska and Newland Archer must sacrifice their ideal of love, since she is married (and subsequently, he) and the scandal of divorce is unthinkable. On two occasions Archer is prepared to defy convention and achieve his happiness, but he is deftly forestalled each time by May Welland. She first cagily advances their wedding date, then, two years later, announces — somewhat prematurely, it would seem — her pregnancy. And the marriage holds up — "the same black abyss yawned before him" — even if May's pressure bears on the angles whose sharpness Archer had most wanted to keep. From the beginning she had represented stability, comradeship, and the "steadying sense of unescapable duty," and she continues to represent these. Duty wins again.

The Countess and Archer constantly try to rationalize about their position, to convince themselves that their sacrifice of happiness produced greater good, but it is difficult to agree with them. One Wharton critic, Marilyn Lyde, does suggest that Archer, by never submitting mentally to the dullness of his group and by channeling his continued spiritual devotion to Ellen into a positive passion for civic reform, manages to give meaning to his life.[9] But this seems too rosy a view. Archer's life had certainly been routine from beginnning to end, and the dullness of his surroundings, one feels, must have worn off upon him. Moreover, always a contemplative and dilettante, he did not prove very effective in his reform work. The best that one can say of Archer is that he did not indulge in an ignominious surrender to convention — he does not blindly follow its commands in the later stages of the book as he had at the outset — but surely he is a defaulting hero, one well aware that he had missed the "flower of life."

Perhaps a faint hope that the generation to follow Archer will battle more valiantly with convention is adumbrated near the novel's end. Archer speaks of the attitude of his son Dallas, one reflecting a lack of concern about the past and a feeling of being very equal to the present. But if he admires his son's boldness, Archer is still rather suspicious of him and of his ideals, and one surmises that Mrs. Wharton entertains equal reservations about the possibly more honest but probably less graceful new generation.

The Age of Innocence, like the majority of Mrs. Wharton's novels, and, indeed, like the majority of novels of manners, is a well-constructed work of fiction, subscribing, one might readily say, to the author's dictum that "every great novel must first of all be based on a profound sense of moral values, and then constructed with a classical unity and economy of means."[10] Mrs. Wharton places her "situation" before us, a conflict between group and individual standards, then develops it crisply. Beginning in a lively manner, offering "signposts" in the form of revelatory little scenes along the way, then mounting to a striking and ironic climax, she creates a focused yet naturally unfolded story. The narrative in *The Age of Innocence* falls into two segments: the events leading up to the setting of the marriage date, and those following, with the climax occurring when the marriage is saved at a threatening point later on. A quiet denouement ensues, the account of Archer's visit to Paris with his son thirty years after the novel's principal incidents, and his refusal at this time to see Madame Olenska. The "overness" of the affair is thus lightly accentuated. Throughout the novel, the affair, or "situation," remains central, and lying behind it the dissection of a certain social sphere.

Contributing to the sense of unity is the author's reliance on the restricted point of view as the means by which the story is told. Most of the action is channeled through Newland Archer, who appears in almost every scene and whose viewpoint on these scenes very much coincides with that of the reader. What the reader knows and thinks of Ellen Olenska, for example, is pretty much what Archer knows and thinks. The novel is given reality, intensity, *and* suspense by this device, with the question of the actual character and status of Ellen — and thus the larger question of whether society or the individual is "right" — remaining in doubt for a long time.

Mrs. Wharton tells her story in a style that is pungent, facile, and witty — again, one ventures to say, all but a requirement of this particular genre, which demands a sophisticated manner of writing in order to preserve its urbane air. The novel abounds, for one thing, in similes and metaphors, arresting in the satiric picture they conjure up. Thus, Mrs. Manson Mingott's appearance: "a flight of smooth double chins led down to the dizzy depths of a still-snowy bosom . . . with two tiny hands poised like gulls on the surface of the billows." Or, the eight tall ushers at a wedding, gathering themselves like birds or insects, preparing for some migratory maneuver. Often the figures of speech deliberately "come out of" the world under surveillance: the younger architects beginning to protest against the brownstone "of which the uniform hue coated New York like a cold chocolate sauce"; Ellen Olenska crouching among the festive ripples of her dress like a stricken masquerader.

Mrs. Wharton employs similarly appropriate patterns of imagery in the novel. I have already spoken of the recurring anthropological images of totems, taboos, rites, and rituals, a group which accentuates, as Viola Hopkins says,[11] the ethnocentrism of Newland Archer's world and perhaps shows its "civilization" to be unflatteringly primitive. Another cluster of images centers about the van der Luydens, the Pharaohs of the New York social structure, and, as such, described as sovereign and sacerdotal. They are also associated with "dead" images, however — "cold," "frozen," "icy," "mausoleum," "shrouded room" — and appropriately, since they rule a dynasty that is falling. One also finds religious imagery mockingly assigned to the "principles" that the van der Luyden world worships, the "deity of Good Form," Etiquette as an idol, May Welland a "tutelary divinity," and Taste as the chief of the gods.

The balanced sentences that predominate in the novel often contain flashing ironies (Mrs. Welland "signed a haggard welcome;" Mrs. van der Luyden shines on Ellen "with the dim benevolence which was her nearest approach to cordiality") and/or an epigrammatic cast ("our legislation favors divorce; our social customs do not;" "the worst of doing one's duty was that it apparently unfitted one for anything else"). The diction supports the syntax in conveying the book's ironic flavor, especially when Mrs. Wharton overstates (Mrs. Mingott's bedroom is on the ground floor "in *flagrant* violation of all the New York proprieties") in order to mock the social legalism of the Knickerbocker group, using the serious word for trivialities, or the one with moral overtones for conventions.[12] Some of the proper names may symbolize ironically, too: Archer as the ineffectual bowman, Ellen a misplaced Helen, May as innocence, overlapped, here, with conformity.[13]

The work as a whole is highly spiced with satire, Mrs. Wharton's observations tingling sharply: the German text of French operas sung by Swedish artists, translated into Italian for the clearer understanding of English-speaking audiences;. Americans wanting to get away from amusement even more quickly than they want to get to it; Mrs. Archer never traveling without a complete family pharmacy; Mrs. Mingott admiring impulsiveness — if it did not lead to the spending of money; Miss Sophy Jackson saying something conciliatory when she knew that she was planting a dart. And so on. The choice of words is clever, the use of the periodic sentence allows the irony to hit full force, and the whole sentence-paragraph sequence flows smoothly and naturally.

With its consistently ironic style, precisely delineated characters and settings, and carefully worked-out theme, *The Age of Innocence* qualifies as an excellent novel. More particularly, it qualifies as an excellent novel of manners, being devoted to so thorough a discussion of the mores of old New York. The stagnancy, the snobbery, the intellectual limitations, above all, the unhappily pervasive pressure of convention present among the aristocratic leaders force Mrs. Wharton to mingle considerable censure with her mild regret at the waning of their power.

Most of Edith Wharton's novels and stories repeat the pattern of *The Age of Innocence,* exploring the "museum world"[14] of gentlewomen and lawyers, living "in uniform streets of chocolate house fronts" just above Washington Square, "a small, sober, proper, tightly knit society."[15] The interest of this world, according to Robert Morss Lovett, lies in the opportunity it offers for intensive personal relations and poignant human intercourse within the forms and ceremonies of social life. In studying these, Mrs. Wharton is "in the highest sense a novelist of manners,"[16] deploying before us an aristocracy with a common language and tastes and with a distinguished and ornamental ancestral background. In her description of the archaic society of *The Age of Innocence,* as seen above, she frequently uses the concept of the tribe, thereby emphasizing the "apartness" of this class, an apartness that it attempted to preserve by inbreeding and by deliberate exclusion from its environment of alien elements. Her twice-told tale of the wasting away of this class in the face of the plutocratic assault carries immense conviction, for "she knew the reality of class as no theoretically Marxist or social egalitarian can know it — in her bones. She knew that the difference between rich and poor, between the socially protected and vulnerable, are more than mere forms or illusions, that they are the realest of realities."[17]

If always concerned with the "entrenched" New Yorkers, Mrs. Wharton, in some of her fiction, removes them from their native habitat and transplants them to Europe, thus following the example of James and Howells. In England, and to an even greater degree in France, she found happy points from which to explore the subject of manners. Her attitude toward the subject is precisely revealed in *A Motor-Flight Through France:*

> Never more vividly than in this Seine country does one feel the amenity of French manners, the long process of social adaptation which has produced so profound and general an intelligence of life. Every one we passed on our way . . . all these persons . . . took their ease or pursued their business with that cheerful activity which proceeds from an intelligent acceptance of given conditions. They each had their established niche in life . . . And this admirable *fitting into the pattern,* which seems almost as if it were a moral outcome of the universal French sense of form, has led the race to the happy, the momentous discovery that good manners are a short cut to one's goal, that they lubricate the wheels of life instead of obstructing them. This discovery — the result, as it strikes one, of the application of the finest of

mental instruments to the muddled process of living — seems to have illuminated not only the social relation but its outward, concrete expression, producing a finish in the material setting of life, a kind of conformity in inanimate things — forming, in short, the background of the spectacle through which we pass, the canvas on which it is painted, and expressing itself no less in the trimness of each individual garden than in the insistence on civic dignity and comeliness so miraculously maintained, through every torment of political passion, every change of social conviction, by a people resolutely addressed to the intelligent enjoyment of living.[18]

Her approval of the French "passion for form and fitness"[19] and its "long practice of manners"[20] is evident, for example, in her novelette *Mme. de Treymes* (1907). To be sure, the contrast drawn here between Frenchmen and Americans reflects — as it does so often in James, also — a qualifiying of the virtues of each, the impeccable but corrupt French nobles offset by the morally good but socially inept Americans. If the scales tip finally in the direction of the latter, yet Mrs. Wharton is obviously intrigued by many features of French aristocracy, its tight family organization, mysterious solidarity, network of accepted prejudices and opinions, and strong sense of tradition, and she makes fully apparent the charm and grace of one of its representatives, Mme. de Treymes. Although the French aristocracy can produce dissoluteness and unfortunate patterns of living such as the "made" marriages that cause the participants, that is, Mme. de Treymes, to seek lovers, it avoids the "social darkness" so evident at the dinner given by the American expatriates the Boykins — all crude talk and too fancy dishes.

Despite her appreciation of the lure of French social life, Mrs. Wharton did not find American expatriates, such as the Boykins, fitting into the scene very happily. The Riviera set, described in novels such as *The Mother's Recompense* (1925) and *The Gods Arrive* (1932), fare badly, often carrying to

Europe their undesirable traits and not appearing to acquire much gloss in the new setting. Most of them are futile escapists, or arrivistes taking the grand tour because it's the thing to do, anyway. Thus, in *The Mother's Recompense:*

> They were all there: the American Consul's wife, mild, plump and irreproachable; the lovely Mrs. Prentiss of San Francisco, who "took things" and had been involved in a drug scandal; . . . the Consul's sister, who dressed like a flapper, and had been engaged during the war to a series of American officers, all of whom seemed to have given her celluloid bangles; and a pale Mrs. Marsh, who used to be seen about with a tall tired man called the "Colonel," whose family-name was not Marsh, but for whom she wore mourning when he died, explaining — somewhat belatedly — that he was a cousin. [P. 28]

In such a faintly Bohemian and certainly not very charming world, the novel's heroine Kate Clephane, long exiled from New York because of a decided marital indiscretion, lives out her life, preserving a bare modicum of the forms to which she had been accustomed — willing to domicile herself in a cheap hotel but unwilling to sacrifice her maid. "One couldn't afford everything, especially since the war, and she preferred veal for dinner every night to having to do her own mending and dress her hair."

The arty crowd depicted in *The Gods Arrive* appear in an even less attractive light, as do those who cultivate them, the Mrs. Glaishers and Mrs. Blemers, stupid nouveaux riches, who, panting after the latest thing, begin to buy "Picassos and Modiglianis, to invite friends to hear Stravinsky and Darius Milhaud, to patronize exotic dancers, and labor privately (the hardest part . . .) over the pages of *Ulysses.*" Given the conjunction of fake aesthetes like Lorry Spear and celebrity hunters like Mrs. Glaisher, Mrs. Wharton can be savage indeed. Well aware of the merits of French artists and intellectuals (and, incidentally, impressed by their assured social position),[21] Mrs. Wharton doubly regrets the shallowness displayed by would-be American artists and intellectuals living in, but not blending into, the French milieu.

Occasionally in her fiction Mrs. Wharton moved, not eastward to Europe but westward to America's great plains, a region that she — knowing nothing at first hand about it — rather stridently described as a vast desert, the source of the philistinism fast descending on the American scene. So, the hero of *Hudson River Bracketed* (1929), Advance G. Weston, is born into the world of narrow religion, bad cooking, bastard architecture, dull amusements, and a pervasive go-getting spirit that is Euphoria, Illinois.[22] As quickly as possible, he moves east, first to his cousins' family mansion on the Hudson, then into the fashionable and artistic circles of New York. The only thing to do with the West, in Mrs. Wharton's opinion, is to leave it.

Ill content with the American Middle West and uneasy with at least the expatriate version of the European scene, Mrs. Wharton for the most part followed Henry James's advice to be "tethered in native pastures," thus confining herself to the "backyard of New York," and reporting, in novel after novel, on the assault of the new millionaires on the old Knickerbocker society. Knowing full well that invaders and defenders were bound ultimately "to bury their hatchet in a noisy, stamping dance," she yet found pleasure in treating and re-treating the "assault," for she sensed "the rich possibilities for satire in the contrasts afforded by the battle line in its last stages and the pathos of the individuals who were fated to be trampled under the feet of those boisterous truce makers."[23]

The House of Mirth (1905) offers an early example, the novel unfolding the tragedy of Lily Bart, a young lady brought up in "society," but lacking the necessary money to retain her place and therefore forced into the unenviable role of a social parasite. Applauded by her "group" if she amuses them, but condemned or ignored when she is compelled, for financial reasons, to seek the protection of the outer fringe, she twists and turns and eventually succumbs, finding suicide the only way out, destroyed by the heartless society that has molded her. Not that Lily is absolved of personal responsibility. She has demonstrated the moral flaw of social ambition and, though unwilling to play the game in society's way, disdaining its shabby compromises and yielding to impulses that vie with her "most gifted conformity,"[24] she still cannot give up society. Hers is a hard decision — made doubly so by the strength of heredity and environment that have shaped her — but it is her decision. She *could* have sacrificed the "house of mirth" for the "republic of the spirit."

While unfolding Lily's conflict between the claims of "sense" and "spirit," the author lays out the social topography against which the conflict is posed, the settled aristocracy over here, the moving plutocracy over there. As a student of manners, Mrs. Wharton is able to "fix" both groups, the former, tepidly devoted to family, form, and culture,[25] the latter, more concerned about the distribution of wealth and the social privileges resulting from it. Mrs. Wharton very effectively dramatizes the plutocracy's social-climbing adventure, outlining a "hundred shades of aspect and manner"[26] as she describes how its representatives are engaged in determining their status in society. The climbing action of the plutocracy suggests society's pyramidal structure, and indeed *The House of Mirth* indicates several gradations. Mrs. Wharton explores, with Proustian exactitude, the world of the great country houses at the apex; that of the Gormers, lower on the pyramid, people rich enough to be ultimately accepted but still at the stage of having to fill their home with hangers-on; lower still the bogus intellectual world of Carry Fisher; and lowest of all the gilded hotel environment of the demimondaine Norma Hatch.[27] Significantly, money is the common denominator at all levels.[28]

Mrs. Wharton judges the scene she surveys, approving of the sweetness and responsiveness to beauty of Lily Bart, while objecting to the hypocrisies to which she is forced to resort; admiring the mind and sensitivity of Lawrence Selden, while objecting to his knuckling under to society's authority; accepting as desirable the taste and sense of continuity of the aristocracy, while objecting to its twisted values — to the elite "piety is a comic virtue"[29] — and its meanly self-protective attitude.

The book's well-bred surface does not conceal its dark texture. The plight of its half-belonging, half-rebelling protagonist produces a somber reaction and reminds the reader that the novel of manners "can register both the surface of social life and the inner vibrations of spirit that surface reveals, suppresses and distorts."[30] The subject of "civilization and its discontents" — to use Freud's phrase — does not promote levity.

Successor to *The House of Mirth, The Custom of the Country* (1913) follows the former's lead in toning down the comic note as it deals with the standard Wharton topic of societal realignments. Shifting, in her choice of protagonists, from defender (Lily Bart) to invader (Undine Spragg), Mrs. Wharton grimly — almost too grimly — delineates the "climb" of Miss Spragg, all the way from Apex City to Paris. Quietly disposing of her first husband before moving on to New York, Undine, in the latter locale, manages to marry again, an old-school New Yorker, Ralph Marvell. Though thus equipped with social position and a respectable establishment, Undine hungers for greater scope and so goes on to Paris and into a third marriage, with the French nobleman Raymond de Chelles. Eventually the wheel turns full circle, Undine returning to her first husband, Elmer Moffatt, now very wealthy as the "Railroad King." Ironically, she still falls short of satisfying her unquenchable ambition for power and position.

The rampant state of the new materialism is mirrored in the meteoric rise of Undine Spragg. Very harshly Mrs. Wharton depicts her as amoral, unsentimental, conscienceless, and cheap,[31] yet with society now constituted as it is, she can forge ahead unimpeded. Mrs. Wharton has concluded that the "custom of the country" decrees money to be the open sesame, with social convention now transmogrified into a superficial veneer of good manners, which hardly mask an essential vulgarity. The main characteristic of the social structure of the day, Mrs. Wharton implies, is instability, its hierarchy being rearranged on a simple pecuniary basis, thus leaving the field open to the social adventurer.

Inevitably disturbed by this phenomenon, Mrs. Wharton, in her subsequent fiction, looks to the ordered past and nostalgically — though the satiric edge is always there[32] — summons up the pre-assault era in such works as *The Age of Innocence* and *Old New York* (1924). The latter, a collection of novelettes (*False Dawn, The Old Maid, The Spark,* and *New Year's Day*), is devoted to picturing the 1840-1870 world of formidable brownstone mansions, academies of music, and "downtown" — the vaguely described place of business, where people, it would seem, seldom had to be. It is a world of sober precedence — the grandmother's carriage preceding the aunt's — of order and form, of leisure, and of a fair amount of taste. Houses are carefully appointed, clothes are carefully chosen, dinners are carefully given.

From the novelettes the reader learns of the self-assured nature of the New Yorkers, their clannishness, their adherence to custom (betrothals, weddings, and funerals all have their pattern — the mourning crape at a precise length — in this "most totem-ridden of communities"), their narrow point of view, and their esthetic limitations. However charming the surface, those polished manners, and tasteful ceremonies, the environment exudes an airless atmosphere. Delia Ralston in *The Old Maid* sees the walls of her own grave in her surroundings. Attitudes are reactionary, family pressure is too intense, the values are often distorted (if society would not condone drink and dishonesty, it did condone almost everything else, including the double standard of morality, hypocrisy, and snobbery), and the culture is decidedly barren. No one read the books in his library, and the creative intelligence was actively distrusted. Such a world was destined to succumb.

And so it did, capitulating rapidly to the plutocracy after the Civil War. The old society had possessed a varnished shell, but one that covered a materialism as permeating as that evident in the richest parvenu. The money motif dominates, as has been pointed out, in *The House of Mirth* and *The Custom of the Country.* In the former the victims are those, like Lily Bart, weak enough to care for the luxury but too fastidious to play the game. In the latter the victims *do* play the game; Claire Marvell yields to the invader Peter Van Degen and learns to repent "in the Van Degen diamonds, and the Van Degen motor [which] bore her broken heart from opera to ball." If perhaps more masked in *Old New York,* still the money motif is discernible, and the class barriers are demonstrably breaking down. Everyone, even the Wesson clan, now goes to the parties of the shoe-polish heiress Mrs. Struthers.

Mrs. Wharton continues her discussion of the amalgamation of the aristocracy with the plutocracy in *The Mother's Recompense,* where one sees the union accomplished under the heading of the "new tolerance." When Kate Clephane returns to America, after many years abroad, she is impressed by the sense of change[33] in this essentially "manner-less-age." Mrs. Lanfrey's yea or nay was almost the last survival of the old social code, and, though the Clephane, Drover, and Tresselton clans are still in dominating positions, even they have been forced to modify their views in order to maintain those positions. The ancient matriarchal rule has given way to that of youth, a bland and too uniform youth, as Mrs. Clephane sees it, and certainly a more tolerant one, sanctioning divorce and other variants from the rigid pattern of yore. Mrs. Clephane recognizes some merit, and so does Mrs. Wharton, one senses, in the veering away from "all the unintelligible ritual with which they [had] barricaded themselves against the alarming business of living," but she entertains doubts as to whether the lives of the *new* generation are not equally "packed with futilities." It would appear that the merger of the old and new societies has cost each its true character and has introduced an inane composite face.

This somewhat petulant disdain for the "modern age" marred Mrs. Wharton's later novels (e.g., *Hudson River Bracketed* and *The Gods Arrive*), most critics agreeing that her treatment of the aristocracy's yielding to the predatory arrivistes grew into a sour caricature. But her last novel, the unfinished *The Buccaneers* (1938), proves a late-in-the-day exception. In this interesting and amusing tale, the Wharton touch returns, and a new-found sympathy with the parvenus considerably mitigates the caricature. Looking backward from the mid-thirties, the author regards the invasion of the "buccaneers" forty years earlier as perhaps a healthy movement, for, awkward, uncultured, and superficial though they were, still, they introduced new blood and vitality into both the effete New York society and into the English aristocracy as well. The charming invaders are now sanctioned by Mrs.

Wharton, especially Nan St. George, a happy blend of the new world conjoined to a sensitive appreciation of the tradition and continuity of the old.

As in her previous fictions, Mrs. Wharton is careful to set the scene, first the summer resort Saratoga "at the height of the racing-season," then the English fashionable world of country houses and baronial estates. To Saratoga, adventurers like the St. Georges, the Clossons, and the Elmsworths flock, their presence suggesting the changing social patterns. One could hardly tell a lady from an actress, "or-er-the other kind of woman; and society at Saratoga, now that all the best people were going to Newport, had grown as mixed and confusing as the fashions." In an atmosphere of swayed fans and iced refreshments, there sat rocking on the hotel verandas, amid the tall white columns of the portico, which so often reminded cultured travelers of the "Parthenon at Athens (Greece)," the wives of the plutocrats, anxiously brooding over the problem of launching their daughters into society. About them flitted these very daughters, Virginia and Nan St. George, Conchita Closson, the Elmsworth sisters, exhibiting the collective grace of the "American girl," the world's highest achievement — Mrs. Wharton's tongue is only partly in her cheek. Their mothers — or, rather, their fathers — had the money (though one could be up one day and down the next, as the secret gods of Wall Street decreed), but the girls very much needed some "social discipline" before they could enter the precincts of the Four Hundred.

The necessary social guidance will be provided by one who turns out to be Mrs. Wharton's focal character, Laura Testvalley, an Anglo-Italian governess of much experience and unlimited savoir faire. Miss Testvalley, not very much attracted to her first American employers, the Parmores, who, if they are New York's crème de la crème in their own opinion, represent at best to Laura a milieu of retired Colonials at Cheltenham or the household of a minor canon in a cathredral town, moves on to the "new people," who will pay more, and who will provide a comparison of the manners and customs of the new and the not-new that "might be amusing." She soon finds herself drawn to her charges, whose prettiness and verve compensate for their lack of style and finesse.

The scene eventually shifts to London, as the American girls, following the lead of Conchita Closson who has managed to ally herself to an English lord (of very little worth), seek the entrée into society that has been denied them in New York. Aided by Miss Testvalley and by a fellow American, Jacky March, whose "narrow front door led straight into the London world,"[34] the "new band of marauders, social aliens though they were," make a big splash, relying on their beauty and their naturalness (Miss Testvalley wisely advises her covey of Daisy Millers to act in their own way — "That will amuse them much more than if you try to copy them") to carry them through. Soon they are attending the Queen's Drawing Room (infinitely more impressive than a New York assembly), beautifully dressed and enjoying themselves immensely, and later, established in a cottage on the Thames, they draw the lords and ladies — mostly the lords — to their side. Miss Testvalley follows the "Runnymede revels" with a keen eye: "The invasion of England had been her own invention, and from a thousand little signs she already knew it would end in conquest." The young men soon saw that the girls must be treated with the same respect, if not with the same ceremony, as English girls of good family, and they courted assiduously. The cottage at Runnymede became "an outpost in a conquered province."

The girls find their husbands — titled ones for the most part — and plunge happily into the London social swim, "Belgravia and Mayfair, shooting parties in great country-houses, and the rest of the fashionable routine." The effects of the "conquest" are not altogether fortuitous, however. Conchita Closson, soon discontent with Lord Richard Marable, goes about openly with her lover Miles Dawnly. Virginia St. George becomes enslaved to the dull, half-asleep Lord Seadown Brightlingsea, absorbed in questions of rank and precedence, and "actually in awe of the stupid arrogance of her father-in-law and bewildered condescensions of Lady Brightlingsea." Only Lizzie Elmsworth, marrying Hector Robinson, a member of the plutocracy like herself, seems sure of much happiness.

Mrs. Wharton is most concerned with the marriage of Nan St. George to the Duke of Tintagel, a marriage that appears the best of all but which proves the least workable. Nan, far more sensitive than her fellow Americans and more in key with the British love of tradition — "At least life in England had a background" — is the most receptive to the English atmosphere, but her husband, if superficially typifying glorious old Albion, turns out to be an incredibly stuffy and empty individual, and their marriage is loveless and hollow. Nan *should* have married Guy Thwaite, one who is slightly less blue-blooded but infinitely more intelligent and worthy. Mrs. Wharton's working plan for the uncompleted portion of *The Buccaneers* reveals that Nan will run off with Thwaite to South Africa, thus utterly defying convention but very possibly achieving happiness. The novel would have become morally as well as socially radical!

Equipped with the double setting of England and America, *The Buccaneers* can register, in Jamesian fashion, some instructive international contrasts. The American social scene, whether at the Saratoga hotels where the parvenus live a vapid existence or at the New York mansions where the already-arrived live an equally vapid existence, appears rather bleak. Those inhabiting it worry about the proper set,[35] about clothes, "those tight perpendicular polonaises bunched up at the back" and the "outrageously low square-cut evening gowns" that the Paris dressmakers were sending over, and about other equally frivolous concerns. At first glance the English social scene has a far more attractive cast. Behind it lies tradition, as embodied, for example, in the ancient walls and ancient trees of Honourslove, the Thwaite country home, "thick with webs of memory." The more impressive estates, such as Allfriars, Inigo Jones's most triumphant expression of the Palladian dream, look palatial, and the way of life within them is ordered, gracious, and cultured. However, most of the inhabitants of the "palaces" prove scarcely less vacuous than their American counterparts. The wastrel Lord Richard Marable, the stupid Lady Bright-lingsea, the egocentric Lord Brightlingsea, turning about "busily in the empty shell of his own mind," the socially arrogant and spiritually poor Lady Churt, the weak Ushant, Duke of Tintagel — they are an unattractive lot. If they know how to give a shooting party, if they grasp the meaning of institutions and understand the hundreds of minute obser-vances that form the texture of an old society, still, the British aristocracy have decidedly material standards (Lady Brightlingsea objects to her son's "entanglement" with Lady Churt only because it is so expensive), and they place far more emphasis on forms than on moral values. The Americans seem rooted in a more austere tradition, clinging more firmly to honesty and integrity. Behind the surface gush lies modesty, behind the bumptiousness, a lack of sham.

But all this is perhaps taking *The Buccaneers* a little more seriously than it should be taken. The book's mood is that of comedy, and so it remains, even if a serious moral problem was to be introduced into the unfinished section. Mrs. Wharton pleasantly satirizes the English and the Americans: on the one hand, the pallid Miss Parmore, a young lady "finished" by Miss Testvalley but "whom Nature seems scarcely to have begun;" on the other hand, the flustered Lady Brightlingsea, whose face "always grew plaintive when she was asked to squeeze one more fact — even one already familiar — into her weary and overcrowded memory." British provincialism is mocked, as is American gaucherie. Mrs. Wharton is particularly severe toward the Duke of Tintagel, so permeated with his stultified notions of dukedom (producing an heir is the sole "purpose for which Dukes make the troublesome effort of marrying") that he cannot appreciate his charming bride, Nan St. George, an American "free spirit."[36]

The exploration in *The Buccaneers* — as in its predecessors — of the "art" of manners involved all the resources of Mrs. Wharton's formidable technique. *The Buccaneers* is as craftsmanlike a performance as *The Age of Innocence*, and the same might be said of *The House of Mirth*, of *Old New York*, and of most of her other work.

Mrs. Wharton is skilled, for one thing, in sharply defining her settings, Washington Square, the Faubourg St. Germain, and even Oubli-sur-Mer, the not quite fashionable Riviera resort. Exteriors are minutely described (the Halston Raycie country home, formerly a settler's cottage, thus appears: "no one could have detected the humble outline of the old house in the majestic stone-colored dwelling built of tongued-and-grooved boards, with an angle tower, tall narrow windows, and a veranda on chamfered posts, that figured so confidently as a 'Tuscan villa' in Downing's 'Landscape Gardening in America' "), and interiors as well (the Correggio room at Longlands, or Fred Landers's comfortable old drawing room with its many armchairs, Steinway piano, and the family Chippendale), and both the "in" and "out" views tend to reveal the character of the inhabitants. Mrs. Wharton does not permit her love of landscape and informed interest in architecture to run away with her; instead she makes the scenic details always conform to relevance and thus obeys her own dictum set down in *The Writing of Fiction:* "The impression produced by a landscape, a street or a house should always, to the novelist, be an event in the history of a soul." Scene functions integrally, then, in helping to define character.

Selection and balance contribute to the sense of form in Mrs. Wharton's fiction, to the well-made novel effect, and nowhere more readily than in the structure. In *The House of Mirth,* for example, a careful sense of design is apparent, with the first chapter establishing various strands of the theme,[37] with the large cast of characters kept in controlled relationships, and with the focus on the theme — the house-of-mirth/republic-of-the-spirit juxtaposition — sustained throughout. The restricted point of view, first Lily Bart's, then Lawrence Selden's, maintains the proportion, since it channels events through one or the other of the two principals.

Mrs. Wharton remains in perfect control of her characters, too, pinpointing their outward appearance by a few salient details, and granting insights into their mental processes as well. Sillerton Jackson's narrow mask and withered pink cheeks (*New Year's Day*) epitomize this superannuated *arbiter elegantiae,* whose well-tailored figure crops up in more than one of Mrs. Wharton's novels. Lizzie Hazeldean's phil-andering minister father is likewise hit off by the description of his snowy head, unctuous voice, and edifying manners, which he carried "from one cheap watering-place to another, through an endless succession of sentimental and pecuniary entanglements," The dowagers in prunella sandals and low-necked sarcenet and the beautifully mannered, albeit vapid, old gentlemen flock vividly through the novelist's pages.

More time is naturally devoted to the protagonists, who, as multifaceted individuals, usually seem more lifelike, for example, Lizzie Hazeldean in *New Year's Day* or Kate Clephane in *The Mother's Recompense*. Often these people are posed against the group, as Mrs. Wharton examines one of her favorite subjects, the rebel at odds with the "clan."[38] So, Ellen Olenska, so Lewis Raycie, or Hayley Delane, or Lizzie Hazeldean. Too good for their society in many ways, yet shaped by it, they become relatively unhappy victims, and the reader, since the characters are actualized for him and made, in a modest way, to seem tragic, "identifies" with their plights and feels sympathy. Mrs. Wharton shares this sympathy, though not permitting it to blunt her incisive analysis of the "victims."

Her style may well give the most conclusive evidence of Mrs. Wharton's workmanship, since it provides, almost constantly, the properly witty and tart tone — Meredith's comic spirit — that her novels of manners demand. In poised and chiseled sentences she maintains the slightly — and sometimes more than slightly — ironic note from beginning to end. Her sentence pattern is often periodic, the point, usually in the form of an epigram, coming at the end. The rather elaborate sentence structure of the narrative portions is counterbalanced by the simpler dialogue sequences, of which there are a great many. Mrs. Wharton knows human speech, the rather formal talk of the old clubman, the more slangy philistine conversation, the patter of the culture clubs, and the jargon of the studios. The dialogue is expert not only in its naturalness but also in its providing crisp exposition and dramatic continuity.

Diction as well as syntax contributes to the success of the prose. The figurative language abounds, the images appropriately belonging to the world they evoke. One finds such similes and metaphors as these: "The room looked at him like an alien countenance composed into a polite grimace." Hylton Davies "had the soul of a club steward." "Such opinions as she had were imposing and substantial; her mind, like her house, was furnished with monumental 'pieces' that were not meant to be disarranged." The play of wit is constant and yet not merely clever. When Mrs. Wharton describes "the meditative rigidity of fashionable persons listening to expensive music," she succinctly if obliquely comments on their hypocrisy and suggests their values. In the balanced phrase, "it was typical of my mother to be always employed in benevolent actions while she uttered uncharitable words," the verbal dexterity impresses, but the character is also defined. The most frequently appearing pattern of imagery, the anthropological terms (so prevalent, as already indicated, in *The Age of Innocence*) serve as arresting descriptions but also make abundantly clear the hidebound nature of this "ancient" society, composed of huge, imperious clans governed by inexorable laws. This concept of inflexibility is further supported by the "icy" images (e.g., the "glacial neatness" of Mrs. Peniston's drawing room in *The House of Mirth*) so often assigned to the aristocracy. Equally in keeping are the pirate-on-the-high-seas images attached to the plutocracy in *The Buccaneers*. "Band of marauders," "outpost in a conquered province," "the healthy hardships of the road," "gales whistling through one's mental rigging," Miss March "on her watch-tower" — the phrases scintillate but, at the same time, harmonize with the book's subject, the plutocrats' invasion of England.

Certainly, then, Mrs. Wharton's style is more than merely decorative. The cleverness of her remarks — "The meeting between her mother and her betrothed had been thickly swaddled in layer on layer of non-conducting, non-explosive 'family'"; "The Drovers and Tresseltons were great at acting in concert, and at pretending that whatever happened was natural, usual, and not of a character to interfere with one's lunch" — does not belie their penetration.

If Mrs. Wharton's work has been relegated to the "archeological shadows," as Diana Trilling says with regret,[39] it does not deserve to remain there, for, within her admittedly narrow range, she performs in a masterly way, coolly observing, poignantly recording. Few can surpass her social appraisal: her reproduction of environment — the Sargent portraits, the rare, flowering plants, the minutiae of costume — to symbolize qualities of period and class; her employment of characters as social types, for example, the Marchesa di San Fedele of *Twilight Sleep,* impoverished unlike her New York cousins, but "still a useful social card. . . . a means of paying off her social scores;" the generally high style of her "dance upon the Aubusson carpet."[40]

It must not be forgotten, moreover, that she puts her study of the social fabric to serious use. Delving behind the forefront of social life — behind such apparently lightweight concerns as declining invitations and social ostracizing — to the level where manners reveal moral stress and faulty codes of conduct, she uncovers the inadequacy of human beings, leaving us, finally, with a despondent sense of life. This seems to be her personal vision,[41] and her appraisal of society — the lighter moments notwithstanding — would seem to warrant the vision.

NOTES TO CHAPTER 6

1. Vernon Loggins views the line of succession in this way: "William Dean Howells kept step with James in turning out novels of manners, but at every step James overshadowed him. And James overshadowed all of his numerous successors, except perhaps Edith Wharton, his pupil. Her fiction shows the old code of social relationships in its decline. So does the best work of Ellen Glasgow" (Vernon Loggins, *I Hear America* [New York: Thomas Y. Crowell Co., 1937], p. 178).

2. Stow Persons's phrase nicely corresponds to one that Edward Wagen-knecht assigns to James, that manners are "the outward signs of an inner spiritual grace" (Edward Wagenknecht, *Calvalcade of the American Novel* [New York: Henry Holt & Co., 1952], p. 163).

3. "My instinct as a story-teller counselled me to use the material nearest to hand and most familiarly my own. . . . The novelist should deal only with what is within his reach" (Edith Wharton, *A Backward Glance* [New York and London: D. Appleton-Century Co., 1934], p. 206).

4. Annette Baxter, in an interesting article comparing Wharton's New York with Howells's Boston, suggests that the new moneyed set in New York was able to "pressure" far more successfully than the corresponding set in Boston (see Annette K. Baxter, "Caste and Class: Howells' Boston and Wharton's New York," *Midwest Quarterly* 4 [Summer 1963]: 353-61).

5. Words like *tribe, rite, ritual* (the first of November "household ritual"), *totem,* and *taboo* (concealment of the bridal night location as one of the most sacred taboos of the prehistorical ritual) run through Mrs. Wharton's work, as they do through that of some of her successors. The novelist of manners antici-pates the cultural anthropologist.

6. Still another social group, European society, is touched upon in the novel. A pehaps more corrupt (see *The Age of Innocence,* p. 256), but certainly more sprightly and stimulating contingent, as Mrs. Wharton sees it. She does more with the European setting in other novels, e.g., *The Reef* (1912).

7. Witness her sharp satire on the artsy-craftsy type in *The Gods Arrive* (1932).

8. She was very knowledgeable about such subjects as landscape gardening and house furnishings, in fact, collaborated on a book, *The Decoration of Houses* (1907). The "poet of interior decoration," Edmund Wilson has called her (see Edmund Wilson "Justice to Edith Wharton," included in Irving Howe, ed., *Edith Wharton, A Collection of Critical Essays* [Englewood Cliffs, N.J.; Prentice-Hall, Inc., 1962] p. 23).

9. See Marilyn J. Lyde, *Edith Wharton: Convention and Morality in the Work of a Novelist,* (Norman, Okla.; University of Oklahoma Press, 1959), pp. 81ff.

10. Quoted in Blake Nevius, *Edith Wharton: A Study of her Fiction* (Berke-ley and Los Angeles, Calif.; University of California Press, 1953), p. 31.

11. See Viola Hopkins, "The Ordering Style of *The Age of Innocence*," *American Literature* 30 (November 1958): 354 ff.

12. See ibid., p. 350.

13. See Edwin M. Moseley, "*The Age of Innocence*: Edith Wharton's Weak Faust," *College English* 21 (December 1959): 156-60.

14. Alfred Kazin, *On Native Grounds* (New York: Reynal and Hitchcock, 1942), p. 74.

15. Louis Auchincloss, *Edith Wharton,* University of Minnesota Pamphlets on American Writers, no. 12 (Minneapolis, Minn.: University of Minnesota Press, 1961), p. 8.

16. Robert Morss Lovett, *Edith Wharton* (New York: Robert M. McBride & Co., 1925), p. 45.

17. Diana Trilling, "*The House of Mirth* Revisited," *The American Scholar* 32 (Winter 1962-63): 114.

18. Edith Wharton, *A Motor-Flight Through France* (New York: Charles Scribner's Sons, 1909), pp. 28-29.

19. Ibid., p. 97.

20. Ibid., p. 76.

21. Mrs. Wharton always wanted their American equivalents to enjoy a similar position. However, though her profound belief in the importance of the artist class must be respected, her picture of its world too often reflects dilettantish values, which do not strike one as a healthy substitute for those of Fifth Avenue.

22. Similarly described is Apex City in *The Custom of the Country*, and other Wharton tales (e.g., *New Year's Day*) contain unflattering references to "Westerners."

23. Auchincloss, *Edith Wharton, p. 12.*

24. Trilling, "*House of Mirth* Revisited," p. 118.

25. It cared about culture, however, as Irving Howe reminds us, "as a static and finished quantity, something one had to possess but did not have to live by" (see Irving Howe, *A World More Attractive* [New York: Horizon Press, 1963], p. 50).

26. See Nevius, *Edith Wharton*, p. 62.

27. Mrs. Wharton, it has been suggested, makes use of architecture as an objective correlative, both for the characters' inner lives and also for the changing social values of the time (see James Gleason, "Edith Wharton and the Architecture of Life-Style" [Talk given before the Midwest Modern Language Association, Milwaukee, Wisconsin, October 1970]).

28. The novel repeatedly demonstrates that the aristocracy is almost as much concerned with money as the plutocracy. Mrs. Wharton sees the single standard of financial success beginning to prevail, and bringing a subtle corruption in its wake.

29. Trilling, "*House of Mirth* Revisited," p. 122.

30. Howe, *A World More Attractive*, p. 52.

31. "No amount of association with cultivated persons or of exposure to the art of Europe can ripple the surface of her infinite vulgarity" (Auchincloss, *Edith Wharton*, p. 24). Mrs. Wharton really makes Undine so awful that one fails to see how she could have had allure for so many men.

32. Christof Wegelin finds less of the "inward gaze" in her than in her mentor James, for she more often "remained out in the nipping and eager air of satire" (Christof Wegelin, "Edith Wharton and the Twilight of the International Novel," *The Southern Review* 5 [Spring 1969] : 399).

33. Mrs. Wharton's short story "Autre Temps" stresses this theme, the "present fluid state of manners." The character Franklin Ide says that "it would

take an arbitration commission a good many sittings to define the boundaries of society nowadays."

34. The middle-aged Miss March, having gained a firm foothold in English society, ushers her fellow Americans into this "marriage-market," very much in the manner of Henry James's Mrs. Medwin, though with less mercenary motives.

35. A pleasant exception is Mrs. Closson, who "really could not see that there was much difference between one human being and another" — but she came from Brazil.

36. Christof Wegelin conceives of her as exemplifying, in her happy combination of humane individualism *with* a sense of discipline, a favorite Jamesian theme that "in social relationships 'manners' are economy" (Wegelin, "Edith Wharton and the Twilight of the International Novel," p. 417).

37. Mrs. Wharton once said, "The conclusion of [a] tale should be contained in germ in its first page." Quoted by Walter Rideout in his discussion of *The House of Mirth* included in Charles Shapiro, ed., *Twelve Original Essays on Great American Novels* (Detroit, Mich.: Wayne State University Press, 1958), p. 151.

38. The social misfit is clearly a type to which novelists of manners are drawn, affording them, for one thing, a fine opportunity to dissect the society into which their characters do not fit.

39. Trilling, *"House of Mirth* Revisited," p. 113. James Tuttleton also regrets the ignoring by many of Mrs. Wharton's artful weaving of the web of custom and manners, her reconstructing, "archeologically, as it were," the social world of her youth. The "old ways," he says, may deserve, like an archeological find, to be exhumed, inspected, renovated, and put to creative use (see James W. Tuttleton, "Edith Wharton: The Archeological Motive," *Yale Review* 61 [Summer 1972]: 562-74).

40. See Millicent Bell, *Edith Wharton & Henry James* (New York: George Braziller, 1965), p. 139.

41. In the words of Millicent Bell, "Irony and detachment, her way of meeting her own fate, was her artistic mood" (ibid., p. 311).

7

Ellen Glasgow

*E*DITH Wharton's "immemorial tale of aristocrat and merchant in a capitalistic society, their mating, mutual accommodation, reconciliation,"[1] was told more than once by her contemporary, and in many ways fellow spirit, Ellen Glasgow. Though employing a different background — Old Virginia rather than Old New York — and emphasizing to a lesser degree the newer half of the "mating," the plutocracy, Miss Glasgow found equal delight in presenting the contrast in manners that results from a drawing of class lines. She also expressed a measure of regret as she saw the blurring of the old distinctions, as the Southern cavalier aristocracy receded before the clever but pushing and quite charmless "New South." Basically loyal to the tradition of which she was a part, at the same time Miss Glasgow freely satirized its shortcomings — again like Mrs. Wharton. Their blend of detachment and sympathy lends a particular poignancy to their accounts of the aristoleisure-class culture.

150

In her many novels Miss Glasgow confined herself very much within the boundaries of her native state of Virginia,[2] depicting a society still living in the shadow of the Civil War, believing in the chivalric legends of its history, and personifying a rather faded gentility and sterile culture. The society had preserved some worthwhile traditions, to be sure, a firm sense of "noblesse oblige," of courage and dignity, of business integrity, and of graceful living, but at the same time it had encouraged less desirable propensities. Perhaps the chief of these was its worship of the Southern lady, an unhappy cult since it introduced so many undesirable consequences — the frozen marriage and double standard, a lack of frankness, a false modesty.[3] Almost equally unfortunate were the excessive devotion to caste (a belief in the lordly privileges owed to "rank"), the presence within the caste of vanity and evasiveness, and its demonstration of stagnant intellectuality. Miss Glasgow, always smarting from the scorn accorded to the "bluestocking" in her social sphere, frequently spoke out against the antiintellectual tone of the "Old Dominion." Virginius Littlepage, her protagonist in *They Stooped to Folly*, had the standard attitude. "All the learning required to make a Southern gentleman was comprised, as every Littlepage knew without being told, in the calf-bound rows of classic authors and the Prayer-Book of the Protestant Episcopal Church."

Though almost all of Miss Glasgow's novels reflect to some degree this Southern aristocratic tradition, only a few fall precisely into the novel-of-manners pattern. Pointing the way were the earlier works, *Virginia* (1913) and *Life and Gabriella* (1916). Several years later, the excellent trilogy, *The Romantic Comedians* (1926), *They Stooped to Folly* (1929), and *The Sheltered Life* (1932), climaxed her efforts. In the trilogy, most notably, Miss Glasgow gives a history of the Upper South, its customs and traditions, and its persistent

adherence to a precise code of manners. Disliking its pretension and false sentiment, but admiring its principles and
its charm, she is unwilling to condemn it outright, and so
she offers a critique written in a spirit of "thoughtful laughter."
Rather more serene than Mrs. Wharton about the human race,
she remains gently ironic as she outlines the passing into
limbo in the post-World War I years of the "planter aristocracy."[4]

The novel *Virginia* sounds many notes that Miss Glasgow
will strike again and presents a cast of characters that will
likewise grow familiar. The cast includes the protagonist
Virginia Pendleton, a sheltered young lady brought up in
narrow provincial patterns; her mother, one of the many
rather sad examples of shabby gentility; Miss Priscilla Batte,
the indomitable but incomplete old maid; Mrs. Payson,
the somewhat "horsey" lady who doesn't quite belong; Mrs.
Tom Peachey, the self-sacrificing wife; and, finally, several
masculine illustrations, of both the old, courteous but
imperious Southern gentleman and the new, untutored
middle-class businessman. These characters suggest some of
the strengths but more of the weaknesses of the post-Civil
War Southern way of life. The author assails their shortsighted
attitude toward education, for example, especially education
for women. Miss Batte, the head of the Dinwiddie Academy
for Young Ladies, possesses dubious qualifications for her
post. "The fact that she was the single surviving child of a
gallant Confederate general, who, having distinguished
himself and his descendants, fell at last in the Battle of
Gettysburg, was sufficient recommendation in the eyes of
her fellow-citizens." Her emphasis falls heavily on "moral
education," firmly rooted in "such fundamental verities as
the superiority of man and the aristocratic supremacy of the
Episcopal Church."

Throughout the novel Miss Glasgow attacks such antediluvian beliefs, particularly regretting that the "old order" seems so static, so obsolete and outgrown. The Pendletons and their fellows recognize, to be sure, that change is in the air — "from where she stood in High Street, she could see this incense to Mammon rising above the spires of the churches, above the houses and the hovels, above the charm and the provincialism which made the Dinwiddie of the eighties" — but they resist the change, seeing not the provincialism but only the charm of the past, not the "progress" but only the materialism and aridity of the future. Miss Glasgow scoffs at their ostrichlike attitude but pities them, too.

Again, in *Life and Gabriella,* Miss Glasgow unfolds a world slowly dying at the roots, and beset by similar problems, a philandering male populace and distressed feminine gentility. Jane Carr Gracey, a willowy but faded belle, tries to hide an unfortunate marriage. Fanny Carr must cope with indigent ladyhood. The Peterborough sisters, ancient spinsters, live "in the beautiful and futile pretence of keeping up appearances." The impractical "old school" type, Arthur Peyton, gets nowhere. His replacements in the "newer school," having "progress, push and punch," do indeed get somewhere, but not where one would necessarily want to go. The novel's heroine, Gabriella Carr, wisely breaks away from her environment and moves to New York. When she returns home, having continued to cherish a romantic dream about Richmond's charm, she finds the dream dispelled, and eventually she marries a member of the new generation, the rough but virile Ben O'Hara.

Clearly this is a sign of the times. Family portraits and antique silver, charming manners and facile conversation, are not enough. Money, as always, makes the mare go, and the money has now left the hands of the old families, to rest — as yet uneasily — in the hands of the parvenus. The description of Mrs. Carr's home — Miss Glasgow is fond of the decaying-house symbol — indicates the social dislocation:

> The house, a small brick dwelling, set midway of an expressionless row and wearing on its front a look of desiccated gentility, stood in one of those forgotten streets where needy gentlewomen do "light housekeeping" in an obscure hinterland of respectability. Hill Street, which had once known fashion, and that only yesterday as old ladies count, had sunk at last into a humble state of decay. Here and there the edges of porches had crumbled; grass was beginning to sprout by the curbstone; and the once comfortable homes had opened their doors to boarders or let their large high-ceilinged rooms to the impoverished relics of Confederate soldiers. Only a few blocks away the stream of modern progress, sweeping along Broad Street, was rapidly changing the old Southern city into one of those bustling centers of activity which the press of the community agreed to describe as a "metropolis"; but this river of industrialism was spanned by no social bridge connecting Hill Street and its wistful relics with the statelier dignities and the more ephemeral gaieties of the opposite side. [Pp. 11-12]

A feudal society, which had been delightful but also ridiculous and indeed paralytically dominating, no longer exists in Richmond (which masquerades as "Dinwiddie" or as "Queenborough" in Miss Glasgow's novels), but the nouveau-riche atmosphere replacing it seems, to Miss Glasgow, a questionable improvement.[5]

The Romantic Comedians also stresses the gradual disintegration of the Virginia aristocracy — that world of mammies and "Missy's," mimosa and myrtle, magnolias and moonlight — but the author's focus on a January-May theme produces less the note of a social history of the South and more the sparkle of a comedy of manners mocking universal human foibles. The "company of happiness-hunters" whom she describes seems to Miss Glasgow "little better than a troupe of romantic comedians," for each expects personal gratification in a world that could not possibly accommodate them all. The protagonist, Judge Honeywell, serves as the leading example. A "great lawyer but a perfect fool," the judge, after the death of his wife, makes a beeline, not for his contemporary and longtime friend Amanda Lightfoot, the Southern lady par excellence, but rather for youthful Annabel Upchurch, the postwar flapper par excellence. Marriage to Annabel predictably proves disastrous, but the judge, even so, may not have learned his lesson. At the end of the book he seems to be turning again from Amanda and toward his young nurse. Love, or, more precisely, the sexual impulse, tyrannizes over the constructive impulses of the mind.

Employing irony as the essence of her comic vision, Miss Glasgow exposes her characters. The egocentric Judge Honeywell fails to distinguish between his conduct and the actual motives for it. The equally egocentric Annabel may be free from moral duplicity but is also free from responsibility. The hypocritical Amanda Lightfoot devotes her life to maintaining a front. The deceptive Mrs. Upchurch hides her corrosive cynicism. The most forthright and least self-deluded of them all, Edmonia Bredalbane, fares best in the author's hands.

In recounting the humorous interactions of various temperaments upon each other, Miss Glasgow both underlines the universal aspects of this human comedy and at the same time shows the conditioning effects of the particular environment, the conservative and provincial Tidewater society. Amanda Lightfoot, as the "Southern lady," epitomizes the society. "A pressed leaf that has grown faded and brittle," she mingles virtues with shortcomings. "Serene, unselfish, with the reminiscence of a vanished day in her face and figure, she belonged to the fortunate generation of women who had no need to think, since everything was decided for them by the feelings of a lady and the Episcopal Church." If patient, gentle, and well-bred, yet "never once has she dared to be herself, and," says Annabel Upchurch, "she hasn't dreamed that courage to be yourself is the greatest virtue of all." In turn, the judge epitomizes the Southern gentleman. Aristocratic in appearance, charming in manner, skilled in his profession, the very "pattern of chivalry," he is also an "old fool," narrow — "tolerant of any views that were not brought into vocal conflict with his own" — and humorless as well. His outspoken sister, Mrs. Bredalbane, reminds him, "The trouble with you, Gamaliel, is that you did not have enough sense of humor to stand the strain of being a Judge and an old Virginia gentleman combined."

The hidebound and duty-bound[6] world of Gamaliel Honeywell and Amanda Lightfoot has receded in the postwar years, however. Thinks Amanda pensively, "If the world continued to grow away, not only from God, but from good breeding as well, what . . . could be trusted to keep wives contented and the working classes in order?" The signs of disintegration are many, for example, the "once aristocratic and now diminished length of Washington Street" merging into the "ostentatious democracy of Granite Boulevard." If Judge Honeywell is more clear sighted about the change than Amanda, recognizing that the community of which he was a part had "lost the faculty of self-criticism and stiffened into a gelatinous mould of complacency," he doesn't relish it very much either. "Though he tried his best to become modern and devoid of the sense of responsibility, the traditions in which he had been brought up were always ready to strangle his efforts."

"Queenborough" in the twenties provides many manifeatations of a different social order, the codes of beautiful behavior loosened, morals declined, and manners all but vanished. Annabel Upchurch personifies the new generation — honest, devoid of sham, but also graceless, irresponsible, shallow. Her group has shaken off many of the constricting trammels but has found few positive values with which to replace them. Their minds are "sprightly" but "not troubled by convictions."

Miss Glasgow views the social turmoil with a satiric eye, thus giving *The Romantic Comedians* a proper consistency of tone and mood. The contrast of the Old and New South, the picture of the genteel code at bay before the industrial revolution, provokes in her a rueful response, illustrating as it does, from both directions, man's follies, but she maintains a lightness of touch in describing the contrast.

Her epigrammatic style complements the tone and, in its hint of artifice, as Frederick McDowell has pointed out,[7] befits the brittle texture of the comedy of manners. Succinct descriptions of character contribute to the effect, as that of Mrs. Bredalbane, she of the strong, plain features, with genuine humor frolicking with an artificial complexion, and a mountainous bosom, "from which a cascade of crystal beads splashed and glistened." The unconventional and bouncy Edmonia Bredalbane contrasts with the prim and ladylike Mrs. Upchurch, who "coos" when she speaks and "flutters like a pigeon before it settles for crumbs," and who is given to small black velvet hats "resting like a benediction on her fluffy grey fringe." These and other portraits in the novel — the octogenarian Don Juan, Colonel Bletheram, of pompous figure and empurpled features, for example — are more than lightly tinged with malice.

Miss Glasgow aptly describes places as well as people. So, the house of Judge Honeywell, "a collection of brown-stone deformities assembled, by some diligent architect of the early 'eighties, under the liberal protection of Queen Anne," and including a baptismal font of a porch. The reader is again reminded of how, in the novel of manners, setting functions as an integral element. The judge is defined by his house, as he is by his membership in select clubs, the Archeological Society and the Episcopal Church.

In keeping with its sardonic treatment of the postwar age, the book is dotted with terse comments on the social scene. Mrs. Bredalbane, guilty of an indiscretion in her youth that had ostracized her to Europe,[8] finds her "scarlet letter" regarded by Annabel's generation "less as the badge of shame than as some foreign decoration for distinguished service." The virtue of perfect behavior lies, the author tells us, not in its rightness, but in its impenetrability. Amanda Lightfoot, a master of perfect behavior, constantly testifies to its inscrutability. "There had been so many occasions in Amanda's past when the social moment, the very surface of manners, had depended upon the facility with which she could look both pained and pleasant at the same instant, that she had learned to achieve this unnatural union with the utmost dexterity." The queenly, impassive type, like Amanda, is, however, becoming as extinct as the pterodactyl. The Annabel Upchurches are not hemmed in by traditions, by exact rules of conduct and reticences of "breeding" as Amanda and her friend Cordelia Honeywell had been.

With considerable suavity — the occasional astringency notwithstanding — Miss Glasgow makes her statement, in *The Romantic Comedians,* about the changing times — as well as about the vagaries of the emotional life — the amusing *and* saddening spectacle of an elderly man yielding to his impetuous desires. And she finds a witty style and a relatively dispassionate tone the proper means for unveiling the story of the replacement of the "first families" by the "second families," who had perhaps expanded the South's horizons, but had failed to introduce genuine social well-being.

In the successor to *The Romantic Comedians, They Stooped to Folly,* Miss Glasgow again resorts to faintly sardonic laughter, as she debunks another myth, and, in incidental fashion, remarks about the "new look" of the postbellum South. Here she shifts her target from the illusion of perpetual youth to the myth of the fallen woman. Describing the seduced woman of three generations, from Aunt Agatha Littlepage, who retired with her shame to a third floor bedroom, to Mrs. Dalrymple, who lived down her shame if not quite establishing her respectability, to Milly Burden, who never felt any shame, Miss Glasgow makes the changes in tastes and values perfectly clear.

While showing the demolition of the myth throughout the successive generations, the author criticizes the strictures and hypocrisies that had initially encouraged it, the shams of conventional social morality of late nineteenth century Virginia. At the same time she does not seem altogether satisfied with the freedom of twentieth century mores. Thus, the book becomes another illustration of the author's divided attitude, her distrust of the suffocating complacency and fallacious culture of the "Kentucky colonel" type, but her equal distrust of — and sharper scorn for — the Rotarian type flourishing in the New South. If, as the character Louisa Goddard remarks, "nothing was worth all the deceit, all the anguish, all the futile hope and ineffectual endeavor, all the pretense and parade, all the artificial glamour and empty posturing of the great Victorian tradition," yet the charmless, Booster-like new tradition does not provide an adequate replacement. The move from a society controlled by ritual bondage, arbitrary law, and older people to a society controlled by youth and pragmatic freedom does not represent a significant advance.

Despite the somber undertones to be detected in an account of progress that is not progress, *They Stooped to Folly* manifests by and large a comic spirit. This is demonstrated in many ways, among them the character sketches that enliven the novel. There are, in the younger generation, such types as these: Curle Littlepage, "a popular young man, without charm, but as loud and bright and brisk as the New South"; his far more intelligent and sensitive but decidedly misanthropic older brother Duncan; his humorless sister Mary Victoria; the ineffectual would-be "artist" Martin Welding; and the waifishly charming Milly Burden. The latter appeals as much as any, yet her physical attractions and forthright demeanor are more than offset by her brazenness and lack of pride and grace, defects that predominate, according to Miss Glasgow, among the young people.

The older generation includes several examples of old-style feminine gentility: Victoria Littlepage, the "average woman of good will";[9] the whining fundamentalist Mrs. Burden; the handsome and capable but slightly congealed spinster Louisa Goddard. In juxtaposition stands the ever-suspect Mrs. Dalrymple, "too alluring for her widow's weeds, to which she imparted a festive air by the summer bloom in her cheeks." Another contrast is offered in the two brothers, Virginius and Marmaduke Littlepage, the former representing the man of position, the Southern cavalier,[10] the chivalric gentleman, whereas the latter is the unconventional artist. It is perhaps significant that Miss Glasgow makes Marmaduke much the most engaging character in the book, and really the most "civilized" man, that is, the most truly charitable and generous. Certainly he outshines the conventionally good figures such as Virginius and Victoria Littlepage, their daughter Mary Victoria, and the holier-than-thou Mrs. Burden.

Stooping to folly, Miss Glasgow indicates throughout the novel, has not been confined to any age, and so it is that she gaily satirizes the social scene both past and present. The "codes" and "rituals" — Miss Glasgow, like her fellow novelists of manners, frequently resorts to such terminology — of the aristocracy no longer support them very well, moral platitudes having decayed, the ideal of chivalry being discredited, and, important too, much of the money having evaporated ("few people can afford to marry into the best families because they are all so impoverished"). The reader observes Victoria Littlepage's acceptance of bootlegging: "All the more prominent pillars of the society in which she lived supported the institution of bootlegging; and custom, which breaks laws and makes morality, had reconciled her law-abiding instincts to this ubiquitous lawlessness." One also sees her generation's acceptance of the plutocracy: "Into this circle, which grew duller as time and tide encrusted the conversational platitudes, there entered occasionally a new member, whose prerogative of wealth only those too poor to profit by it had ever disputed."

The "arrivistes" and the young people generally breathe fresh air into that dull circle, it is true, but their hardness and flippancy, bad manners and lack of taste do not, on the other hand, recommend themselves. Just as intellectually provincial — the "readers" like Martin Welding are an exception — and cheaper in speech and style, the present generation, substituting wealth for gallantry as a title to fame and ignoring personal dignity, do not replace the forsaken standards with sturdier ones: "Modern life," to Virginius Littlepage, and to Ellen Glasgow, too, "appeared without dignity and even without direction, an endless speeding to nowhere."

A felicitous style, marked by rapier thrusts and polished phrasing, supports Miss Glasgow in her delineation of Southern life. With the precise word she will, on the one hand, skewer a pretension, on the other, intimate the "candlelight charm."[11] A concise phrase will define a background, the quiet impressiveness of the "Brooke mansion" underscored, for example, by her speaking of its "very simple *and* very expensive bedrooms." Miss Glasgow employs still other seemly tactics: the balanced epigram (Marmaduke Littlepage was too sure about his ancestors to be particular about his acquaintances); the cool and scrupulous observation ("In the severe discipline of marriage Mr. Littlepage had cultivated the habit of looking at his wife without seeing her"); the appropriately commonplace figure ("Mrs. Burden wore an agitated frown, as if her moral fiber had suddenly become unbuttoned"); and the ironic description (Mrs. Dalrymple, who had been blessed with sex attraction, "would have preferred, as she grew older, a moderate amount of card sense or even a strong religious belief").

They Stooped to Folly succumbs to flaws, one feels: a too petulant treatment of the younger generation, an excessive reliance on epigram, a playing on the surface of its theme rather than delving deep. Yet it must be said that, in creating a mordant sense of the social reality of the South, and in evoking the "brilliant air of the mind,"[12] Miss Glasgow notably succeeds. The myths of the fallen woman and of chivalry generally[13] — such merely "formal patterns of inherited opinions" — are proved hollow, but so, too, are most of the idols of the "contemporary mannerless youth," which prefers "to order its culture, as it ordered its Battle Creek health foods, from the most convenient greengrocer." Miss Glasgow does not deliberately play favorites in her account of the Southern social tradition.[14]

The decline of this antebellum tradition is most sharply emphasized in *The Sheltered Life,* in which novel men and women "who have survived a tradition and yet adhere to its code . . . call attention" to that tradition, "itself threadbare, sometimes a little cruel, often patently ridiculous."[15] Central embodiment of the tradition is the beautiful "sheltered" lady Eva Birdsong, obviously born out of her time. So, too, her husband, the gay philanderer George Birdsong. They and their neighbors, the aristocratic Archbalds, can only regret — they can't prevent — what is happening to them, as the code fails to support them. Their decay is ironically accentuated by the factory stench that pervades their homes, their only weapon against it Mrs. Archbald's "pretending" it away.

The novel may be regarded as a moving study of social decomposition,[16] with almost every character as a case in point. Judge Archbald was married to a woman he did not love, forced into this formal marriage because he had compromised her by being found alone with her after midnight. Aunt Etta represents the fearless but lonely spinster gentlewoman. Eva Birdsong, the last example of ideal Southern womanhood, is intelligent enough to grasp the sad implications of her code, for example, the double standard, yet is committed to it. Mrs. Archbald indulges in rigid genteel resignation as she watches the old families being smoked out by the nouveaux riches and their factories. George Birdsong's charm does not compensate for his deceit, nor for his poverty — no longer a badge of honor as it had been directly after the Civil War. Even the new generation, represented by Jenny Blair Archbald, is affected; Jenny Blair, having so far led the sheltered life of a young Southern girl of good family, may expose herself to evil — her "affair" with Mr. Birdsong — with no clear realization of what she is doing.

The decomposition of the Old South is tangibly shown throughout the novel by the symbol of the diminished grandeur of Washington Street, reduced by the industrial conquest of Queenborough.

> Here they [the old families] had lived, knit together by ties of kinship and tradition, in the Sabbath peace that comes only to those who have been vanquished in war. Here they resisted change and adversity and progress; and here at last they were scattered by nothing more tangible than a stench. [P.6]

But these "first Families" made themselves an easy prey to the plutocratic invasion — largely because their values had grown false or misshapen. They sanctioned the superficial, endorsing, for example, the notion that nothing was worse than a homely woman. They scorned the intellectual, assuming that a "man" hunted rather than wrote poetry. They encouraged pretense: if Mrs. Archbald ever spoke the truth, Miss Glasgow records, "it was by accident, or on one of those rare occasions when truth is more pleasant than fiction." When her sister-in-law Isabella married the "plebeian" Joseph Crocker, Mrs. Archbald expeditiously put the genealogists to work to find some "family" for him. She — and those of her sphere — even condoned immorality, choosing to look the other way at miscegenation.

To be sure, Miss Glasgow redresses the balance to some degree, indicating the appeal of the vanishing aristocracy, its pleasant customs, beautiful women, and gracious living. Its "savoir vivre" is cheerfully exemplified in the sketch of Judge Archbald's surroundings, his library with its ruby leather and English calf, Brussels carpet and wood fire, his handsome gardens, his well-trained servants, a picture considerably more engaging than the "neutral as asphalt" tint of modern life. Yet the constrictive images, of the "sheltered life"[17] closing in, or of the "suffocating grasp of appearances," dominate the novel and cause the reader to place more faith in the younger generation, neutral or no. If Jenny Blair Archbald lacks Eva Birdsong's queenliness and repose, she has considerably more vitality. If John Welch lacks George Birdsong's urbanity and winning personality, he possesses honesty and "the rare gift of moral indignation."

The clash of generations in the novel is accentuated by the observation post extablished by the author as she "regards" her material. Miss Glasgow, who planned most of her novels in terms of point-of-view characters (e.g., Judge Honeywell in *The Romantic Comedians* and Mr. and Mrs. Littlepage in *They Stooped to Folly*), uses a double focus here, first presenting the "vision" of Jenny Blair Archbald, then that of her grandfather — in a section mostly devoted to summoning up the "deep past" — then, in the final long section, a combination of both points of view. The youth-age contrast helps descry the Southern social tapestry, the employment of an hourglass, as it were — the action sifted through one way and then another — proving a most effective device in probing the aristocratic decline.

In chronicling the manners of the "Old Dominion," Miss Glasgow, one must conclude, performs with tremendous skill. It has been said that the

> comedy of manners requires precise observation of manners, a sense of form, a detached point of view, wit and charm, the ability to make little things interesting and, above all, a civilized society. It requires also the ability to see beneath and beyond details to . . . the eternal verities.[18]

Miss Glasgow fills the bill. Her novels are cleverly written, well made, and consistently ironic in tone. They also dissect a civilized society — looking beneath the "enamelled surface" of "beautiful behavior" in Tidewater Virginia — and, in the process, expose the eternal verities. The author, knowing what the code of beautiful behavior leaves out of account, makes it perfectly evident that "morality" consists of something more than taking the important "step from the Baptist Communion to the Episcopal Church." The disoriented ethics of both the older and the newer generations do not satisfy, no more than the hypocrisy that the graceful social usages of Southern ladies and gentlemen only partially veil. Miss Glasgow loves her South, but she examines it with an impartial eye.

This examination proceeds — pleasurably enough for the reader — in the spirit of high comedy. As Miss Glasgow notes the effect of the monster "change" in Virginia,[19] the widening breach between manners and a significant morality, "the laughter, even when muted almost to a compassionate silence, is still there."[20]

NOTES TO CHAPTER 7

1. Alfred Kazin, *On Native Grounds* (New York: Reynal & Hitchcock, 1942), p. 79.

2. Echoing both James and Mrs. Wharton, Miss Glasgow said: "We write better . . . when we write of places we know, and of a background with which we are familiar" (Ellen Glasgow, *The Woman Within* [New York: Harcourt, Brace and Company, 1954], p. 129).

3. Alfred Kazin tartly describes the effects of the myth: "Pure womanhood, raised in pure ignorance, married off for the purest of motives, came to pure disaster" (Kazin, *On Native Grounds*, p. 261).

4. In *A Certain Measure*, Miss Glasgow, in speaking of the Southern lady, defines her attitude: ". . . and because I admired them, somewhat pensively, as one admires the rare art of a finer period, I have tried to interpret this vanished lady with sympathy, though not entirely without the cutting edge of truth which we call irony" (Ellen Glasgow, *A Certain Measure* [New York: Harcourt, Brace & Co., 1938], p. 78).

5. As Louis Auchincloss amusingly puts it, "If she shuddered at Thomas Nelson Page, she shuddered more at *Sanctuary*" (Louis Auchincloss, *Pioneers and Caretakers: A Study of Nine American Women Novelists* [Minneapolis, Minn.: University of Minnesota Press, 1965], p. 58).

6. Says Mrs. Bredalbane in reply to her brother's comment that he has tried to do his duty: "That is the trouble with all of you in Queenborough, especially the women. You look as if you had lived on duty and it hadn't agreed with you."

7. Frederick P. W. McDowell, *Ellen Glasgow and the Ironic Art of Fiction*, (Madison, Wis.: University of Wisconsin Press, 1960), p. 166.

8. The stereotyped view of Europe as a hotbed of iniquity prevails in Queenborough, as Miss Glasgow more than once gleefully points out. Judge Honeywell, despite many summers abroad, remains convinced that there is "a foreign bent in morality" and never modifies his opinion that Europe was the proper haven for his sister after she had committed a moral faux pas. Edmonia had been happy there, certainly, perhaps in part because "my respectability increases with every mile of the distance I travel from Queenborough."

9. See Glasgow, *A Certain Measure*, p. 244.

10. Their father was perhaps more truly the Southern cavalier, "a Virginia gentleman of Georgian morals but Victorian manners, who had found it less embarrassing to commit adultery than to pronounce the word in the presence of a lady."

11. Frederick J. Hoffman, *The Modern Novel in America, 1900-1950* (Chicago: Henry Regnery Co., 1951), p. 65.

12. McDowell, *Ellen Glasgow and the Art of Fiction*, p. 183.

13. Miss Glasgow would label chivalry a "myth" when it is no longer rooted

in moral idealism.

14. One strongly suspects, of course, that, were she really forced to choose, she would prefer the pleasing social manners of Mrs. Littlepage and the still quite well-regulated world of Mr. Littlepage.

15. Hoffman, *The Modern Novel in America, 1900-1950*, p. 68.

16. See Kazin, *On Native Grounds*, p. 263.

17. "The sheltered life is also the life of willful blindness" (Louis Auchincloss, *Ellen Glasgow*, University of Minnesota Pamphlets on American Writers, no. 33 [Minneapolis, Minn.: University of Minnesota Press, 1964] p. 32).

18. N. Elizabeth Monroe, "Ellen Glasgow," in *Fifty Years of the American Novel*, ed. Harold O. Gardiner (New York and London: Charles Scribner's Sons, 1952), p. 53.

19. "To preserve tradition in our own century," Louis Auchincloss reminds us, "has been a pretty desperate affair" (Auchincloss, *Pioneers and Caretakers . . .*, p. 4).

20. Auchincloss, *Ellen Glasgow*, p. 30.

8

John P. Marquand

A natural ally of Ellen Glasgow, John P. Marquand follows her lead in many respects. His novels are similarly devoted to exploring the ways of the "old stock,"[1] though he substitutes New Englanders for Virginians. Like Miss Glasgow, he also views his group with a mixture of aloofness and identification, both attracted and repelled as he links the group's worse qualities, provincialism and puritanism, with its better ones, dignity and "stewardship." Again like Miss Glasgow, he functions as a serious craftsman, demonstrating a fine sense of milieu, an acute insight into character, an awareness of the well-made novel pattern, and considerable technical skill.[2] The two writers, in thesis and in manner, fall easily into line behind James and Howells and Mrs. Wharton.

Though long regarded by many as suspect, because of his association with the "slick" magazines and because of his large reading audience, Marquand should be given his due, both as an accomplished writer and as a perceptive student of manners. Employing the comedy-of-manners formula in order to expose various aspects of the American social scene, he focuses on what is perhaps a backwater, the Boston of the Brahmins, yet finds universal significance therein and presents questions and answers relevant to all. He thus imitates his predecessors in lending depth to his social satire, in using "modes of social intercourse as a way of expressing moral attitudes."[3]

The New England region in which most of his novels are set and the tradition-bound aristocratic class inhabiting the area, he knew very well. Indeed, he belonged to both. Though born in Wilmington, Delaware, he came from a Boston family of ancient lineage, and his principal realm, as everyone knows, is the world of the "proper Bostonian." A grandnephew of the Transcendentalist Margaret Fuller, and a member of a family that had lived near Boston for two hundred years, Marquand, from his childhood on, was surrounded by portraits of colonial ancestors, family heirlooms, and talk of bygone days. He was not, at the same time, surrounded by a great deal of affluence, the Marquands, in his younger days, bordering on shabby gentility and living in a somewhat straitened way. As a consequence, Marquand, though attending Harvard, had to work his way through and live in off-campus rooms, and he did not belong to any clubs — let alone the "final" ones. Such experiences enhanced, one surmises, his sense of "not belonging", and they were to lend an edge to his pen when it was used to describe this world later on.

After intermingling forays into advertising and journalism with some army service, Marquand, in the post-World War I period, settled on a writing career, and, as a magazine contributor, became an almost instant success, producing such sprightly and popular stories as the Mr. Moto series for the *Saturday Evening Post.* When he turned to longer and more serious work, for example, *The Late George Apley* (1937), he was not immediately accorded much critical attention, and only quite recently has he come into his own as more than a potboiling lightweight, as, in fact, a social novelist of great talent.

Of the many factors contributing to his success as a "social novelist," a central one is the tone of the author, an appropriate blend of sympathy and detachment. Toward the Apley, Lowell, Sedgwick Boston he maintained — even after marrying a Sedgwick — an attitude mingling affection with resentment, appreciation with dissatisfaction.[4] Indeed, a bemused cynicism conditions his view of the world as a whole, thereby introducing into his fiction a perpetual note of gentle irony. This mood works well for Marquand, since the mocking temperament lends a healthy spice and the moments of tenderness an unforgettable poignance to the novels.

Marquand combines his Montaigne-like skepticism with other weapons that are suitable for the novelist of manners. That which makes him particularly deserving of the manners label is his subject, the presentation of a particular social class from a definite point of view, and the showing of the power of that class over its members. This class is, for Marquand, often the Bostonian aristocratic one, a group on which he concentrated especially in the earlier Apley-Wickford Point-Pulham series of novels. So accurate was his rendition that the Beacon Hill contingent was sure it could pick out and identify characters, in *roman à clé* fashion.[5] Some people even managed to imply that to find one's self in a Marquand novel was equivalent to being listed in the Social Register.

It should be remembered, however, that if Marquand's work has a regional flavor,[6] he is still dealing with universal types in his fiction, not simply with Back Bay Bostonians.

His major novels present as their protagonist "everyman," "Everyman" armed with a large measure of worldly success, to be sure, but an "everyman" not confined to any one geographical area. Marquand believes that "human nature is about the same, whatever the environment,"[7] and has his anthropologist Malcolm Bryant, in *Point of No Return* (1949), declare that the people in Clyde, Massachusetts and in Borneo are closely akin. If this seems a mite stretched. surely one is ready to agree that the citizens of Chicago's North Shore resemble those on Boston's North Shore, that the inhabitants of Grosse Point, Michigan resemble those of Chestnut Hill, Massachusetts. Furthermore, those prosperous suburbanites, in their finding cause to doubt themselves and their values, seem not too far removed from the man in the street. The "rentier" type, just as much as the subdivision dweller, is engaged "in search of perspective"[8] in an attempt to examine his life profitably, to discover, if possible, some sense of individual integrity in a spiritually bankrupt society.

The tone assumed by the author in treating this different but not too exotic social group (not nearly so exotic as the "*very* rich" who are Fitzgerald's special province) reflects a blend of the satiric and nostalgic, an uneasy combination, one would think, yet one that works for Marquand, as it has previously worked for Wharton and Glasgow. He manages like them, to "keep astringent in . . . potentially weepy air,"[9] commenting quite sharply on contemporary mores that displease him, for example the cocktail party pat-ter of the Fairfield County "intelligentsia," but also tempering even the roughest blasts with pity. His attitude toward the George Apleys is essentially one of tolerance; he laughs and admires, and he finally concludes, "They will never become, I hope, entirely extinct."[10]

An examination of Marquand's best-known, and in many ways his best, novel, *The Late George Apley,* may serve to illuminate his attitude and to indicate how precisely he operates within the novel-of-manners bounds. The book presents, Granville Hicks has said,[11] a study of the mechanisms by which a social class enforces its standards and achieves the conformity of its members. George Apley, ineffectually rebellious — understanding neither fully enough nor in time — is finally and firmly pinned into position by the society to which he belongs. As a doubting individual,[12] he wins the sympathy of the reader, who may laugh at Apley's often ridiculous attempts to do the "right" thing, but who at the same time admires his willingness to fight for certain principles at the risk of opprobrium. One follows the struggle in Apley, his first period of passion and doubt, the "straying youth" in love with Mary Monahan, succeeded by a yielding to the impact of conventional society, parental pressure forcing him into the mold, and then by an uneasy acceptance, as he never rids himself of lingering doubts about whether he has pursued the proper course.

Family, class, and locality are at the center of George Apley's universe. The consciousness of antecedents, of the group to which one belongs, of the place where one lives dominates his thinking. Throughout the novel the traditions of aristocratic Boston are clearly outlined, forms stemming from an "undeviating discipline of background," some of them meritorious, some considerably less so. The positive attributes include a refreshing simplicity, family loyalty, and a sense of continuity. The latter can lead, of course, to an unhealthy inflexibility. Lives are lived out in generation after generation according to a quite rigid pattern. An Apley goes to Mr. Hobson's School, to Papanti's dancing class, to Harvard — there had been an Apley at Harvard in every generation since 1662 — then enters the legal profession or joins a brokerage firm, marries a cousin, enrolls in clubs such as the Berkley or Province, supports charities like the

Boston Waif Society, and collects, more out of duty than out of pleasure — "everyone in a certain position owes it to the community to collect something" — art objects, perhaps Chinese jades and bronzes. Meanwhile, the female Apley goes to private school or is tutored, attends dancing class, is admitted to the Sewing Circle, waits for a cousin to marry her, then joins the Thursday Afternoon Club and Friday Waltz Evening group, and manages her household in town and country. Such was the course of the George Apleys, and such, George hopes, will be the course of the John Apleys of the next generation, with only minor changes, slowly accomplished, allowed.

Many and many a "proper Bostonian" follows the established pattern, and thus a tight little circle is formed. So compact is the group of Boston "cousins" that the entry of outsiders can very seldom be effected — the "intermediate stations" in New York, which, Mrs. Wharton felt, lent some social mobility to the scene, having no counterpart in Boston. According to *The Late George Apley*'s narrator, Horatio Willing, there is nothing unnatural in this "concentration." Every human being tends to conform to the social demands of a group, to be preoccupied with his own circle. Does this automatically spawn snobbery? No. The intense congeniality of one's group, the unique community of ideas prevailing, result in a common attitude toward life and contentment in association. Why should the members look further? Terribly smug though Horatio Willing is, his point, the tendency to seek one's group, has validity — as any sociologist would tell us. The effect of such seeking, however, must be taken into account, an inevitable narrowing, a cliquishness, a stultifying ingrown quality. When a Bostonian goes abroad, he stays with other Bostonians, in London, in Paris, in Rome. George Apley, as a young man, questions this habit — how strange, he thinks, that, instead of gaining much impression of different cultures, we have succeeded in transferring our own momentarily on every place we have visited — but in his later years he accepts the practice. Rome is delightful, particularly when one's own group is along. Another example may be found closer to home. A Bostonian marries within his circle, even — after the consanguineous pattern — within his family. A key incident in *The Late George Apley* is George's rejecting Mary Monahan in favor of Catherine Bosworth, the not beautiful, the too managerial, but the well connected. Marriage proves "a damnably serious business around Boston," as his uncle warns him, for one marries the family as well as the bride. George says, while waiting at the altar, "Well, this is the end." The "end" of his move toward emancipation it is; he is inexorably caught in the social fabric of Boston tradition, spending his subsequent years with Bosworths and Apleys at the same summer resorts (the Cleveland people at Mulberry Beach meet only the servants), at the same European capitals, at the same dinners and balls and Thanksgiving reunions. The provinciality of the "circle" does indeed startle!

The Late George Apley testifies, then, as to the hold of the Back Bay-Beacon Street world on its members, with the book's protagonist, after something of a struggle, succumbing to his environment. Horatio Willing sees George's changing from "erratic" to "sound" as altogether desirable, the wish to establish one's self in a firmly entrenched environment being a commendable one, and George, therefore, deserving congratulations for allowing his "inherited instincts" to come to the fore. But the reader is more apt to view the change as a capitulation rather than a finding of one's self. When Apley makes his "proper" marriage and accepts his position in the closed circle, especially when, years later, he endeavors to mold his son along similar lines ("for better or worse we are what we are; don't try to be different"), he appears in a much less attractive and less sympathetic light.

Author Marquand is responsible, of course, for our rather divided feelings about his protagonist, choosing, in order to mock some of the "values" of the Apley world, to place his "hero" in awkward, even foolish positions. George Apley thus appears as an outrageous snob in wishing to exclude Marcus Ransome from his club.[13] Again, he seems naively self-centered in requesting his son to ask permission to leave his military post so that he may telegraph his Aunt Amelia, urging her not to remove the rose bushes from Hillcrest. Similarly, Apley's excessive patriotism during World War I — denouncing the "Irish element" as pro-German — becomes silly chauvinism, and his actions in interfering in his cousin John's attempt to divorce his wife and in having cousin Hattie's body removed from the family burial lot make him look pompous in the extreme.

Eventually George all but out-Apleys an Apley. His petty concern about every minute detail of his Milton estate illustrates his reversion to type, as do his stuffy letters to the *Boston Transcript,* or his eagerness to have his son appear at Hillcrest early for the annual Thanksgiving rite, so that he could contribute ideas for pencil and paper games, or his desire to have John rather than the hired man shoot the squirrels that are plaguing Hillcrest — it would "look better." Insignificant are the problems and confined the boundaries — the Middle West is a place "I have never seen nor ever want to" — of Mr. Apley's existence.

Yet, as the reader looks closely at George Apley's character, his attitude, like Marquand's, remains respectful, however tinged with amusement his respect may be. One is bound to recognize that Apley represents many of the good qualities of his "class" and that this class has praiseworthy features. George Apley displays "guts," according to his son, or "discipline" in the more genteel terminology of Horatio

Willing. In him can be seen a conscientious sense of public spirit, a recognition that the possession of wealth involves the responsibility of using one's resources to benefit the community — supporting those "waifs," or indigent old sailors. One practices "noblesse oblige." Again, while embodying the dignity and restraint of his caste, still, George Apley will speak up courageously when he feels the occasion demands it, attacking Prohibition for flouting the rights of the individual, or defending *Lady Chatterley's Lover* as a work of art rather than of pornography.

The reader's sense of his worth is aroused early in the book when he manifests signs of revolt against his environment, and it lingers even after the rebellion is quelled. He is endearing as he protests against the "rigors of blue-nosed bigots" and as he falls in love with Mary Monahan, and as he insists upon writing his own paper — not enlisting the services of a Harvard instructor — on "Jonas Good and Cow Corner." He is poignant as he admits to having stood more on his own two feet in college than he ever has since, or as he tries to avoid the adjustments to his environment, or as he seeks to know his children's generation, or to accept change, or even to like New York! When he examines his life objectively near its end and notes how he has conformed to the "obligation of convention and the fabric of the past," he cannot say that he likes the life very much. The reader doesn't like it very much either, and feels that son John's counsel to his sister to "get out of this" makes very good sense, but he also feels that Eleanor's opinion that her father was a "really splendid man" makes sense too.

The Late George Apley displays the satiric mood that seems most appropriate for such a comedy of manners. The form that Marquand has chosen, a parody of the "life and letters" biography, with stuffy Horatio Willing as the "editor," lends itself particularly well to satire. As Marquand has himself pointed out, the main character can thus be illuminated not only by his own letters and those of his family and friends but also by his fictitious biographer who has arranged the letters. The latter, of course, often provides the wrong slant, being himself pedantic and vain and bigoted — thus seeing Apley's rebellions as "erratic moods" or "high-strung" idiosyncrasies — but no one else could evoke the stifling Brahmin air more readily. The mannered style, as well as the "memoir" form, contributes to the burlesque, Marquand assigning to Willing a long-winded pomposity that is trite, stilted, and more than a trifle flowery.

One is always conscious, of course, of the author's irony lurking beneath the novel's surface, Marquand indulging in mockery of Horatio Willing all of the time, of the Apley family much of the time, and of George Apley some of the time. To cite examples: Horatio Willing remarks on the sensible Bostonian propensity for staying at the Belmont when in New York; the hotel is "near the theatres and closer still, by good fortune, to the Boston train." George Apley's mother, a "woman of taste," admires Rosa Bonheur and H. W. Longfellow. George's father, with the best of intentions. tyrannizes over his household — "we were all more afraid of Father on Sunday than any other day of the week" — crushing his daughter's spirit to such a degree that she becomes "mental," and nipping his son's iconoclasm in the bud.

With such "hits" Marquand's "memoir" sharply defines the Apley world, making sport of its limitations and amusing foibles (the Apley and the Bosworth families' turning the naming of the first grandchild into a fierce vendetta is a case in point). The author is serious, however, in regretting the seeds of decay he senses in the New England aristocracy. Behind the poised self-assurance, behind the graceful facade, lies what? Much of the vigor, energy, and adherence to principle of earlier generations seems to have dissipated. "It may be, like the Chinese, that we are finally ending in a definite and static state of ancestor worship, that the achievements of the past are beyond our present capacities." George Apley, cast in the Boston mold, does not fully realize his "present capacities," and it looks as if his son John must escape to Texas in order to do so.

In many ways *The Late George Apley* forecasts the remainder of the Marquand canon. Its contrast of the values of the past with those of the present, with a tipping of the scales toward the former; its selection of a central figure described by Marquand himself as the "badgered American male — and that includes me — fighting for a little happiness and always being crushed by the problems of his environment;"[14] its note of fatality; its double vision ("If I use satire, I try to use it kindly"[15]); and its quietly effective style — all these aspects will reappear as Marquand goes on to tell "much about the manners and the social patterns of post-WWII American life and, first and last, [to provide] a moral judgment of the quality of that life."[16]

The later Marquand novels continue the examination, so neatly begun in *The Late George Apley,* of tradition, family, and place — the "weight of one's total heritage"[17] — the elements in the "social pattern." Repetitiously but knowledgeably, and always with skill, grace, and control, Marquand maneuvers his way through his subject.

In particular, he devoted the rest of his career to proving that class lines can still be marked out — at least in New England, where lower, middle, and upper classes mingle but do not coincide. While juxtaposing the three groups in novel after novel, he usually set his sights upon the "uppers" or "upper-middles," composing a series of fictional biographies of the generals, trust officers, tycoons, playwrights, news commentators, and Brahmins old and new who constitute these classes. Their lives are used to advance the thesis that the past inevitably hangs over one's head, often like a miasma, never permitting him to be free of the social distinctions bred into him in his childhood. The Marquandian "hero" is always, to a degree, conditioned by his earlier environment. Perhaps snubs received as a youngster have intensified in him an ambitious drive for status, or perhaps, like the Brahmins, he resigns himself to never escaping from the frame in which he was placed at birth. Whatever form the reaction takes, one's subsequent course appears partly determined.[18]

Three of Marquand's earlier novels, *The Late George Apley*, *Wickford Point* (1939), and *H.M. Pulham, Esq.* (1941), sharply record the impact of a distinctive environment, that of the Boston upper crust, upon their central characters. George Apley has been seen settling down, after a muffled revolt, "to a life of bird watching, civic duties and an arid satisfaction of denouncing a new world,"[19] finally petrified by the dead weight of his class's tradition. Jim Calder and Henry Pulham were also caught in the vise of a social system and fatalistically settled for a very qualified contentment — "nothing was ever perfect and nothing ever could be." Weaker protagonists than Apley, Calder in his cynicism and Pulham in his lack of imagination, their plight moves the reader only slightly. He is impressed, however, by their creator's skill in investing with depth and glamor the social background against which their stories unfold — the web of insular Wickford Point and the net of polite Boston — and in suggesting the dramatic, as well as comic, possibilities of their situation.

After this triumvirate of novels Marquand took a new tack, dealing with individuals who had moved away from the New England locale, even if they usually failed to escape entirely from its influence. His problem now was to create a hero who would still be strongly molded by environmental circumstances and yet would possess the ability to strike out on his own and to achieve "success" in a larger frame of reference. As his solution he chose to switch from the Boston Brahmin to the "gentleman hero of the suburbs,"[20] the "genteel and conscientious routineer,"[21] living out a dullish life but usually evincing some solid strength of character in the process.

Though many a Marquand protagonist fits this role, Bob Tasmin in *So Little Time*, for one,[22] the most appealing example is Charles Gray of *Point of No Return*. A young man with the mobility that enables him to move easily from small town to big city, he leaves his class-conscious background behind — almost — and successfully negotiates his "point of no return." The book, probably Marquand's most mature novel, offers a graphic and at the same time moving account of that "badgered American male," the upper-middle "every-man" fighting for a little happiness. When Charles Gray receives his business promotion, the vice-presidency of the Stuyvesant Bank, around which the plot hinges, will he also receive genuine satisfaction, or has the uphill struggle, involving obsequiousness and a frequent distortion of values, been worth it? There is the irony of doubt amidst prosperity.

The novel's theme is developed in three sections. The nine-chaptered Part 1 focuses on the current situation, the supposed tussle between Charles Gray and Roger Blakesley for the vice-presidency vacancy. In the eyes of the world, Charles Gray, whether he wins the tussle or not, would seem successful: he is a competent banker, he has an attractive home in Westchester, he loves his wife and two children. Yet the novel's opening pages hint at a vague rebellion in him, a disturbed feeling that life is contrived and rather shoddy, a series of apples to be polished. When his wife Nancy makes a plea for the happy family unit as offering comfort, and for their "belonging" in the Sycamore Park world as consoling too, Charles grants their solace, as he does his satisfaction in the details of his job. But the business of getting ahead — and success in the modern world means the possession of money, purely and simply — is such a cutthroat and petty process (one twits Roger Blakesley about his electric razor in the presence of their boss, Tony Burton, knowing that the latter does not approve of electric razors) that Charles cannot rid himself of a feeling of malaise. As he goes along on his "one-way ticket," he keeps asking himself whether it *is* worth it. The family, yes, but the brave new world of the Oak Knoll Country Club and Sycamore Park, well, no. Still, he goes along, of course, trying not to feel tied down like Gulliver among the Lilliputians, and, at this particular time, trying to feel confident that he will win the vice-presidency, and more "success."

In the long second section of the novel, the scene shifts from Westchester County to Clyde, Massachusetts, Gray's boyhood home, and in a lengthy flashback Marquand recounts his protagonist's youth. The reader is thus permitted to see how the present is a projection of the past, how events in Charles Gray's earlier days led to his achieving his current status. At the root of his ambitious drive for financial reward and attendant security had been the example of his father, a conspicuous material failure. Though the latter obtained prosperity for a time, he lacked the necessary carefulness to retain it, thus reducing his family to genteel poverty and himself to suicide. Thereafter Charles carefully cultivates success, avoiding the obvious approach of Jackie Mason, writing prize essays on his hero Andrew Carnegie, but also avoiding the haphazard approach of Mr. Gray. This led him from dead-end employment in a local company to E. P. Rush's, a gentlemanly Boston brokerage firm, and eventually to the even larger world of the Stuyvesant Bank in New York, where, with a "priestly, untouchable, ascetic" devotion to business and with considerable financial acumen, he continued to forge ahead, until reaching the point of no return, the vice-presidency opportunity.

Another motive in Charles's upward drive had been Jessica Lovell, a Clyde girl, with whom he fell in love at the beginning of his business career. Since Jessica belonged to the town's aristocracy and Charles to the bourgeoisie — the haute bourgeoisie, but still the bourgeoisie — the latter had a gap to bridge, persuading Jessica's father that he was both socially and monetarily acceptable. When Charles lost Jessica, more, it must be said, because of Mr. Lovell's inordinate love for his daughter than because of Charles's failure to prove himself or to seem socially assimilable, the loss, coupled with his father's suicide, only stiffened the young man's resolve to get ahead.

The final section of the novel returns to the present, though the locale remains, for the moment, Clyde, which Charles Gray visits, after an absence of many years, on banking business. In calling upon his old neighbors the Masons, Gray realizes that Jackie Mason, successful in a local business, a leader in the community, and about to marry Jessica Lovell, has pursued a career more than partially parallel with his own. If Charles's had been followed in a far larger world and with far greater financial rewards, yet it has involved similar hard and fast rules of "buttering up" the right people and seems to be reaching a similar preordained and sterile ending. The harder one pursues happiness, the less liberty he has, and even the less chance of securing happiness. Back home in New York, and driving with his wife to dinner at Tony Burton's, where he anticipates hearing whether the vice-president's position will fall to him or not, Gray certainly doesn't feel happy. The struggle in which he has been en-meshed seems so petty, the values so childish, the attrition of personality that results so unfortunate. When he learns from his host that the position is his, he only feels dull and very tired. His life could be no other way, but his state is one of uneasy acceptance. The "hero of the suburbs" or the "Apley Agonistes" finds sadness in the victory and in the not very blissful status quo for which one settles in "our times."

What makes the theme of *Point of No Return* effective is its embodiment in a sympathetic and wholly credible protagonist. Most readers will share Nancy Gray's feeling that she is married to a "damn nice man," or the more objective judgment of Malcolm Bryant that Charles is a good type with lots of guts. Having a tough mind that enables him to get ahead, he balances this with a sensitive disposition that makes him question the process. Certainly the fair share of virtues that he displays, intelligence, humanity, perseverance, sincerity, would seem to entitle him to lead a life less filled with what Thoreau would have called "quiet desperation."

Yet could he have changed the pattern? Could he in this crucial instance have tossed up his job and said it was the happiest day of his life? Surely not and have remained in character, that of the average man, conditioned by the frame, by the cobwebs from the past, by the notion of family responsibility, by the obligation of convention. He must, like most of us, rest content with a modicum of happiness.[23] His sense of loss, hemmed in by the "system" and irritated by the annoyances of its competitive infighting, should be measurably lessened by his increased understanding — one must pursue "bundles of hay," but not with the assiduousness of an ass — and by his preservation of a strain of individuality, even if it is only the mild revolt of wearing a soft shirt to the Burton dinner. Charles Gray accepts himself — and it is not merely resignation.

The sociological aspects of the novel have some bearing on the theme and certainly contribute to its reflection of manners. In writing the book Marquand had in mind a study of his old hometown Newburyport ("Clyde") made by

W. Lloyd Warner and a team of Harvard sociologists and social anthropologists in the early 1930s. A Yankee City series of six volumes resulted, based on the premise that class distinction underlay the typical "Yankee City." As Warner put it:

> [Classes are] two or more orders of people who are believed to be, and are accordingly ranked by the members of the community, in socially superior and inferior positions. . . . A class society distributes rights and privileges, duties and obligations, unequally among its inferior and superior grades. A system of classes, unlike a system of castes, provides by its own values for movement up and down the social ladder. In common parlance, this is social climbing, or in technical terms, social mobility. The social system of Yankee City, we found, was dominated by a class order.[24]

In *Point of No Return* Warner appears as the anthropologist Malcolm Bryant, and his study as "Yankee Persepolis" (the "place that worshipped memories'), a dissection of the town of Clyde. If granting merit to the Warner-Bryant research, Marquand still feels that it will never know as much about Yankee City-Clyde as a native like Marquand-Gray knows,[25] and so he parodies, to a degree, the anthropological picture. Malcolm Bryant's sociological lens sees correctly that the Irish and French Canadian and Italian and Polish elements in the town will never have the same status as the old English stock, yet he doesn't see that among them all an easy surface camaraderie, fostered in the small-town atmosphere, will prevail. Charles Gray's pastoral lens, on the other hand, does reveal this. Actually, both sociological and pastoral views possess limitations, Bryant's scientific detachment becoming the "unselective curiosity that goes with a closed mind" — Malcolm knows all about research methods but very little about human nature — and leading to oversimplified conclusions, whereas Charles Gray's nostalgic backward glance brightens the picture considerably.

Bryant's investigations do uncover, Marquand would admit, many home truths about Newburyport-Clyde, especially in their revelation of its social stratification, so precise that one can find not only upper-, middle-, and lower-class, divisions, but also upper-upper, middle-upper, lower-upper, and so on! Everyone is "placed," from Lovells to Masons to North Enders, from lawyers to druggists to servants. A beautiful, static, organized community, Bryant calls it; "my God," he exclaims with scientific zeal, "a wonderful town." The rigidity of the class barriers can, of course, be dissolved occasionally, *if* one possesses social mobility. So Charles Gray, with a college education, good manners, an instinct for the right clothes, could have moved from the middle to the upper class, an end that would have been accomplished by marriage to Jessica Lovell. Instead, as it happened, he moved out of town.

It is worth noting, however, that Charles remained in the upper-middle frame even after he had progressed to more expansive horizons than those provided in Clyde. In Nancy he married a "Spruce Street," not a "Johnson Street," girl, and in Westchester they found themselves in middle-class environs, belonging to Oak Knoll rather than ultraexclusive Hawthorn Hill, and living in the Sycamore Park development rather than at Rogers Point. The "chain" seems everywhere apparent, in small-town Clyde or in suburban New York or in the City itself, for example, the Stuyvesant Bank hierarchy; in fact, Malcolm Bryant concludes that society is similar everywhere — in Clyde, in New York City, also in Borneo. He takes delight in pointing out the resemblances between Clyde and primitive societies — the tribal rituals such as the Fireman's Muster and the Confessional Club (an old men's council, with the women hiding in the kitchen) — and probably would be willing to find them in the more sophisticated **New York** world, perhaps the Tuesday evening club dances or the Stuyvesant board meetings. Marquand, while slightly mocking Bryant's overeager classification, yet shares a belief in the complexity of the social structure and in the presence of subtle gradations of class stratification.

Since Charles Gray and others in the novel are molded by the social context, the importance of their backgrounds cannot be minimized, and hence setting becomes a prominent element. To this the author devotes considerable attention, first evoking for us the New York-Westchester, urban-sub-urban world. He minutely describes the Gray home in Syca-more Park, tasteful and pleasant, if hardly commensurate with the quietly luxurious estate of the Anthony Burtons at Rogers Point, nor with the lavish Park Avenue apartment of the wealthy Whitakers — "an environment in which [Charles] could move gracefully . . . but one in which he could never live." In addition to houses, exact details are furnished about the commuter train, the country club, the big city bank; in every one of these, Marquand observes, the sense of a social hierarchy — one's train seat, one's bank desk showing his status — can be discerned. In paying such loving attention to his "sets," the author intends to define his characters[26] and their place in society as well as to offer decorative material.

Marquand also recalls, in brilliant fashion, the small-town atmosphere of Clyde. The reader clearly visualizes the Historical Society, the various churches of the town, for example, the Unitarian Church, wonderfully simple in its architectural design. He also may contrast the comfortable but unpretentious Gray home on Spruce Street with the stunning row of "Captains' Houses" on Johnson Street, climaxed by the formal Federalist loveliness of the Lovell mansion. Downtown, in the messy Dock Street business district, are located less attractive buildings, such as the shabby Wright-Sherwin plant and the seedy — but ivy-covered — old Clyde Inn.

Authenticity and charm are lent to the setting by the touches of local color: the natives' waiting for the east wind off the ocean to freshen up a mid-summer muggy day; the Baptist church bell infallibly ringing after the Congregationalist; bittersweet cocoa for supper; the uncomfortable but antique Windsor chairs; and the local idioms, like "tonic" for "pop," Decoration Day for Memorial Day, "go 'round with" for "go steady."

Many of these descriptions of locale are tinged with satire, a favorite Marquand weapon, and often in evidence in *Point of No Return.* Examining the social aquarium, where vanity and pretensions flourish, the author speaks in an urbanely lethal way that provokes from the reader a hearty — or, more frequently, a rueful — laugh. The conference room at the Stuyvesant Bank is adorned with old prints of Broadway; the bank is ancient enough to cultivate a tradition, and, after all, the State Street Bank in Boston has its ship models. At the Tuesday night Oak Knoll dinner-dance one shifts partners often, for business reasons, and one never dances too long with reputation-tarnished Bea Merrill. Charles Gray's father John labels Dartmouth: ". . . a small college, and yet there are those who love it. His marks are bad enough, and he likes football, but if he can't get into Harvard or Yale, why not Amherst or Brown?" Poor Dartmouth! Charles learns not to mention it at E. P. Rush's, where all the "team" came from Harvard, and from the final clubs too. Charles is uneasily accepted at the brokerage firm, but he is accepted. Harvardians are democratic — after three years on the varsity crew a young man was spoken to by all except the number seven oar. Boston — as well as Harvard — provinciality is mocked, John Gray locating Kansas City on the Mississippi, and speaking of the "hiatuses" in a Kansas education. And Clyde, with its Mrs. Smythe-Leigh drama group, its "quaint" Pine Trees Fireman's Muster, its worship of local poetess Alice

Ruskin Lyte, is satirized as well. Charles Gray may invest the town with romance and nostalgia, but Marquand is not so "queer" about it as he.

The author, in fact, exhibits a disillusioned tone throughout the work. New England appears in a rather uncharitable light (Clyde is hardly a "wonderful town," with such as the desiccated Mr. Lovell in the forefront, and love and ambition frustrated), and the alternative, the upward, mobile "company life," seems even less attractive, the world of business success being devoid of spontaneity, with individuality reduced almost to zero. Anxiety dominates this world, even the private realm of the home and family being poisoned by the compulsions of a career. Charles Gray's final victory, as stated above, is hollow; it is a settling for the half-loaf.[27] The book's sharply ironic ending points up Marquand's cynical feelings. Do you suppose, asks Tony Burton, that Roger Blakesley thought he was being considered for the vice-presidency? Now that you mention it, Nancy Gray replies, I think perhaps he did — a little.

The author's skeptical treatment is illustrated in his handling of character, especially of the lesser figures whom he "scores off" very adroitly. For example: the Whitaker family, faintly decaying aristocrats. Dorothea Gray, Charles's too positive and humorless sister. Her fiancé, Elbridge Sterne, metallurgist, who knew about brass and that was all. Tony Burton, the very model of a model banker gentleman. Jackie Mason, the typical small-town boy, with his slickly brushed hair, carefully knotted tie, and suit "too aggressively brown."

The principal characters, appropriately, show greater complexity, and consequently more verisimilitude. Charles's two "loves," Jessica and Nancy, contrast nicely, the former seen more attractively in a young lover role (she is not terribly pretty and certainly is father-dominated, yet she has great charm, and one knows why the affair is never completely over for Charles), the latter as the trim, efficient wife, perhaps too efficient and "hard," but suffering, in the glimpse the reader has of her, under the strain of the bank-job crisis, and so reflecting a veneer that doesn't really conceal her genuine love for her husband. The latter must be considered an appealing protagonist, a man who is bright, perceptive, very likeable, even if "not quite so nice as he used to be." He is unselfish and keeps his promises. If he must use caution and discretion and must rely on the instinct to please, he still won't "crawl." In other words, he retains his principles even in an unprincipled world and even if the edges of his personality become a tiny bit frayed. His father, John Gray, is the book's most fascinating character, and one of Marquand's very best. Though deplorably unstable and basically selfish, he is also charming, witty, and lovable. Moreover, the more positive values of kindness and spontaneity are his as well. If he is the one who left his family all but unprovided for when he committed suicide, he is also the one who charters a boat for a month and takes the townspeople out sailing. While serving as a foil for his more stodgy but more upright son, he functions as a delightful, eccentric but believable character in his own right.

Marquand puts these characters through their paces and tells his story with the cool, supple dispatch that readers have come to associate with novelists of manners. One evidence of his skill is the carefully modulated dialogue with which the novel is generously sprinkled. Marquand tailors the conversation to the speakers while at the same time getting across necessary exposition, or underlining important relationships between individuals, even underscoring the theme. A case in point might be the book's opening discussion between Charles and Nancy Gray: expository, characterizing, and thematic, all in one.

Marquand's style is not particularly dressed up with

figures of speech, but when they appear they vivify the scene, chiefly because they "fit" the world being described. Thus, the Stuyvesant Bank officers, like Charles Gray, sit in a bastion, fronting for the executives who were higher in the scale, "like a knight and a bishop on a chessboard." Thus, Roger Blakesley cultivates acquaintances and contacts as "scientifically as a market gardener could start young tomatoes." Or, the uneasy friendship between Charles and his father is like that "between two lawyers who had argued in court and dined together afterwards." Or, living in Clyde was like walking through spiderwebs without any spiders. Invisible strings kept getting around you, brushing across your face. Precise, if deliberately prosaic, images these are, and they sometimes, as in the case of the last one, the spiderweb, have symbolic implications.

Throughout the book the author carefully selects his words to place a scene before the reader completely, yet without wastage. The weird, setting-back-the-clock visit of Miss Sarah Hewitt to the Grays illustrates, as do the interviews, filled with tension, between Charles and Mr. Lovell, or the final scene, the Burton dinner. To maintain the suspense and at the same time the naturalness of such episodes calls into play many of the writer's resources; indeed, these are on display throughout the book, which reflects a lambent play of wit and humor and a keen sense of *le mot juste.*

Marquand's subsequent novels continued to concentrate upon the disturbing effects of a class-conscious background, or the anxieties accompanying the move from small town to big city, or the insecurity born of a sense of impermanence, isolation, and inferiority occurring even among the well-to-do. Varying slightly from the pattern is *Melville Goodwin, USA* (1951), whose protagonist, General Goodwin, shows less self-doubt than his counterparts in the Marquand canon, and who is less affected by his up-country New Hampshire origins, and more satisfied with his role in life.

This novel interests the reader primarily because of its exploration of a new environment, the Army world. New, yes, but not very different, Marquand quickly tells the reader, from business and professional circles. Class relationships remain as clearly drawn in the service as in the "real" world, the rigid caste lines seen, of course, in terms of the rank-rating hierarchy. The Army resembles a tightly knit corporate organization, with parallels to the senior and junior executives, the secretarial staff, and so on. Rank has its privileges, at the Officers' Club or at the Commissary. Social life is carefully outlined, with the smart "top-drawer" wives wisely following their bible, *The Army Wife*. Conformity prevails, fawning is practiced, a sense of lost freedom is pronounced. General Goodwin has done things by the book — military histories are *his* bible — and has been conditioned like everyone else.

On the other hand, Melville Goodwin, if a type, is, Marquand emphasizes, a good type. His simplicity and certainty indicate honesty, if also dogmatism, and his courage and decency offset his narrowness. The journalist Sid Skelton, interviewing Goodwin for a *Time*-like profile, comes to respect him heartily, for the General's "monumental assurance" turns, for Skelton, into "splendid assurance," and it shines brightly when contrasted with Skelton's own uncertainty and shopworn integrity. Marquand wishes, one feels, to establish the point that an individual should become fully conscious of his own identity, its strengths and its weaknesses, and should then cling to a faith in himself and in his capacity to "operate" in the world. This is an encompassable goal, for, though society vitally affects it members, it does not tyrannize over them.

Marquand's last novel, *Women and Thomas Harrow* (1958), offers proof that the author remained at his old stand to the end. In this work he turns to the world of the theater, telling the story of dramatist Tom Harrow, one who, like many an earlier Marquand creation, has been "trained" by his past and has reached the "point of no return," the hour when there is "so little time," and the questioning of one's "success" begins. The book reports again that, under the dictates of social sanction, "life is loss."[28]

In its account of Tom Harrow's life,[29] the novel deals with three areas, the domestic, the materialistic, and the artistic, in each of which the protagonist has shown confusion, with varying degrees of misfortune resulting. In the first place, he has been involved in domestic problems, as his three marriages clearly suggest. His first wife and true love, Rhoda, divorced him during World War II, preferring a marriage to very wealthy Presley Brake and thus an absolutely gilt-edged security. On the rebound he attached himself briefly to the fascinating but very self-centered actress Laura Hopedale, who gave very little love and subsequently demanded very much alimony. His third and current wife, Emily, loved his position and money rather than his person, and their marriage has grown increasingly shaky. The outside chance, presented near the book's end, of a return to Rhoda is ruled out, in part because, despite a lingering love, the past cannot be recaptured.

Tom Harrow has been at fault in shortsightedly choosing rather "bitchy" wives, and also in not dealing with them properly — in not fully recognizing that marriage is a reciprocal relationship. Nothing probably could have been done about Laura Hopedale, but, with Emily, Tom is partly to blame, having never chosen to face issues with her. Whenever a showdown was indicated, he resorted to ironic dialogue instead of explanation or self-assertion. With Rhoda, the blame must also be shared, for Tom made no endeavor to correct her overinsistence on wealth and security, nor did he put his foot down when occasion required. For all his intelligence and charm he allowed too many "scenes," with corroding consequences.

Since Tom Harrow's domestic troubles usually stemmed from money problems, the materialistic area blends into the domestic. A tremendous drive for money and security motivates most of the characters in the novel, most strikingly Rhoda, compensating for an impoverished childhood, but also Tom. When given the chance, Rhoda heads unerringly for the old-rich Bramhalls and the new-rich Hertimes. Though Tom prefers "living" to security, he also loves Rhoda and doesn't object to the Scott Fitzgerald atmosphere either, and so he trails along, into the Palm Beach-Riviera world of the "securest sort of solidity." Eventually Rhoda shakes him off, unable to stand his habit of now and then throwing away safety — his going off to fight in the war — and always suspicious of his unstable theatrical associations. Money was involved in his subsequent marriages, too, Emily, for example, wanting a well-established older man as a husband. In most instances the push for financial security effects a sad decline in human relations.

Granting that Tom Harrow has met with failure in matters domestic and materialistic (at the novel's opening he is facing severe financial losses through an unwise theatrical venture), yet he would at first glance seem to have encountered more success in the artistic realm, and thus a measure of compensation. His career as a playwright has been distinguished, including many aesthetic as well as financial triumphs, and establishing for him "a niche in the history of American drama." Marquand gives us a distinct impression of Tom's knowledgeability, not only of the writing, but also of the casting, directing, and producing of plays. Equipped from the outset of his career with originality and flair, he had quickly acquired professional competence and had only occasionally veered from the maintenance of high standards. At the present time, however, he seems to have passed his peak, having become rather too slick, and he must also look back upon certain plays written with movie adaptation — and money — in mind. He says of his talents at the very end of the book that "he was a mediocre playwright who was occasionally a good one" — far behind his idols, Sophocles, Shakespeare, Molière, and behind Ibsen, Shaw, and O'Neill as well.

The stocktaking seems a sorry business then. Tom has barely, if at all, maintained personal and professional integrity and dignity, and he looks upon his life as a downward slide, a gradual chipping away of one's values and eroding of one's "niceness." Thus, there echoes throughout the book a "where has everything gone" refrain, youth, love, money, even the artistic skill having evaporated, leaving Tom with the conviction that his life has been a "dingy, inexpert production."[30]

Most readers will view Tom less harshly than he views himself, however, for, if he has often succumbed to conventions, and if he has been caught up in the drive for security, and if he has proved uxorious and unstable, yet he has shown many positive attributes — loyalty, honesty, generosity, intelligence — and he has done many "right things," such as serving in the war, refusing the return of Rhoda's divorce settlement to tide him over the financial crisis, and not seriously trespassing on his work. One sympathizes with him in his endeavor to "know himself," to recognize the limitations of the blueprint of his life, and to assess its virtues and its weaknesses.

Though *Women and Thomas Harrow* at first seems less demonstrably a study of manners than Marquand's earlier efforts — mostly because the reader often lingers in a very specialized world here, that of the theater — yet the book, on closer examination, reveals a sense of class structure and of the mores of various social levels. Like the standard Marquand hero, Tom Harrow belongs to the upper-middle level, though his status has been made slightly uneasy by the early loss of his parents and by a lack of financial resources; his dipsomaniacal father had been more charming than breadwinning. Brought up by an uncle and aunt — who were themselves unsure of their "position," being Johnny-come-latelies in the New York "brownstone" world — he remains something of an outsider, despite attendance at a fashionable boarding school and a good college and despite having his name appear on the debutante "extra man" list. Besides, the unconventional has already cropped up more than once in his life, first when he spent two years at a public high school in a small town (living with his mother's sister, at a time when finances were at an ebb), and second when he chose to become an employee of a theatrical agency after completing his education. His subsequent embarkation upon a career as a playwright made him, of course, irrevocably suspect in the eyes of his Harrow relatives and others, who recognized only stocks and bonds or the law as legitimate professions. Tom is actually a socially mobile person — like Charles Gray — who could fit quite easily into almost any world, that of Broadway, that of the old rich and of the new rich — though he's not too happy in either of these — and even that of the small-town middle class. To be sure, his former classmate at the Clyde High School, Jack Dodd, would never be on easy terms with him, yet Jack, and others who have remained in Clyde, accept Tom — as they will never accept his wife Emily.

The rigidity of the social structure is best seen in the glimpses of the town where Tom spent part of his youth, a town called, as in other Marquand novels, Clyde. One is emphatically told that everyone knew about everyone else, and everyone knew where everyone else fitted in the undeviating social order. A settled, structured community lies before the reader. Tom's relatives, Judge Fowler and his family, belong at the top, together with the residents of Johnson Street, whereas in the middle are located such townspeople as the Brownes, parents of his first wife Rhoda, and at the bottom come the Italians and other inhabitants of the "South End." One is "fixed" by the house in which he lives, by the manners he displays, by the clothes he wears. Tom's so "carelessly beautiful" attire, as Rhoda describes it, quite distinguishes him from her father in an overpressed, double-breasted suit. The chain in Clyde is firm. Fortunately for Rhoda, she is — unlike her parents — almost as mobile as Tom, having beauty, a refreshing frankness, wit, and a decided adaptability, and thus, with a little coaching, and having moved away from Clyde, she deftly progresses in an upward direction.

The class pattern prevails in the larger world as well as in Clyde, with similar characterizing features defining the levels. Rhoda and Tom penetrate the upper-class circles, visiting their beautifully appointed houses in New York, Palm Beach, or on the Cap d'Antibes, adopting for themselves the correct because "ostentatiously simple" attire, and acquiring the gracious manners, for example, the ability to "stage" a well-ordered dinner party, one with a table setting of fine china and silver and an unfussy centerpiece, and with a good pièce de résistance such as rare roast beef, and the proper wine to accompany it. Such a world champions tradition, loving the permanence of old law firms, enjoying genealogical explorations, delighting in historical associations. Tom's nostalgic evocation of "old New York" with its serene mansion-and-club life, or even of "old Clyde" in the days of the lamplighter, hand-cranked telephone, and kitchen coffee mill reflects this fascination with the past.[31] The aristocracy, in short, epitomizes grace and charm and, above all, assurance. As Rhoda Harrow says of the duPonts — no matter what happens, there they are. Tom's theater friends may be infinitely more creative and talented and interesting, yet they'll always be at a slight disadvantage in confrontation with the duPonts and Bramhalls — for "there they are."[32]

Marquand does not overlook the snobbery, narrowness, and intellectual limitations of this segment of society,[33] and can be satiric about the manners question — as in his amusing contrast of Southampton with Easthampton, the latter having "More to Start With," and deliberately preserving the "Dear Old Things" in order to maintain its edge. He is prepared to catalog the weaknesses as well as the strengths of the "smart set" and the "Old Guard," but, whether praising or blaming, he wishes to insist on the paradoxical presence of a class hierarchy in "democratic" America.

Just as in *Point of No Return,* setting plays a key role in *Women and Thomas Harrow,* helping to outline the social framework.[34] The shabby old seaport town of Clyde, not very successfully modernized by the plastic facades on Dock Street, looms up before the reader from the early pages of the novel on. If giving a down-at-the-heels impression as a whole, yet it is dotted with attractive buildings and homes, such as the Congregational Church, defiant in its simplicity (and making Tom Harrow feel closer to the truth than he had ever felt at Notre Dame or Chartres), or the lovely Federalist mansions built "in the best McIntyre tradition." Tom's carefully restored house, with its graceful Corinthian columns, Seabury front door, and precisely appointed interior — like the American Wing in the Metropolitan, Emily Harrow unsympathetically declared — complete with prayer-closet-converted-into-bathroom, its beautiful formal gardens in the rear, and the coachhouse-became-study, is representative.

Less appealing, but important as characterizing their inhabitants, are the pedestrian frame dwelling of the Brownes and the aggressive-looking "late Currier and Ives vintage" home of Aunt Edith Fowler, the latter characterful if not overly tasteful.

Touches of the elegant world of Park Avenue, Palm Beach, and the French Riviera are provided in the novel, too, varying from the picture of the Hertimes' domicile in Palm Beach — a place that "King Midas would have understood" — to the description of the solid New York home of the Howlands with its rooms done in heavy fumed oak, to that of the massive Jacobean offices of Arthur Higgins. Paying, as always, special attention to interiors, Marquand lovingly itemizes the contents of Judge Fowler's library or Tom Harrow's dining room. Through such means he richly authenticates his background.

The characters populating the novel authenticate the background as well, especially the minor ones who occupy the back of the stage. These are often gently mimicked by the author, for example, Walter Price, the theatrical agent, seedy, bibulous, a congenital liar, a sponge, yet not without charm and not without shrewdness either. Also from the theatrical world come actors, producers, secretaries — usually talented, hardworking people, if a bit showy. Small-town types like Jack Dodd of the "arboreal service," Mr. Browne, the owner of a stumbling Ford agency, and Mr. Godfrey with his "How Happy Are You Inside?" sermon topics, are needled by the author, especially the latter, who runs his church as if it were a sort of spiritual service station, and who talks a great deal about motivation, adjustment, and the subconscious but not very much about God.

"Society" in its various gradations can be seen through the individuals in the book. The "climbers" range from Mrs. Browne, who, to her perpetual dismay, has climbed *down* from her youthful Rhyelle mansion eminence, to Aunt Mabel and Uncle George Harrow, never quite self-assured, to the also still slightly parvenu Hertimes. Wealth, like good Burgundy, needs maturing. Securely fastened at the top one finds the Bramhalls and, almost as securely, Presley Brake — the possessor of a Bentley with a wooden inlaid instrument panel. Snug in her niche, outside the fashionable world but in an eminently respectable one, is Aunt Edith Fowler. Not at all snug in *her* niche is Emily Harrow, the "little Hoosier girl" now the wife of an eminent dramatist but still so uncertain that she is always overbraceleted, seemingly carrying "as much as she possibly can on her person in case things may become difficult again." The fluid Rhoda Brake — née Browne, and once Rhoda Harrow — easily adapted herself to the upper echelons, and when the reader sees her in the final sequence of the novel, she seems the perfect portrait of what she had wished to become, the high-society girl. Even if she is just a bit outdated already, as Marquand ironically notes — too close to the Jamesian *Portrait of a Lady* or an Edith Wharton girl to be wholly accepted in the present scene; there would be no one of her type this year at El Morocco or the Stork — still, the hall porter at Claridge's would have rated her very highly, "and, by God, he would have been exactly right."

These portraits in *Women and Thomas Harrow* are obviously etched with a fair degree of acerbity, Marquand delighting, as usual, in exposing man's foibles. People *and* things provide him with manifold targets: from the litter in city streets in the present day of packaged goods to Hollywood director Egbert Rhinestein, who is "all the time thinking wide-screen"; from the gastronomical and spiritual mediocrity of national life to the fringe of useless intellectuals present in the entertainment fields; from the horrors of the new fin-tailed car to the questionable contributions of "forward-moving beauticians." As Marquand thus comments on the present era, he often nostalgically wishes for the earlier, more graceful age.

It is, finally, a pleasure to watch Marquand the stylist at work in this, as in his other novels. Again the reader encounters the deft characterizing phrase, the ironic insight, the sensitive ear for speech, the appropriate image, the amusing understatement, the brisk allusiveness. There is Emily Harrow, changing from sweetness to sternness by making her kimono less like a peignoir and more like the draped gown of a Roman matron. And there is young Hal Harrow, ex-Naval Reservist, possessing the Navy's young-officer stamp but not quite the "Annapolis patina." Marquand makes the past "unwind like ticker tape." He sends Emily Harrow "off the rails on the curve of her own garrulity." When youthful Tom Harrow feigns skill in fixing lobsters in order to impress his girl, Marquand calls it "a prediction, not an established fact." Older Tom Harrow he describes as writing "an impromptu script for the benefit of cabana-domiciled royalty." The varied stylistic effects — theater idiom, drawing-room dialogue, descriptive passages of Balzacian exactitude, tart observations — are authoritative and persuasive and very much in keeping with the mood and tone of the book.[35]

Thus, Marquand functions as a clever purveyor of the comedy and drama that derive from the interplay within and among the "classes" in American society. Mixing his poignance with acidity, he both sympathizes with and laughs at man's vanity, snobbery, and general limitations. Though his "heroes" do not attain tragic proportions, and though their lives contain little "poetry," nonetheless, Marquand attributes values and standards to them, for example, George Apley's firm idea of responsible service or Charles Gray's unwillingness to sidestep truth, and in the process he reveals himself to be more committed about man-in-society than some critics have been willing to grant.[36] While always aware of the possibility of uncertainty in moral judgments and of the complexity inherent in most situations, and thus avoiding black-or-white pronunciamentos, he nevertheless "stands for" certain principles and attitudes, for taste and social grace, for a benevolent concern for others, for the ordered (not the crippling) community. With the social novelists who preceded him, he shared the belief that the manners of an age must be evaluated, and perhaps corrected, in terms of such fixed principles and attitudes. Moreover, he considered these standards to remain real even in the "changing market for manners,"[37] and even if they were more often honored in the breach than in the observance.[38]

Very possibly deserving Nathan Glick's tribute — "our most accomplished novelist of manners"[39] — Marquand probes and illumines as well as entertains, and, with a wonderful sureness of touch, unveils the nuances of the social hierarchy.

NOTES TO CHAPTER 8

1. Herschel Brickell, "Miss Glasgow and Mr. Marquand," *Virginia Quarterly Review* 17 (Summer 1941): 405.

2. These, says Leo Gurko, are the attributes, after all, of a great novelist. See Leo Gurko, "The High-Level Formula of J. P. Marquand," *The American Scholar* 21 (Autumn 1952): 443.

3. Chester E. Eisinger, *Fiction of the Forties* (Chicago and London: University of Chicago Press, 1963), p. 289.

4. One should bear in mind, for example, Marquand's own comment about his character George Apley: "In conducting Mr. Apley through the trivialities of his years I confess I was startled to discover when I left him that he amounted to more than I intended" (the statement appears in his preface to the 1940 edition of *The Late George Apley*).

5. A game Marquand would decry, he having explicitly said (in his preface

to *H. M. Pulham, Esq.*) that "living men and women are too limited, too far from being typical, too greatly lacking in any universal appeal to serve in a properly planned piece of fiction."

6. Every writer, Marquand has remarked — and he sounds like James, Wharton and Glasgow as he does so — is limited by the area of his experience. He could perhaps write about China, but not with the feeling and conviction of Kipling and Conrad, nor could they, conversely, write with the same conviction about Boston (see J. P. Marquand, "Apley, Wickford Point and Pulham," *The Atlantic* 198 [September 1956] : 73).

7. Ibid., p. 74.

8. The phrase used by Robert W. Cochran to describe what he sees as Marquand's major theme (see Robert W. Cochran, "In Search of Perspective: A Study of the Serious Novels of J. P. Marquand", [Ph.D. diss. University of Michigan, 1957]).

9. William James Smith, "J. P. Marquand, Esq.," *Commonweal* 69 (November 7, 1958): 149.

10. Marquand, "Apley, Wickford Point and Pulham," p. 72.

11. Granville Hicks, "Marquand of Newburyport," *Harper's Magazine* 200 (April 1950): 103.

12. Again the not-quite-belonging protagonist is utilized by the novelist of manners, who finds substance for drama in the struggle between personal ideals and the dictates of society.

13. Ironically, he acts on good instinct, blackballing Ransome because the latter wishes to use the club to further his business connections, not for the purposes of friendship for which it is designed.

14. C. Hugh Holman, *John P. Marquand*, University of Minnesota Pamphlets on American Writers, no. 46 (Minneapolis, Minn.: University of Minnesota Press, 1965), pp. 6-7.

15. Quoted in ibid., p. 28.

16. John Gross, *John P. Marquand* (New York: Twayne Publishers, Inc., 1963), p. 18.

17. Eisinger, *Fiction of the Forties*, p. 29.

18. Stewart Benedict, in a recent article on Marquand, agrees in finding determinism in his work. In fact, he goes much farther than I am willing to go, declaring that "with the exception of Dreiser, Marquand is perhaps the most rigidly deterministic author who has thus far written in America in this century" (Stewart H. Benedict, "The Pattern of Determinism in J. P. Marquand's Novels," *Ball State Teachers College Forum* 2 [Winter 1961-62]: 60). The general outlines of personality of a Marquand character, Benedict says, are irrevocably fixed at a very early age, with the details filled in during youth by environmental influences over which he can exercise no control. Moreover, once the pattern is set, the individual cannot change it.

Although conceding that the environmental influences (region, family, education, financial standing, life work) are strong indeed in Marquand's work, I would not regard them as absolute. If man is conditioned in various ways, he is still free to participate in shaping the direction his life will take. Marquand's major thesis is that his protagonists *do* participate — in that they examine themselves and their lives. Some, of course, achieve greater self-awareness and show more growth than others, and are therefore more free of the deterministic pattern.

If Marquand is fascinated by determinism (as phrases in his novels — "you become a type," "ominous sort of destiny," "the frame where life had placed you," "the inevitability of Greek tragedy," "there is some needle inside everyone which points the way he is to go without his knowing it" — also suggest), he does not go so far as to present it as a consistent philosophical and psychological position.

19. Louis Auchincloss, *Reflections of a Jacobite* (Boston: Houghton Mifflin Co., 1961), p. 144.

20. Ibid., p. 146.

21. Frederick I. Carpenter, *American Literature and the Dream* (New York: Philosophical Library, 1955), p. 62.

22. Tasmin is "identified" by Marquand as "a member of the well-stocked club group which was indigenous to the Eastern seaboard and which had a culture stemming from the British upper middle class — a group with good manners and one which had trained itself in several generations of security."

23. Says Robert Haigh, Gray is "a patient Griselda in a pin-stripe suit. Not happy; not unhappy either" (Robert F. Haigh, "The Dilemma of John P. Marquand," *Michigan Alumnus Quarterly Review* 59 [Autumn 1952]: 23).

24. Quoted in Hicks, "Marquand of Newburyport," p. 101.

25. Cf. Nathan Glick's comment, "Certainly, on his native grounds, Marquand is more than a match for any battery of sociologists" (Nathan Glick, "Marquand's Vanishing Aristocracy," *Commentary* 9 [May 1950]: 441).

26. For example, Charles Gray's very neat bedroom, in his boyhood home, indicates his slightly priggish nature, whereas his father's book-strewn and most untidy study suggests his intellectual and careless, and, by indirection, endearing nature.

27. See Hicks, "Marquand of Newburyport," p. 108.

28. Many critics have declared that Marquand "writes the same novel over and over again" (Haigh, "The Dilemma of John P. Marquand," p. 20), but perhaps it is more accurate to say that Marquand has treated with variety and subtlety one major theme (see Cochran, "In Search of Perspective . . . ").

29. The "life" is unfolded by means of the customary Marquand flashback rather than by a straight chronological method, thus emphasizing the customary Marquand thesis of the impingement of the past upon the present. In weaving past and present together so deftly, Marquand gives himself room for many subtle and illuminating comparisons and contrasts.

30. In such terms (appropriately drawn from the theater) Tom sums up his life — the running through a series of scripts written by Providence, he says, not by himself. This phrasing again calls to mind the deterministic flavor of Mar-

quand's work. "Providence" directs one's activities; more specifically, environment molds one. Yet Marquand remains, as it were, an environmentalist-with conscience, not allowing man to resign responsibility. Within the frame of necessity he can do a great deal, overcoming some of the barriers to happiness, even finding, sometimes, a measure of spiritual solace.

31. In contrast, Rhoda Harrow and the nouveaux riches to whom she is particularly drawn do not cherish the bygone days. Not having a mentionable past themselves, they would choose to forget it.

32. Novelists of manners often stress this self-assurance quality of the very rich, Marquand, Fitzgerald, and Auchincloss serving as cases in point. Though the latter may not subscribe to the myth established by Fitzgerald that the rich are very different from the rest of mankind, believing that only their money makes them stand out (see James W. Tuttleton, *The Novel of Manners in America* [Chapel Hill, N. C.: University of North Carolina Press, 1972], p. 253), still, he does emphasize their poise and security.

33. He echoes Edith Wharton in hinting at the intellectual shortcomings of "society," and in posing an artistic world against it. His "artistic" world, that of the theater, is much more carefully realized — auditions, rehearsals, tryouts, after-theater parties — than hers, however, and also seems more worthwhile.

34. Marquand asserted in his last book, *Timothy Dexter, Revisited*, that "environment is more interesting than the man."

35. Nathan Glick speaks of Marquand's prose as having the flat, polite, unexcitable rhythms of gentility and suburbia, that is, low in pitch "but perfectly suited" (Glick, "Marquand's Vanishing Aristocracy," p. 439).

36. See Michael Millgate, *American Social Fiction: James to Cozzens* (New York: Barnes & Noble, Inc., 1964), p. 184.

37. Glick, "Marquand's Vanishing Aristocracy," p. 440.

38. See Gross, *John P. Marquand*, pp. 170 ff.

39. Glick, "Marquand's Vanishing Aristocracy," p. 435.

9

Practitioners, 1920 - 1960

*A*MONG the immediate predecessors and contemporaries of Marquand were a group supporting the historical development of the manners genre. Novelists like Sinclair Lewis, Carl Van Vechten, F. Scott Fitzgerald, James Gould Cozzens, and John O'Hara also chose to treat of the role of manners and its relationship to moral vision. They, too, talked of the everyday realities of social spheres, of the place of religion (absent!) and of culture (all but absent!), of kinds of businesses and entertainments, and of American-European associations. They, too, often showed the effects of the past on manners and values, as they made inquiry about the continuance and impact of social "norms."

Sinclair Lewis, for one, impinges upon the novel-of-manners tradition in much of his fiction, taking as he does a particular segment of society — the *middle* middle class — and elaborating on its forms, rituals, and characterizing features. His protagonists are usually strongly conditioned by their social situation, which indeed often affects their destiny, and Lewis sets forth a careful study of the way of life within that social situation.

A recent biographer of Lewis, Sheldon Grebstein, has described him as "superbly a novelist of surfaces, of manners and mores, and only occasionally a novelist of morals and of the heights and depths of human experience."[1] An accurate summation, one feels. Lewis's best work records, with very explicit details, the surface view of the middle class, the great bulk of the American populace between the masses and the "nobs," the fiction indicating the class's status symbols and its canons of taste.

One may cite Lewis's famous character creation, George F. Babbitt, as the prototype: the Babbitt who uses the same caterer and bootlegger as his neighbor, gives the same kind of dinner, relies upon the same number of mechanical gadgets, and belongs to the same clubs — not the most select. Lewis mocks Babbitt's hypocrisies, his cultural limitations, and his trivialities, through making up for this unflattering list in part by suggesting at the same time Babbitt's kindness, loyalty, and basic decency. When Babbitt sheds his tribal opinions and evaluations — temporarily — his creator even bestows some affection upon him, an affection that blunts the satiric attack.

Generally speaking, of course, Lewis's indictment of the Middle Western bourgeoisie is severe, as his early, country-shaking *Main Street* (1920) testifies. Here Lewis has chosen, in Carol Kennicott, an "outsider" protagonist, one who views her world with a little more perception than Georgy Babbitt views his. Though Carol is basically solid middle class herself, she has a cultivated family background and big-city veneer that enable her to recognize the limitations of Gopher Prairie. The town has few redeeming features. Its "broad straight, unenticing gashes" of streets "let in the grasping prairie." Along the streets appear the Minniemashie House with its fly-specked windows, the Rosebud Movie Palace, and the Bon Ton Store. An emblemizing home is the one to which Carol's husband, Dr. Will Kennicott, brings her:

> A square smug brown house, rather damp. A narrow concrete walk up to it. Sickly yellow leaves in a window with dried wings of box elder and snags of wool from the cottonwoods. A screened porch with pillars of thin painted pine surmounted by scrolls and brackets and bumps of jig-sawed wood. No shrubbery to shut off the public gaze. A lugubrious bay-window to the right of the porch. Window curtains of starched cheap lace revealing a pink marble table with a conch shell and a Family Bible. [P. 44]

Gopher Prairie proves a grim locale, unattractive during the hard winter, during the muddy spring, during the close heat of summer.

Mrs. Kennicott is bothered by this depressing backdrop, and even more troubled by the individuals who people the scene. The men of the town are concerned with making money or with hunting, the women with playing bridge or with making futile stabs at "culture" — covering the English poets in a one-hour session of the Thanatopsis Club. Confronted with so many "savorless people," Carol fails with the dramatic association, the library board, even with the more sensitive individuals like Vida Sherwin or Guy Pollock, who have been bitten, as the latter admits, by the "Village Virus." The few unconventional figures such as Fern Mullins or Miles Bjornstam are driven out of town. Gopher Prairie insists upon its "unimaginatively standardized background, sluggishness of speech and manners, rigid ruling of the spirit by the desire to appear respectable."

After a period of escape to Washington (and even there one finds a "thick streak of Main Street"), Carol returns to Gopher Prairie and her wifely duties. She must settle for the love of her sturdy and capable husband and the affection of a circle of friends, which afford a measure of compensation for the constricting and ugly environment.

Without much stylistic pretense, Lewis yet renders his scene vividly. His figures of speech are properly graphic: "towns as planless as a scattering of pasteboard boxes on an attic floor," the Clark house "as shiny, as hard, and as cheerful as a new oak upright piano." His repetitions, as Mrs. Dawson's "bleached cheeks, bleached hair, bleached voice and bleached manner," effectively characterize, and his descriptive phrases — the dignified poverty of the Congregational parsonage, Lyman Cass's pinnacled, dark-red, hulking house — have the value of pointedness. Less commendable is the author's strident tone, apparent in such scenes as that of the Beavers' convention, and less commendable, too, is the overdone dialogue, so extravagent as to suggest that Lewis's fabled skill at mimicry can sometimes fail him.[2]

Occasionally Lewis trained his sights on a class other than the "booboisie." *Dodsworth* (1929) deals with the aristocracy — at least the "aristocracy of Zenith dancing at the Kennepoose Canoe Club." Presenting the story of automobile manufacturer Sam Dodsworth and his flighty wife Fran, Lewis first poses them against their Middle Western big-city background. Living in a comfortable if slightly florid home — one that is, it must be granted, more tasteful than that of brewer Herman Voelker, a dwelling of many turrets, colored glass windows, and lace curtains — and leading the community in social and cultural affairs, the Dodsworths should be but aren't altogether satisfied. Fran in particular feels that they have "drained everything that Zenith can give us." As a consequence they depart on an extended European trip.

This change of locale[3] gives Lewis the opportunity to indulge in the international contrast so popular with novelists of manners. Suave Britishers like Major Lockert, his cousin

Lord Herndon, or Sir Francis Ouston of Woughton Hall appear to advantage beside the "American Captain of Industry." At least, they do in the eyes of Dodsworth's socially conscious wife. Sam feels discomfited at arty teas and tedious dinner parties, "unable to understand the violent differences between an Oxford man and a graduate of the University of London, between a public school man and one who abysmally was not." When Fran assures him of the inestimable benefits of European civilization, he clings to his Americanism, even to his "American materialism."

As the scene shifts to the Continent, Fran continues to adapt to "foreign ways," seemingly more readily than Sam. However, despite her remarks about liking the "civilized amusements" and "traditions" of Europe and abhorring the "thinness" of America, she looks upon Europe purely as a social adventure, as offering her a chance to play the dashing role of "The Sophisticated American Lady Abroad." In fulfilling such a role, she spends her time cultivating the Duchesse de Quatrefleurs and Count von Obersdorf. Her husband, on the other hand, enjoys appraising European customs or touring through the art galleries. Far more sensitive than his wife — to whom "painting, like all 'culture,' was interesting only as it adorned her socially" — he clearly profits from his gallery-going. At the same time he recognizes more quickly than Fran the genuine article among their titled acquaintances, sensing, for example, in the Princess Drachenthal, a "reality of breeding." one which distinguishes her from some of their other "amateur headwaiter" friends. Sam evaluates his European experiences with much more intelligence than Fran, seeing the "tiny, unchartable differences" — and the larger ones, too — between Europe and America.

By the time he encounters Edith Cortright, an American expatriate of charm and penetration who has happily adapted her American heritage to European living, he seems prepared to accept the best of both worlds. When he is at length freed of Fran, he marries Mrs. Cortright and presumably settles down contentedly in her, or similar, quarters, quite ready to appreciate a habitation on the order of the Palazzo Ascagni, where there was a "suggested quietness, a feeling of civilization grown secure and placid through generations." Dodsworth feels certain that "in this most Italian Italy he might without apology still be a most American American."

Always the satirist, Lewis, in *Dodsworth*, mocks those on either side of the ocean: the go-getting president of the Unit Automotive Company, Alex Kynance; shallow expatriates like Lycurgus (Jerry) Watts; social "arranger" Mme. de Pénable; the German professor Braut, who lectures Fran "as though she were a rather small seminar." Of the two principals, Fran and Sam Dodsworth, the former is much more sharply attacked, her dilettantish personality being clearly exposed in Lewis's tart phrase, "an unsurpassed show-window display but not much on the shelves inside." Lewis obviously prefers Sam Dodsworth, even if the author is willing to define him unflatteringly as one who was "extremely well trained in not letting himself do anything so destructive as abstract thinking." No one really comes off unscathed, the American aristocrat (plutocrat is perhaps the proper term — Lewis calls the Dodsworths "these spoiled children of new wealth") faring only slightly better than his middle-class cousin Babbitt.

In subsequent novels Lewis continued his assault on American life, the fields of medicine, religion, social work, the theater, and so on coming within his purview. He apparently wished to evaluate the behavior patterns of his age, perhaps to correct them in terms of some absolute standards of value, certainly to chastise the mechanized, spiritually inadequate middle class. His technique, as he made his assault, varied little from book to book, consisting throughout of two-dimensional characterization, massive cultural detail, ponderous satire, and a slam-bang style. The comedy-of-manners genre was most precisely echoed in his exact reproduction of locales, for example, country club districts and hotel barbershops, in his reflection of the class structure,[4] and in his extensive reliance upon irony. He paid some attention, too, to the themes prevailing within the genre, those such as the social-climbing experience, the clash of generations, or the pitting of the independent individual against a narrow, stupid society.

It cannot be said that Lewis successfully confronted all the problems posed by the genre, however. He failed, most notably, to satisfy the need for a scintillating style and for noncardboardlike characters, whose actions and relationships will genuinely concern the reader. Despite the truthfulness of his account and the vigor of his execution, he remained the blunt caricaturist rather than the skilled novelist of manners.

Another novelist of the 1920s who looked rather severely at the Middle Western social scene was Carl Van Vechten. His Maple Valley, Iowa, the setting for *The Tattooed Countess* (1924), serves as a replica of Lewis's Gopher Prairie, being equally stultifying and culturally barren. Former hometown girl Ella Poore, returning as Countess Nattatorrini, after many years of flourishing in a smartly cosmopolitan world, is regarded with deep suspicion by the townsfolk. She wears makeup, she smokes, she reads Daudet and Maupassant, she talks of Bernhardt and the Paris theater, and she prefers the company of men, especially young men, to that of women. Though pleased by an item or two on the local scene, the "picking garden" behind the Poore mansion, the fresh raspberries and thick clots of cream for breakfast, the Countess is, on the other hand, oppressed by the gossiping sewing circles and the town's architectural "triumphs" like the new waterworks, and the reader is not surprised when she cuts short her visit and swirls back to the Continent, trailing her magenta tulle and with the only eligible Maple Valley young man in her train. Van Vechten amusingly contributes his bit to the "revolt from the village" pattern, suggesting a lack of viable traditions among the social leaders in this "busybody" world. The expatriate existence to which the Countess returns at least has a polished glow − if hardly moral character.

Van Vechten more frequently located his novels in New York City than in Iowa, actually, and they more closely resemble a Fitzgerald effort than they do one by Lewis. In jeux d'esprit like *Firecrackers* (1925) and *Parties* (1930), he puts the "smart set" through their frivolous paces, indulging in prolonged luncheons at the Moloch Club and more prolonged cocktail hours at the Wishbone speakeasy. The title of the latter novel aptly enough suggests the atmosphere ("a man with an extensive acquaintance could drink steadily in New York from the beginning of cocktail time until eleven in the evening without any more expense than that entailed by car or cab fare"), and Buddy Parsons, who "went to all first nights and debutante parties and vernissages and tried out the new speakeasies before any one knew whether they sold poison or not," is a representative character. As Van Vechten passes over topics such as internationalism ("the English prefer Americans to be eccentric; it makes them feel more secure"), conspicuous consumption, and the boredom of the society figures (devoted to the "great god Vacuum"), he catches the tensely gay mood of the "Roaring Twenties." Characters like Rilda and David Westlake (Zelda and Scott?) exude an air of decadence as they attempt to escape the problems of their marriage by downing quantities of bootleg liquor or lindy-hopping all night at a Harlem ballroom. The author accords to their world a lightly mocking treatment.

One cannot take Van Vechten very seriously as a literary artist, however. His employment of proper names like Campaspe Lorillard and Wintergreen Waterbury, and of a vocabulary filled with words like hyaline, brumous, and appropinquation seems a more sophomoric than adroit technique, and, if he does provide an occasional stylish touch (such as the atmospheric catalogue — "Helen Morgan, Richard Tauber, La Argentinita, Lord Dunsany"), he for the most part reminds one of a Ronald Firbank without the wit.

The infinitely more subtle as well as more stylistically accomplished Scott Fitzgerald also focuses on American "classes" and on a hierarchically structured society of prescribed values and restrained liberty, and thus, like Lewis, he nestles within the novel-of-manners tradition, indeed receiving from Charles E. Shain the accolade, "America's most sentient novelist of manners."[5] In his work conventions and amenities play a significant role, his people have definable manners, a sense of exclusiveness hovers over the scene, and such trappings as velvet evening coats and emerald studs, old china, good wine, well-bound books, and Spanish altar laces appear. His world of the *very* rich stands above that of Lewis's Babbitt and Dodsworth, to be sure, but it is reproduced with a comparable degree of authentication. By means of what Irving Howe calls "brilliant guesses and fragments of envious insight,"[6] Fitzgerald vividly accentuates the social drama stemming from the entangling of social aspiration and romantic love and from a basic incompatibility between classes, and he gives to his treatment the proper note of elegiac incisiveness.[7]

Like many of his predecessors, Fitzgerald often presents the conflict between the old and the new moneyed classes, those whose wealth might be described, says Malcolm Cowley, as solid possession versus those whose wealth might be described as fluid income.[8] On the one hand, there is

Jay Gatsby, with his shadily acquired resources, his pastel clothes, and preposterous mansion; on the other hand, Tom Buchanan, with his familial inheritance, his tweeds, and his tasteful estate. Examining the clash between the two "cultures," Fitzgerald shows how society establishes barriers to be surmounted by the "young man from the provinces" if he wishes to gain entrée into the select circle flourishing in the Princeton eating clubs, the mansions on the North Shore of Long Island, the exclusive Riviera resorts.

This Side of Paradise (1922), Fitzgerald's first novel, introduces the reader to the upper echelon to which the financially and socially ambitious young men aspire. The novelist's protagonist Amory Blaine would seem to have a decided head start in his quest for admittance into this world, for he derives from his father very substantial financial resources, and from his mother, grace, beauty, and social ease. However, Amory is brought up — after his mother had suffered "a nervous breakdown that bore a suspicious resemblance to delirium tremens" — in Minneapolis, and there the "crude, vulgar air of Western civilization first catches him — in his underwear, so to speak." Supported by his code of "aristocratic egotism," Amory fares well enough, though, and, especially after going east for his schooling, fits neatly into the world of men-with-an-aura and of "golden girls" in white palaces. During his years at Princeton "the best of Amory's intellect," Fitzgerald tells us, was "concentrated on matters of popularity, the intricacies of a university social system and American Society as represented by Biltmore Teas and Hot Springs golf-links." He learns, at college, about the social order's rigidities, observing the boys from St. Paul's and Hill and Pomfret eating at certain tacitly reserved tables in Commons, dressing in their own corners of the gymnasium, and "drawing unconsciously about them a barrier of the slightly less important but socially ambitious" to protect them from the friendly, rather puzzled high-school "element." Amory easily attaches himself to the "right people," and he continues to be linked with them after his graduation.

Although intent, in this novel, on stressing the theme of Amory Blaine's emotional readiness for life rather than that of his searching for a niche on the social ladder, Fitzgerald nevertheless reflects the cultural climate, the Jazz Age milieu of "belles" who had become "flirts" and "flirts" who had become "baby vamps," of callow undergraduates and professional prom-trotters. It is a milieu that, owing to the author's informed remarks about houses, clothes, and schools — the various counters in the game of social distinction — emerges clearly, and as a surprisingly stabilized system of manners.

Fitzgerald also brings to his first book the stylistic élan that was to distinguish him: the keen ear for dialogue and the trick of establishing mood with an idiomatic turn of phrase or a popular song refrain; the deftly amusing description of character (Amory's mother "had once been a Catholic, but discovering that priests were infinitely more attentive when she was in the process of losing or regaining faith in Mother Church, she maintained an enchantingly wavering attitude"); the picturesque allusion (Monsignor Darby, clad in his full purple regalia from thatch to toe, resembles a "Turner sunset"); the apt word choice ("Tom D'Invilliers became at first an occasion rather than a friend"). Graceful, lucid, and often slightly acrid, the Fitzgerald prose contributes notably to the exactness of the evocation of the world of the well-to-do.

The Great Gatsby (1925), the most highly acclaimed of his productions, and deservedly so,[9] continues the evocation, indicating how rusty the armor of the aristocracy has grown, how filled with ethical carelessness is the race for status and money. Viewing the book as a novel of manners, one is impressed by the class contrast so central to its theme, that of the aristocracy living on family money as opposed to the plutocracy living on money stained by the sweat of their own efforts. Utilizing a deliberate symbolism of place, Fitzgerald juxtaposes East and West Egg, those two sides of Long Island Sound which offer, the author says, a "bizarre and not a little sinister contrast." In West Egg stands Gatsby's house, "a factual imitation of some Hôtel de Ville in Normandy," mammoth, extravagant, and ostentatious. "Across the courtesy bay," on the other hand, "the white palaces of fashionable East Egg glittered along the water." The Buchanan house, "a cheerful red-and-white Georgian Colonial mansion" with a long lawn "jumping over sundials and brick walks" and with sunken Italian gardens and acres of deep-pungent roses, differs sharply from that of Gatsby. Nick Carraway's quiet little cottage, not trying to be anything in particular, lies elsewhere on the social scale, and, well below them all, comes the apartment on 158th Street in New York in which Tom Buchanan has installed his mistress Myrtle Wilson. Trying to be very much indeed, the apartment has a living room "crowded to the doors with a set of tapestried furniture entirely too large for it, so that to move about was to stumble continually over scenes of ladies swinging in the gardens of Versailles."

At the Gatsby parties the differences are further outlined. Jordan Baker's group preserves a "dignified homogeneity" and assumes to itself "the function of representing the staid nobility of the country-side — East Egg condescending to West Egg, and carefully on guard against its spectroscopic gayety." The "Hornbeams and the Willie Voltaires, and a whole clan named Blackbuck . . . gathered in a corner and flipped up their noses like goats at whosoever came near." Most important, Daisy Buchanan "was appalled by West

Egg, this unprecedented 'place' that Broadway had begotten upon a Long Island fishing village."

When Gatsby arranges to meet Daisy at Nick's house for tea, he provides a "greenhouse" of flowers "with innumerable receptacles" and arrives himself in a white flannel suit, silver shirt, and gold-colored tie. Subsequently taking Daisy on a tour of his own dwelling, he points out the period bedrooms swathed in rose and lavender silk and vivid with new flowers, the dressing rooms and poolrooms and bathrooms with sunken baths, the armoires filled with dozens of silk shirts. Even his car, an elaborate cream-colored affair with a "conservatory" for an interior, suggests the arriviste limitations. The Buchanans, too rich for ostentation, have an easygoing blue coupé; Nick Carraway, scion of a long-established Middle Western family, drives a conservative old Dodge.

Though depicting the 1920s as a kaleidoscopic era, marked by shifting values and moral confusion, still, Fitzgerald implies that social standards and social distinctions remain immutable in the midst of the whirl. The Buchanans can cause discomfort even in the well-bred Nick Carraway ("'You made me feel uncivilized, Daisy,' I confessed on my second glass of corky but rather impressive claret. 'Can't you talk about crops or something?"), and clearly Jay Gatsby can never aspire to membership in their "rather distinguished secret society." Granted that the elegant young roughneck with his romantic readiness of hope, and Nick, too, with his "provincial squeamishness" and "fundamental decency," are worth considerably more than the careless and morally irresolute Buchanans, yet the latter retain their status in this rigorous social system.[10]

Again Fitzgerald develops his man-on-the-way situation with verve and with a properly "smart" style. Whether casually impaling his characters (Tom and Daisy "drifted here and there unrestfully wherever people played polo and were rich together"), or setting his scene (in Gatsby's blue gardens "men and girls came and went like moths among the whisperings and the champagne and the stars . . . and already the halls and salons and verandas were gaudy with primary colors, and hair bobbed in strange new ways, and shawls beyond the dreams of Castile"), Fitzgerald writes with seemingly effortless precision. Using appropriate image patterns of wealth and flutter and rush, relying on pastel colors[11] to convey the impression of an attractive but artificial environment, inserting the revelatory detail, as the guest list at Gatsby's party — one of divorces, deaths, and broken lives — he adroitly chronicles his social history of the twenties, "getting down the sensational display of postwar America's big money" and including "moral instructions on how to count the cost of it all."[12]

The scene shifts to Europe in *Tender Is the Night* (1933), as American expatriates take the center of the stage. Fitzgerald himself, in his statement of the novel's purpose, offered the best short definition of the work: a story devoted to showing a man who is a natural idealist giving in, for various causes, to the ideas of the haute bourgeoisie, and, in his rise to the top of the social world, losing his idealism and talent and turning to drink and dissipation. Placing Dr. Richard Diver, a European-trained psychiatrist but also a small-town clergyman's son, against the Warrens, one of the feudal families of Chicago, Fitzgerald again dramatizes a social conflict. The Warrens inevitably feel that they have "bought" a doctor-husband for the psychotic Nicole Warren. Diver, though marrying Nicole out of love as well as out of pity for her mental state, inevitably comes to feel that "he had been swallowed up like a gigolo, and somehow permitted his arsenal to be locked up in the Warren safety-deposit vaults." Partly corrupted by the standards of the leisure class, but mostly exhausted by the strain of curing his wife, who, ironically, gains strength as he loses it, Diver yields his place as the charming leader of the expatriate clan and eventually sinks into obscurity, deprived of his wife and family and of his career.

Depressing as the subject matter is, in its account of ridiculous duels, dipsomaniacal collapses, and incestuous relationships, the novel still possesses great appeal. As always, the author vivifies his special world of the very prosperous, who are "different from you and me." In the sequence of the book that is "seen" through the eyes of the innocent young movie star Rosemary Hoyt, the graciousness and apparent moral superiority — for example, Dick Diver's fight against egotism and selfishness — of the Diver group are abundantly illustrated. The Riviera setting — Gausse's Hotel still undiscovered by the "trippers," the "bright tan prayer rug of a beach" where the Divers and Norths and Tommy Barban form their own little island, the "intensely calculated perfection" of the Villa Diana, the Divers' home — all this is sharply realized. Fitzgerald unveils the Diver entourage in all its meretricious charm:

> The Divers' day was spaced like the day of the older civilizations to yield the utmost from the materials at hand, and to give all the transitions their full value, and [Rosemary] did not know that there would be another transition presently from the utter absorption of the swim to the garrulity of the Provençal lunch hour . . . Her naiveté responded wholeheartedly to the expensive simplicity of the Divers, unaware of its complexity and its lack of innocence, unaware that it was all a selection of quality rather than quantity from the run of the world's bazaar; and that the simplicity of behavior also, the nursery-like peace and good will, the emphasis on the simpler virtues, was part of a desperate bargain with the gods and had been attained through struggles she could not have guessed at. At that moment the Divers represented externally the exact furthermost evolution of a class, so that most people seemed awkward beside them. [P. 21]

A far cry, this, from the "derisive and salacious improvisations of the frontier."

Wherever the "class" ensconces itself, at the Roi George in Paris, among the "Sturmtruppen of the rich" at St. Moritz, or alongside the "fierce neurotics" on the Golding yacht, it remains a race apart. If too acute to abandon altogether the "contemporaneous rhythm and beat" of "organized fashion," the group generally goes its own way and preserves its reputation as "the most civilized gathering of people that I [Royal Dumphry] have ever known." Eventually, to be sure, the underside of the picture becomes apparent, the "desperate bargain with the gods."[13] Abe North dies in a street brawl, his widow marries a half-caste potentate, the thoroughly decadent Lady Caroline Sibly-Biers rises to the forefront, as Dick Diver, having overdrawn on his intellectual and emotional resources — even his skill with people now a "tarnished art" — becomes a "deposed ruler" and descends to oblivion.

The Fitzgerald "high style," as finished as a Chippendale chair, carries the novel competently along. The reader encounters the tart paradox — "Violet McKisco, the wife of an arriviste who had not arrived"; the colorful figure of speech — a trio of young women with "small heads groomed like manikins' heads, and as they talked the heads waved gracefully above their dark tailored suits, rather like long-stemmed flowers and rather like cobras' hoods"; the barbed adverbs — "she was another tall rich American girl, promenading insouciantly upon the national prosperity"; the atmospheric adjectives — "outside the taxi windows the green and cream twilight faded, and fire-red, gas-blue, ghost-green signs began to shine smokily through the tranquil rain." With a thoroughly practiced pen Fitzgerald records the minute gradations and fascinating surfaces of the expatriate social world. One accepts the picture as decidedly authentic,[14] both in its light and in its shadows.

In thus offering a prevailing theme of the novel of manners, the individual entrapped by his society, and in developing the theme by means of appropriate manners terminology — the "rites of party-giving," the solving of "social problems," the demonstration of "compact social gifts" — and with a high degree of artistry,[15] Fitzgerald belongs to and lends luster to the novel-of manners tradition. His work, like that of those who anticipated him, avoids the cruder manifestation of the social-novel pattern, for, in recording the actions of his society, he endeavors to get at the inner moral experience of his characters. The tragic end befalling Dick Diver, after the blunting of his inherited self-discipline in his wife's world of charming superficiality, inevitably saddens the reader, who is distressed that Dick's facile manners (a "trick of the heart," that is, based on a thoughtful considerateness that led to the shouldering of responsibility) finally failed him. Adding "conduct" to "courtesy," Fitzgerald lends weight and literary respectability to the novel of manners and popularizes it anew.

James Gould Cozzens joins the "clan" in that he singles out a special class of Americans as the subject matter of his fiction. It is the upper-middle professional group that attracts him, the clergy, the lawyers, the mill owners, the military leaders. These form an easily identifiable elite, characterized by adherence to the code of the gentleman, and by employment of certain rituals and routines. Very much conditioned by their environment,[16] they live out their lives according to well-established patterns, observing old traditions, and clinging to firmly defined standards (e.g., "if your word is good only so long as it is comfortable and agreeable for you to keep it. then clearly, you have no regard for your obligations"). The best of them embody many virtues, exemplifying, as "men of reason," intelligence and poise, and, as "concerned" individuals, a willingness to "get angry at what they thought was wrong."

In his major novels Cozzens selects his leading figures from this group, the civic leader in the small city, the military leader on the army base, the prominent clergyman, the established lawyer — in short, the pragmatic, responsible, reasonable individual such as Dr. Bull, Ernest Cudlipp, Abner Coates, Colonel Ross, and Arthur Winner. Partly flawed the "man of reason" may be — subject, perhaps, to snobbery, prejudice, or sensuality — yet his practical wisdom and his "professional" attitude win for him the measured respect of his creator. Cozzens thus favors placing him at the top of the hierarchical organization that is American society. Apparently sharing John Adams's view that ability and privilege run in small groups of families,[17] Cozzens contentedly assigns a major share of community responsibility to families like the Winners in *By Love Possessed* (1957). Intelligent and fair in their judgments, they deserve to lead. The judges, the prelates, the college presidents — those members of the Union League Club — possess qualities of will, imagination, and common sense, which qualify them "as custodians of their civilization and its institutions."[18] Imperfect, yes, these "gold-trimmed Wasps,"[19] yet less imperfect, in Cozzens's view, than the marginal figures, the poor, the uneducated, the Catholic, the Jew, the non-Anglo-Saxon-white.

Since he has chosen their "civilization" — with its insistence on an interlocking society tightly bound by custom — as his "donnée," Cozzens not unnaturally adopts the novel-of-manners formula. His characters fit into a definite sphere, the aristocratic-conservative world of manners, culture, and regulated living. Their milieu is one of clambakes at "Old

Harbor" summer homes, of Yacht Club dances, of Fathers' Weekends at boarding school, with the weight of history — the past is "humanely instructive" — and of tradition clearly felt. Appearing only on the very fringes of this world are such figures as the farmer, the factory worker, the Negro, the artist. Cozzens's technique, as he analyzes this class structure,[20] emanates a high degree of sophistication.

From among his many adroit accounts of upper-middle-class America, one may choose two novels as representative, *Guard of Honor* (1948), his most popular, and *By Love Possessed*, his most controversial. The former is concerned with a special "social landscape," the military scene. Taking place at the Ocanara Air Base in Florida, just before the invasion of Europe in World War II, the novel presents the military class, from privates to generals, reservists as well as regulars, women as well as men. A large aggregation of lives, including such individuals as the youthful General Bus Beal, the embittered because "passed-over" Colonel Woodman (all "whiskey fumes in short explosive puffs"), "flyboy" type Colonel Benny Carricker, Chief Warrant Officer Botwinick, Lt. Amanda Turck, and the focal character Colonel Norman Ross, the collection represents a momentary and rootless society. Yet behind the wartime uncertainty and personal uprooting lies the solid military tradition, which is carefully outlined by Cozzens. The Ocanara Air Base, Officers' Club and officers' quarters, top sergeants' hangout, Personnel Analysis Auditorium, hotel for transients (the "Oleander Towers," a "mixture of Moorish and other Oriental styles"), hospital, hangers and fields — all stand out vividly. One is fully aware, too, of military protocol, the rank hierarchy, the saluting, the studied address to one's superior.[21] If the simple integrity of the best of the "career men," for example, Bus Beal and Benny Carricker, is made apparent, the limitations of the regular air-force personnel, unfortunately a majority group, manifest themselves as well, Cozzens suggesting the "closed corporation" nature and hence the narrowing quality of the military.

The book's protagonist, Colonel Ross, a judge in civilian life and at best a semiprofessional soldier, exemplifies Cozsens's favorite type, the courageous, shrewd, in this case modest, man of reason. An integrated, morally fit individual, Colonel Ross, though not really at home in the Army, acquits himself well, adhering to his creed, "Every man must stand up and do the best he can with what he has." More believable than such a stereotype as Hemingway's Colonel Cantwell,[22] Colonel Ross practices the "art of the possible," facing up, in a thoughtful and sensible way, to the various crises occurring on the base. Through him Cozzens offers a probing — quite often in a satiric vein — of the "guard of honor."

In the course of his probing Cozzens treats of a number of issues: the element of determinism in man's life ("I and my fellows/Are ministers of Fate," says the epigraph from "The Tempest"); the difficulties in acquiring self-knowledge (General Beal "knew no more about himself than most men"); the corruptions of power, the web of interrelationships that complicates any society. As usual, he stresses the need for accommodation and compromise, for recognition of life's moral ambiguities, and for the adoption of a protective stoicism. To be sure, one can never be free of reason's bonds and responsibilities and obligations, for this would at the same time free one from affection, understanding, trust and devotion.

The "probe" is skillfully executed, the author carefully defining characters (from the perennial sorehead Lt. Edsell to the good-natured ladies' man Capt. Duchemin), daubing in the local color (General Beal with his sleeves rolled up, gold crash bracelet, and raunchy cap; the officers' wives rolling Red Cross bandages; Major Post moldering at the "tarpaper post which is Sellers Field"), utilizing a flashback structural pattern and a narrative spiced with informative and often witty dialogue, and relying on a seasoned style (the military base and the neighboring town, "two large diverse and independently directed communities, not merely side by side but actively overlapping and elbowing each other"). *Guard of Honor* is a poignant commentary on the air force world, indeed, by very little extension, on any world.

In *By Love Possessed* Cozzens again insists upon activism, doing-what-you-can, obligation, discipline, and the ethic of responsibility and again assigns the role of executing these principles to the professional elite. This is the corps that must lead its fellows and must maintain society's imperfect but necessary institutions.

Shifting from the "specialized" locale of *Guard of Honor*[23] to his more customary small-city environment, Cozzens now turns his attention to the leading citizens of the "rural county seat" of Brocton. The reader sees their gracious if unassuming country houses, filled with antique music boxes and grandfather clocks, and surrounded by extensive lawns and carefully cultivated gardens. He follows them to their dignified Christ Church — Episcopal, of course — to their rambling summer cottages at a nearby lake, to their unpretentious law offices near the county courthouse. He witnesses their conservatism — Mrs. Pratt's large and costly car, of daffodil color, attracts unfavorable attention — their not-very-well-concealed prejudices against Irish Catholics and Jews, and their strong sense of class barriers — what Water Street boy would not jump at the chance to join the Union League if the opportunity ever presented itself? Cherishing "points of propriety" and "temples of convention," they revel in the "quiet satisfactions of . . . ceremonial power and authority" and firmly defend the status quo.

Cozzens's view of the world is far too Pyrrhonistic, to be

sure, to allow these "natural aristocrats" to escape unscathed as perfection itself. Their competence and assurance can lead to stuffiness and self-satisfaction, as he makes abundantly clear. Moreover, the "In" group is no more immune than the rest of mankind to the god of love, who can, when in "possession," shake the soundest of standards, victimize the most reasonable of individuals. Irrational emotion, imposture, and self-deception ("How dies the wise man? said the Preacher. As the fool") afflict all.

To this novel, as to his others, Cozzens brings very adequate technical equipment. His themes are serious — and gravely meditated. His characters are illuminated by their actions, reflections, and speech, the "professional" figures like the lawyers Arthur Winner and Julius Penrose, the doctor Reginald Shaw, and the judge Fred Dealey having, in their verisimilitude, a special appeal. His structure seems tight despite the spacious outline, for the story line focuses on a series of crucial incidents. His "sets" are drawn with extreme precision, whether it be the county courthouse of attorneys' rooms and jury quarters, or the Christ Church Sunday service with its choir of "not-bad tenors and some by-courtesy baritones." The use of a Jamesian sensitive reflector as his point-of-view character is skillful, as is his employment of symbols (the old French gilt clock reminding one of how the past conditions the present, as its nymph-shepherd-cupid ornamentation underlines the "love" motif). A detached and cool tone heightens the book's irony, and the author's style seems appropriate. Mannered it may be — as many a critic has pointed out — yet the ornate complications serve to qualify and sharpen meanings, the uncommon diction ("armillary sphere") and neat phrases are discriminating, the allusiveness clarifies, however esoteric the reference, and the balanced sentence structure complements the author's rather formal manner. Such a scene as the interview between

Mrs. Pratt and Arthur Winner, a fine set piece of irony, aptly illustrates.

Cozzens presents, in short, very competent pieces of fiction, and ones that give the feeling of a living community. The descriptive details of air base and county seat, the legal and military shoptalk, the next-door-neighbor characters all convey this feeling and create an impressive social density. His best work does indeed lend credence to the notion that the "traditional social novel with its high seriousness and moral urgency is still viable."[24]

Far more often than Cozzens has John O'Hara been discussed as a student of manners and a social commentator, and there is universal agreement that, bearing in mind the constancy and accuracy with which he reproduces the "insignia of social station,"[25] he amply qualifies as a novelist of manners. In fact, it has been said that no one matches him as a social historian.[26]

Considerably less often is he praised for having occasionally delved below the social surface. However, a careful reading of his work reveals, if not a religious or philosophical dimension, nonetheless, the "high seriousness and moral urgency" that I have just attributed to the practitioners of this kind of social novel, his themes tending to extend themselves beyond a superficial account of the cruelty of snobbery to a thoughtful pondering on the futility and tragedy of the waste of life within the social system.

In most of his fiction O'Hara is concerned with a "living community," an even more tightly knit and sharply defined one that that of Cozzens. Many of his novels and stories deal with Gibbsville, Lantenengo County, Pennsylvania — for which one is inclined to read Pottsville, O'Hara's sometime hometown. Perhaps seeking redress against the "no

Irish need apply" social climate prevailing in Pottsville,[27] O'Hara devotes much of his fiction to a clinical dissection of the Gibbsville social system, concentrating on an exposure of the local "aristocracy," the upper-middle-class "country club set." His work outlines its manners and mores, as well as those of the rest of the town, giving an exhaustive — sometimes exhausting — picture of the education of the inhabitants, their clothing and appearance, speech and leisure habits. In presenting this inventory, O'Hara sets off one class against another, indicating the rigidity of social class lines and thus underscoring the excessive degree of social snobbery prevailing in Gibbsville. Snobbery, with its attendant implications, has always attracted the novelist of manners, and certainly O'Hara is as preoccupied with the shelves of society, even with its nooks and crannies, as any in the field.[28] To him, as Louis Auchincloss affirms, the most important item about any character is the "social niche in which he was born,"[29] and it really seems to matter if one belongs or does not belong to the Lantenengo Country Club.

Appointment in Samarra (1934) provides one of the most satisfactory illustrations of the intricacies of the caste system in what O'Hara probably considers a reasonably representative American town. The protagonist Julian English belongs to the social elite of his community of Gibbsville, not only to the Country Club set but to the smoking room crowd of the Country Club set, absolutely the inmost circle. This circle reigns supreme in Gibbsville society, having attended the right schools, adhering to the right religion, and possessing some family background. Seemingly, its members are so secure that nothing could affect their status.

Julian English, however, rebelling against the stifling atmosphere of such a world and unhappy because of a dominating sense of his own futility, commits several tasteless acts — throwing a highball in Harry Reilly's face, taking

Helene Holman out to a parking area, insulting Mrs. Grady, battling Froggy Ogden and the Polack lawyer, and attempting to seduce a society reporter — and these, taken in toto, suffice to alienate him from his fellows. Guilty, because of his excess, of "status derangement," English is subjected to censure by his own clique, and, indeed, to eventual ostracism. With his business, his marriage, and his friendships on the rocks, Julian gives way to a compulsion that has been with him from the first and commits suicide.

O'Hara, in his portrait of Julian English, depicts the disintegration of a frivolous, callous, joyless, weak individual, a snob, a drunkard, and a lecher, yet withal a man of intelligence, some decency, and, surprising though it may seem, an "indefinable winningness."[30] Hereditary influences condition him adversely: his grandfather was a suicide and his father, a cold and selfish man. Julian, if spoiled as a child, found very little love in his household, and a strong sense of snobbishness. Environmental influences affect him even more, the predepression party-party atmosphere of big spending and big drinking. He is surrounded by unhealthy social stratification and racial antagonism, living in a town constituted of hunkeys, schwackies, roundheaders, broleys, the Christiana Street crowd, and, on top, those from Lantenengo Street. Shoddiness exists on all levels, with materialism the primary standard (for upon money depends respectability and social acceptability), and proper manners, even in the highest social sphere, scarcely in evidence — nor "morals" either. The "snubbers" lead lives as corrupt, worthless, and aimless as the snubbed. Julian could not hope to survive.[31]

The "tragedy" of this character is played out against a sharply realized background, O'Hara outlining his stratified world in immensely detailed fashion. The social rites like the club Christmas dance, the status symbols like the proper cars, proper bootleggers, and proper fraternities, and the social positions of the characters — from the Englishes to the Fleiglers to the Greccos — are carefully enumerated. O'Hara lives up to his reputation for professional competence, as he shows off his gift for exact language and the nuances of common speech, and his skill in graphically reproducing an environment. An effective recorder of the social and cultural facets of everyday life he is, exhibiting them with "phonophoto-graphical" accuracy.

Many of O'Hara's subsequent novels are hewn from similar material, works such as *A Rage to Live, Ten North Frederick, From the Terrace, Ourselves to Know,* and *The Lockwood Concern* confronting questions of wealth, power, and status among the upper classes. The novels are filled with the usual O'Hara "artifacts," a painstaking accumulation of details about homes, schools, and clubs, and they are written in the usual terse, unadorned prose.

An interesting variant from the Gibbsville axis, though still concerned with manners material, is *Elizabeth Appleton* (1963). This novel, set in the small college town of Spring Valley, centers its attention on the quest of its protagonist, John Appleton, for the presidency of Spring Valley College, a quest entailing a drive for power and for status. John, as a professor, and with a sound if unspectacular family background, has "position," to be sure, but he is drawn toward the loftier "position" that the presidency would ensure, his unstated motive being a desire to compensate for the feeling of inferiority engendered by the "good" marriage he had made into the exclusive Webster family.[32] The plot thus hinges upon this upward thrust and the attendant husband-wife clash, the adjustments to be made between the small-town intellectual John Appleton and the tennis-playing Long Island society girl, Elizabeth Webster, whom he marries. O'Hara works out the Appletons' problems, domestic and professional, in a quietly effective way and makes of both Elizabeth and John Appleton decidedly flawed yet still worthwhile, and certainly very human, individuals.

The book is strewn with cultural details, brief biographies of members of the faculty, exact pictures of college buildings, vignettes about Model Schools and the entertainment program for college visitors — the omnipresent O'Hara local color. The small-college-town hierarchy is set forth, the faculty circle at the center, surrounded by the rich "Hill" crowd of wealthy alumni, a composite of touchy professors, possessive benefactors, and stuffy trustees.[33]

This social context is unveiled by means of a neat structural pattern of shifting perspectives. A controlled tone of low-keyed irony (e.g., the announcement on the society page of Elizabeth and John Appleton's wedding was inevitably flawed since John had "no clubs, grandparents, no aid to identification") also contributes to the novel's success, as does the author's Marquand-like commentary on the vulgarization of American life, the lack among contemporary individuals of the innate courtesy that underlies all "good manners."

One or two weaknesses interfere, though, or so it seems to me, with O'Hara's *total* performance as a novelist of manners. His tone, for one thing, lacks the urbane note (*Elizabeth Appleton* excepted) that makes the work of his predecessors in the field so right. O'Hara is too often the "mick" — using the James Malloy persona — sneering at the world to which he does not belong and refusing to employ the double lens — what I have earlier called the inside-outside view — which distinguishes the approach of Mrs. Wharton and Marquand, James and Fitzgerald. In the words of Irving Howe, he feels "his way along the provincial outposts of the America that made its money late and fast,"[34] and thus reports with less conviction than those, with a more centralized stance, who had preceded him. He also overloads his work, as they do not, with too many vital statistics of person and place. His style, too, proves serviceable rather than arresting. The sparkling expressions encountered in a book by Louis Auchincloss — "jerry-built castle of evasions," "dousing the candle of scruples," "encasing one's feelings in a cold-storage cellar" — have no counterpart in the O'Hara canon, the figurative language being sparse indeed.

Nevertheless, few authors have so convincingly captured the sufferings of the socially "underprivileged" or the cruelty of the snobbish, and few have offered so comprehensive an account of the deadly war that is, to O'Hara, American social experience. The reader is forced to accept his gloomy conclusion that moral stamina and dignity and "civilized behavior" are often in abeyance in "Gibbsville."

NOTES TO CHAPTER 9

1. Sheldon N. Grebstein, *Sinclair Lewis* (New York: Twayne Publishers, Inc., 1962), p. 8.

2. His caricature of "booster" speech has never seemed to me to represent nearly so accurate a reproduction of midwestern speech patterns as that which one finds in Mark Twain or Ring Lardner.

3. The Dodsworths sail to Europe on the S.S. *Ultima*, minutely described as a floating iron eggshell, complete with roseate music room, a smoking room with a Tudor fireplace, and a swimming pool washing beneath Roman pillars. Lewis like Marquand, revels in details of setting, in this case to accentuate the "moneyed" atmosphere.

4. See the picture of Grand Republic in *Cass Timberlane*; "the early Minnesota had its families with the correct and rigid manners, the Emersonian scholarship of New England. . . . But lesser and brisker tribes like the Wargates had taken their togas."

5. Charles E. Shain, *F. Scott Fitzgerald*, University of Minnesota Pamphlets

on American Writers, no. 15 (Minneapolis, Minn.: University of Minnesota Press, 1961), p. 11.

6. Irving Howe, ed., *Edith Wharton, A Collection of Critical Essays* (Englewood Cliffs, N. J.: Prentice Hall, Inc., 1962), p. 11.

7. He shares with such writers as Wharton, Glasgow, and Marquand the paradoxical yet workable combination of fascination *and* detachment in viewing his "world."

8. In his Introduction to *The Great Gatsby* in *Three Novels. F. Scott Fitzgerald*, ed. Malcolm Cowley and Edmund Wilson (New York: Charles Scribner's Sons, 1953), p. xi.

9. Cf. the comment of Kenneth Eble, "We could restrict its scope to that of the novel of manners and still find the novel an admirable achievement" (Kenneth Eble, *F. Scott Fitzgerald* [New York: Twayne Publishers, Inc., 1963], p. 97).

10. Charles Shain draws some interesting parallels between Fitzgerald's society and that of the present day. "Americans living through a new postwar society," he says, "can no longer feel superior to Fitzgerald's interest in the American greed for fine cars, the right clothes, and the pleasures of the best hotels and off-beat entertainment." In fact, he adds, "American people now seem to be less embarrassed than they once were at the snobbery of large parts of their social system. Contemporary social analysis has shown them how far ahead of his times Fitzgerald was in describing the rigorous systems of status that underlie that rather contradictory American term, the Open Society" (Shain, *F. Scott Fitzgerald*, pp. 7, 8).

11. See Michael Millgate's remarks on the strands of "white" and "gold" interwoven throughout the novel (Michael Millgate, *American Social Fiction: James to Cozzens* [New York: Barnes & Noble, Inc., 1964], p. 119).

12. Shain, *F. Scott Fitzgerald*, p. 35.

13. K. W. G. Cross suggests that the Diver clan has always suffered in contrast with the English and European aristocracy that it imitates. Even at their most charming, the American princely classes lack the moral responsibility of a traditional aristocracy, their society being based simply on money (as symbolized in the novel, perhaps, by Nicole Warren's shopping orgy) (K. G. W. Cross, *Scott Fitzgerald* [Edinburgh and London: Oliver & Boyd, Ltd., 1964], pp. 84-85).

14. Fitzgerald follows the novelist-of-manners penchant for writing about the world one knows. His comments on this subject echo those of J. P. Marquand: "Mostly, we authors must repeat ourselves . . . we learn our trade, well or less well, and we tell our two or three stories . . . as long as people will listen" (from "One Hundred False Starts," quoted in James E. Miller, Jr., *The Fictional Technique of Scott Fitzgerald* [The Hague: Martinus Nijhoff, 1957], p. 83).

15. Sergio Perosa declares that Fitzgerald "dealt with the novel of manners as a major literary form, bestowing on it the same artistic dignity and the same endless care that the Master had given it" (Sergio Perosa, *The Art of F. Scott Fitzgerald* [Ann Arbor, Mich.: University of Michigan Press, 1965], p. 187).

16. The proper study of mankind, says the narrator of Cozzens's *Morning, Noon and Night* (1968), involves learning to understand, thus to manage one's environment.

17. See Frederick Bracher, *The Novels of James Gould Cozzens* (New York: Harcourt, Brace & Co., 1959), p. 144.

18. D. E. S. Maxwell, *Cozzens* (Edinburgh and London: Oliver and Boyd, Ltd., 1964), p. 81.

19. Richard A. Long, "The Image of Man in James Gould Cozzens," *College Language Association Journal* 10 (June 1967): 301

20. The analysis, says Granville Hicks, "might well have been admired by J. P. Marquand," especially in its knowing account of "social distinctions in a small town" (Granville Hicks, *James Gould Cozzens*, University of Minnesota Pamphlets on American Writers, no. 58 [Minneapolis, Minn.: University of Minnesota Press, 1966], p. 12).

21. "You live in one long, very slow intrigue. . . . If the colonel's wife thinks poorly of you, or of your wife, that will do you no good. When some brass turns up, you'd better mind your p's and q's. Years later, you may not be given the assignment you'd like to have because you said or did the wrong thing that day."

22. See W. M. Frohock, *Strangers To This Ground* (Dallas, Tex.: Southern Methodist University Press, 1961), p. 77 ff.

23. Cozzens also chooses a specialized setting as the background for *Ask Me Tomorrow* (1940). Trying his hand at the popular manners theme of expatriation, he places his protagonist Francis Ellery in Europe. However different the background, its influence is felt as strongly here as in the America-set novels. Ellery, viewed very much as the "social animal," is observed warily assessing status and relationships on the Continent.

24. Bracher, *Novels of James Gould Cozzens*, p. 20.

25. Sheldon, N. Grebstein, *John O'Hara* (New York: Twayne Publishers, Inc., 1966), p. 21.

26. This is Matthew Bruccoli's declaration. O'Hara's scope, Bruccoli says, is broader than that of such writers as Marquand and Auchincloss, his closest competitor being Cozzens (Matthew J. Bruccoli, "*Appointment in Samarra*," included in *Tough Guy Writers of the Thirties*, ed. David Madden [Carbondale and Edwardsville, Ill.: Southern Illinois University Press, 1968], p. 130).

27. Critical debate has raged about how "snubbed" O'Hara felt in Pottsville, about the poor-boy-looking-in-the-country-club-window syndrome conditioning his writing. It does seem safe to say that, though his life was by no means socially deprived, he did feel stigmatized by his Irish Catholic background and tended to view the social situation from an outsider's angle.

28. A series of comments in his book *Sweet and Sour* (New York: Random House, 1953) — a collection of newspaper columns — affords most thorough evidence of O'Hara's overwhelming concern with "society":

"Society, I have it on the word of people who don't know anything about it, no longer exists in this country . . . . The truth of the matter is that it is slightly more difficult for the outsider to identify Society, but Society is, if anything, more there than ever."

"I guess I know as much about Society as any author today . . . . In modern Society an author who was not born social has a better chance of observing the upper crust than he would have in Grandpa's day . . . . He will get invited to some Society homes, if not asked to be godfather to the Society children and not tapped for the best clubs . . . . I am not in Society: I'm not even in the S. R., although I was a Dilatory Domicile for one issue, just for the record. But I have quite a few friends in Society, people I like a great deal because they are considerate, well-mannered, kind, undemanding and have their own private hells."

"I am fascinated by the rich and how they live, and I go with them every chance I get . . . . Both the Beaton set and the Beacon Hill billies are tough to write about. Beatonians don't interest me except as minor characters . . . .The Auchinclossers do interest me, and I have abundant information on their habits and their tribal customs, but they interest me so much that it's hard for me to know when to stop."

"For twenty years, off and on, I have been gawking and listening and comparing the results with my findings after a like period of study of small-town country-club life. There is a difference. The small town, like my invention Gibbsville, has it all: the entrenched, the strivers, the climbers, the rebellious. But the big town, by which I mean the Boston-Providence-New York- Philadelphia-Wilmington-Baltimore group, offer [sic] many more of the entrenched, the striving, the climbing and the rebelling to choose from. And of course they're richer. What is particularly nice is that they don't produce novelists. Aside from Louis Auchincloss . . . I can't think of any Insider who has dared to risk ostracism by slipping out messages to the Outside."

29. Louis Auchincloss, *Reflections of a Jacobite* (Boston: Houghton Mifflin Co., 1951), p. 151.

30   Grebstein, *John O'Hara*, p. 41.

31.   In addition to environmental pressures, an element of chance militates against him — and his own character, too, perennially boyish and excessively touchy. He is a poignant figure in his bewilderment, growing concern, moral groping, and slowly developing realization that he is doomed.

32.   The social mobility factor entering into O'Hara's work here and elsewhere provides a link, as Russell Carson points out, with the novel of manners format (see E. Russell Carson *The Fiction of John O'Hara* [Pittsburgh, Pa.: University of Pittsburgh Press, 1961], p. 12).

33.   Charles Walcutt complains, however — unfairly, I think — that "as a novel of manners, *Elizabeth Appleton* shows our social fabric to be so loosely woven that people do not feel it. There are so many levels of wealth, education, status, and morality in the book that these elements do not cohere into a substantial social reality" (Charles C. Walcutt, *John O'Hara*, University of Minnesota Pamphlets on American Writers, no. 80 [Minneapolis, Minn.: University of Minnesota Press, 1969], p. 36).

34.   Howe, ed., *Edith Wharton*, p.12.

10

Louis Auchincloss

*T*HE contemporary novelist most solidly bound to the novel-of-manners tradition would seem to be Louis Auchincloss, one as concerned as his forebears with social schemes and county-and-class, and almost as skilled in analyzing them. Auchincloss is indeed currently being recognized as our leading practitioner of the novel of manners and as an excellent craftsman and deservedly popular writer. His later works, such as *The Rector of Justin,* (1964) and *The Partners,* (1973) have occasioned a host of favorable reviews and endorsing comments and brought attention — somewhat belatedly[1] — to its author as a worthy successor in the Jamesian line.[2]

As one who concentrates on a particular social class, the American "aristocracy," and who suggests the influence of that society over its members, Auchincloss fits readily into the pattern. He, too, gives evidence of a clear understanding of the serious — if uncosmic — problems of upper-class society and chronicles with devastating accuracy the activities of the fashionable world.[3] He, too, perceives that, against its relatively stable background, subtle human relationships, affording both comedy and tragedy, can be neatly studied. He, too, displays fastidious literary artistry in making such a study.

The reader of Auchincloss's work is perhaps first impressed by the author's ability to evoke fully the social milieu that he has chosen for his fictional explorations. The milieu, the Eastern Seaboard world of the well-to-do, is one to which Auchincloss himself belongs. He was born in New York City, the son of a successful lawyer, and spent his childhood years there, and in Bar Harbor, Maine. A graduate of the Groton School, he attended Yale for three years, then transferred to the University of Virginia Law School, taking his law degree in 1941. After spending four years in the Navy during World War II, he returned to civilian life and to a career as a lawyer. Since that time he has interspersed the writing of short stories, novels, and criticism with his legal activities.[4]

Drawing on this background of private school-fashionable summer resort-law office-naval experience in his fiction, Auchincloss thus writes of what he knows well. In so doing, he follows the lead of James and Howells, Wharton, Glasgow and Marquand, carefully confining himself, as they had, to an area with which he was intimately acquainted — all of them perhaps having in mind that superb model Jane Austen, and her "two inches of ivory."

The Auchincloss fictional province, the "great world" of New York's "Four Hundred," stretches from their winter homes, the Fifth Avenue mansions, or the luxurious apartments near Central Park, to their summer places on Long Island ("Easton Bay") or Bar Harbor ("Anchor Harbor"), or, occasionally still, Newport. His protagonists have thus, **grown** up between "town and country," attending Groton

("Chelton") or Miss Hewitt's Classes ("Miss Dixon's"), serving as naval officers or as Red Cross aides in World War II, then entering a solid profession, either the law or suburban housewifery, eventually ending up as rather stuffy dowagers and clubmen. Reese Parmelee, the protagonist of *Pursuit of the Prodigal,* (1959) describes his representative life as a series of compartments, necessarily related: Woodbury Day and Parmelee Cove, St. Lawrence's and Harvard and the Harvard Law School, marriage and the war, then finally Clark, Day and Parmelee, that "legal Escorial."

Auchincloss deftly depicts the manners and mores that prevail in this environment, making one quickly aware of "Social Register" penchants. These include heavy stress on family and the family bond and a reverence for social formulas ("Esther had a feeling that any social formula, once established, should be maintained"). They demand attendance at the proper schools ("Esther regarded the New England church schools as among the absolutely unavoidable, if arbitrary, hurdles which every boy of her world had to take") and selection of an appropriate career (preferably the law — it was a "wonderful mind-trainer" and also a "fine jumping-off point to other careers"). Inflexible are the rules for the products of this WASP-ish, Ivy League-ish locale.

"SOCIETY's" setting has a Park Avenue-Wall Street axis, the female members of the group reveling in the splendor of the uptown world of subscription dances, opera, cocktail parties, and shopping, while the males congregate in the downtown world of "high buildings at the southern tip of a skinny island," where they are engaged solely in "profit." In the summertime they all relax at the somewhat dowdy but comfortable "Easton Bay," though the more sophisticated prefer livelier, "Glenville," and the more arty — a decided minority — prefer "Mog Beach's" artist colony. Whether the scene is a vast and highly organized old-firm New York law office, with its chain of offices, its library, its conference rooms, its secretarial hierarchy, its muted auto-call system, or a vast and lavish "Anchor Harbor" summer residence dining room "so desperately eighteenth century, crowded with porcelain figures of ladies curtseying and little gilt chairs", the setting registers briskly on the reader's vision and is given zest by virtue of the author's slightly mocking description.[5]

The kind of people who inhabit such a world are predictable. There are the wealthy dowagers like Aunt Jo Cummings, who "loved the opera, or at least she loved the opera house." The old-maid poor relations — "they were 'dears'; for six decades they had lurked in the backs of boxes and adored opera." The old-maid rich relations — "In another day and age they would have followed their monarch over the border and dedicated themselves to the drab formality of a court in exile." The lightweight debutantes, like Millie Dessart, who wants to "have a little house in Greenwich and raise two dear little children, only two, a boy and a girl, and send them to small select cocktail parties that are undistinguishable from other people's small select cocktail parties." The archsophisticates like Lucy Hilliard, who, together with her husband,

> served excellent food to which they paid little attention, and excellent liquor to which they paid considerably more. They never, of course, went to church, for they believed in nothing except, very casually, the few principles of social formality which they had not yet discarded. They liked animals and people who liked animals and prided themselves on a tweedy, rustic toughness of mind and manner.[Sybil, pp. 37-38]

A second cousin to the smart Mrs. Hilliard is the avant-garde type such as Edith Kellogg, who, however, "after six or seven bold and striking mannerisms of speech seems to have exhausted the rather meager supply of her charm." Old guard, on the other hand, is a person like Gertrude Farish, who, with her unwavering faith in "style" and interests so "obsessively genealogical," serves as a reincarnation of Edith Wharton's Mrs. Archer.

The men — often relegated to the background in this somewhat matriarchal society — include middle-aged businessmen, lawyers, and sportsmen,[6] dedicated, with few exceptions, to laxity about ethical principles but firmness about the pleasures of eating and drinking, bridge and beagling, and of offering sage advice on matters of which they knew nothing. The younger men of the "proper set" are charming, polished, and bright, and adaptable enough to "get ahead."

A handful of Auchincloss's characters do not fit comfortably into this silver-gilt world, however, and it is these thoughtful and somewhat "odd-stick" types who often serve as his protagonists. Low-pressure heroes and heroines these — does modern fiction contain any king-size heroes?[7] — who stage mild and mildly successful rebellions against the conformity that surrounds them. The group includes, among others, Sybil Rodman, Eloise Dilworth, Timothy Colt, and Reese Parmelee.[8]

The girls are used by Auchincloss to develop one aspect of his favorite theme, the baneful pressure of social convention. Though born and brought up in upper-class society, the Sybil Rodmans and Maud Spreddons don't belong — and don't really want to belong. Bored by the social round of field hockey, teas, and debutante balls, they have always preferred the "library and the quiet life." But parents and friends conspire against so unorthodox a taste and strive desperately to make those just slightly "ugly ducklings" more "normal."

In the hothouse milieu of the "Four Hundred," Auchincloss insists, convention exerts a potent and unhealthy force. For example, family solidarity *must* be preserved, even if the members of the family are incompatible and therefore unhappy together. Maud Spreddon, unable to share in the superficial Spreddon conviviality, stages a rebellious tantrum; in reply to this her mother cries "Darling" and envelopes her in "arms of steel." Sybil Rodman wonders whether she is bound to "fester forever in the illusion that they were a happy, loving family." The answer is yes — the "form" of familial love must be fostered, and all the tribal rites — family dinners, birthday celebrations, christenings — carefully observed.

There are many such forms, and many that are equally empty. Auchincloss's great favorite is the "proper" marriage. In the novel *Sybil* (1952) misfit Sybil Rodman snags the catch of the season in Philip Hilliard, thus pleasing friends and relations, who fail to think of whether the two are well mated. Sybil herself has doubts, knowing Philip's intellectual limitations and shallowness, knowing, too, that even his physical charm is partly limited (she decided that "he was the handsomest man that she had ever seen, knowing perfectly well that he wasn't"). But she is in love and therefore willing to be fooled. The "stiff meaninglessness of the wedding reception" she recognizes, however, and, a few years later, when her marriage is wavering and she is seriously contemplating divorce, she reflects that the mist of convention covering the threatened termination of her marriage is as thick and cloying as the mist that covered its commencement. In each case the "forms" count, not the personal feelings behind them.

When Sybil eventually returns to her husband, she does so partly as an atonement for having viewed Philip in the first place through rose-colored glasses and partly as a fulfillment of a need for order and stability, *not* out of love nor out of duty:

> Life with Philip at least was patterned. It sometimes seemed to her that she was making a life out of the ashes of her love, but there was more left than ashes. There was a grate; there were andirons, indeed there was a whole hearth. [P. 191]

This acceptance of the "pattern " indicates that even the "rebels" like Sybil are bound by society's rules. It should be remembered, though, that she sees her husband for what he is — "as time passed, they developed an easy, if mutually critical relationship" — and that she is no longer overawed by family pressure. On her eighth wedding anniversary, the book concludes, she finally feels free of self-consciousness, and stands, "without fear, without even embarrassment," in the presence of the assembled tribe.

Sybil Hilliard settled for partial contentment in her marriage, and so, too, will Eloise Dilworth in *A Law for the Lion* (1953), Ann Colt in *The Great World and Timothy Colt* (1956), Ida Hartley in *Portrait in Brownstone* (1963), even Harriet Prescott in *The Rector of Justin.* There is at least the comfort of habit or the reasonably appealing "pace of occupied monotony," which suits Ann and Tim Colt. In the drama of domestic strain that is the ordinary marriage, one must expect considerably less than the stars.

If Auchincloss's somewhat "flattened" heroines do not always enjoy married bliss, if they do not always mesh well with the "Seventieth Street crowd," if they do not share its faith in the "healing powers of group activity," if they bemoan its conforming and superficial pattern,[9] neither do his heroes find much comfort in their trust-company, duck-blind, golf-course world — but for somewhat different reasons. Whereas the women resist the pressure of social convention, the men essentially resist the pressure of economic convention. And this constitutes the other aspect of the author's principal theme.

Tim Colt in *The Great World and Timothy Colt* represents

the idealistic lawyer, a man of integrity and principle. Following in the footsteps of his mentor Mr. Knox, another "man of good will,"[10] he pursues a strictly honest legal career. When handling the affairs of George Emlen, however, he becomes involved in money matters having a shady tinge, and though he escapes with his principles intact, he does not escape without receiving jibes from Emlen at the idealism he has shown, such "flights into the wild blue yonder." More disheartening still, Emlen's uncle Sheridan Dale, a partner in Tim's firm, sanctions these "flights" no more than does his nephew, reminding Tim that one cannot "leap from cloud to cloud." Seeing how the land lies, and bereft of the counsel of Mr. Knox — who has, unfortunately for Tim, rather suddenly died — Tim cynically changes course and in some other Emlen family business *is* guilty of legal misdemeanors. When examined in court, he frankly admits his guilt, malfeasance as a trustee, and is prepared to take his punishment, thus righting himself and redirecting his course along the lines of integrity. On his wife's praising his action, however, he declares it to be simply a sentimental, martyrlike act. No, she replies, you've got to hang on to something. And that was truth. "He shrugged. 'A kind of truth. A willed truth.' " You can build on it, he concludes, not I — but her building is perhaps enough for both. In other words, Tim Colt ends by championing a modified idealism; one doesn't expect the ideal, one doesn't find it either, but one must somehow — perhaps ruefully and cynically, but somehow — go on fighting for it.

In *A Law for the Lion* a minor character, Bobbie Chapin, comes closest to assuming Tim Colt's position. Whereas the central male figure, George Dilworth, has a moral code "almost confessedly tied up with the simple American goal of getting ahead," whereas the powerful and prominent Gerald Hunt is "too much a man of the world to find in the application of broad moral rules to individual problems anything but the crudest possible taste," whereas others firmly believe that "you've got to compromise, that's life," Bobbie Chapin insists on higher standards and fights against legal chicanery and shoddy ethical practices. No more than Tim Colt does he expect to reform the world, but one must cling to principles in order to bring a measure of self-content-ment. And this rather thin measure is the best one can hope for in a conformity-ridden, shallow, and materialistically minded society.

Not even that thin measure is granted the leading character in Auchincloss's most somber book to date, *Venus in Sparta* (1958). Michael Farish, unfortunately, has no principles to cling to. In his business life he has achieved success − as the prospective president of the Hudson River Trust Company − but there have been an unsavory episode and a general sense of attrition along the way to this goal. In his personal life he has failed, both as a husband and as a father, largely because of an incapacity to love. Farish ends his dreary "biography of what you think you have to be " by commit-ting suicide. It was not "having to be" things, not the pres-sure of convention that really brought about this act, how-ever, but, rather, a nihilistic attitude, which lay beneath his polished and proper surface from the beginning. Unsuited to the conventional pattern, that is, "never quite on the team," yet without the resources that would have enabled him to break from it − being, in fact, that unhappy combin-ation of a "conformist who believes in nothing" − he can only bring to a close the "cotton-packed box of his exist-ence." Neither social nor economic convention best him in the last analysis, but simply his emptiness. Yet "there was still a lot to believe in in Michael," and thus his wasted life has at least an aura of the tragic about it.

The pattern of rebellion is restored in the successor to *Venus in Sparta, Pursuit of the Prodigal,* and the infinitely more positive hero of this novel, Reese Parmelee, fights against both the social and economic rules that tend to turn one's life into a "slow trickle down a long plateau of anticipated anti-climax." Discontent with the "cozy, gossiping, accepting, even hypocritical" world of New York and Parmelee Cove, he breaks away from this by divorcing his wife and finding greater satisfaction in a second marriage to a non-socially-prominent career woman. Discontent with the not wholly ethical, however respectable, world of old New York law firms such as Clark, Day and Parmelee, he breaks away from this environment, associating himself with a different kind of law practice, one that he hopes is more honest.

The "break" made by the protagonist of *The Embezzler* (1966), a later Auchincloss novel, goes to far greater extremes and takes, as the title suggests, a decidedly disastrous direction. Stockbroker Guy Prime, apparently always restive in the rusty armor of the Long Island-Wall Street aristocracy, indulges in financial peculations on so grand a scale that he is jailed and then must exile himself to Panama — the "particular suicide he had planned so long." Though the method of rebelling, a playing fast and loose with his own and other people's money, cannot be condoned, Guy Prime retains his own kind of honesty as he goes under, refusing last-minute compromises and hypocritical veilings of the facts. Moreover, in his "engagement" with life and in his recognition of the immense shortcomings of the "social cluster" to which, by birth and breeding, he was attached, he arouses sympathy, considerably more than that generated by his old friend Rex Geer, the ruthless man-on-the-make type who replaces him. If "the small pilot light of Guy's idealism had been snuffed out" early in his life, such a light never burned at all within Rex.

Auchincloss's comedy of manners seems almost continually to have darkened, as his heroines, from Sylvia

Tremaine to Sophie Shallcross, are quite violently jerked into conformity, as his heroes, from Beverly Stregelinus to Guy Prime, register a decided uncertainty about society's values. "Out-group" morals appear in almost perpetual conflict with "in-group" ones, and there is a generally widening breach between manners and a significant morality.

"Old New York," it would appear, has taken a decisive turn for the worse since Edith Wharton's day. That self-contained little world of "quiet afternoon calls in brownstone streets, of a mild rubbing of elbows with landscape painters and even Shakespearean actors, of long midday meals of Madeira to which the men came home, of insularity and integrity, of small minds and high principles" has felt the impact of, at worst, out-and-out scoundrelism, at best, blunted moral perceptions. Even the financial probity, on which Mrs. Wharton insisted, has gone, in a world marked by a slow drying-up of moral resolve. Although the "first families" still live by their forms and still command some respect, they have lost most of what constituted their position; as Christians they have accepted atheism, as Republicans, socialism, as snobs, everybody. Reese Parmelee, the escapee, the "prodigal," sums up their uncertainty:

> People no longer waited for the prodigal to return; they chased him, shaking sticks and rattling pans. The old stockade was too tottery to afford a single deserter; they were always engaged now in calling musters and checking rolls. Prodigal? *They* were the prodigals, spending their tiny capital of integrity in the endless task of adapting themselves to the new, anything new. [P. 279]

Surely, one thinks, Reese Parmelee decided wisely in becoming a "prodigal," in fleeing from such an ambiance. Flight isn't easy, however, and his escape, like that of many another Auchincloss protagonist, is imperfect. He cannot shake off all ties with Parmelee Cove, for example, his various family

responsibilities; no more can he be sure of always finding the
right way amid the intricacies of the law. Yet Auchincloss
would have us appreciate Reese's effort, his fighting for his
small, tough belief in his own powers against the world. One
may sometimes retain his spiritual spontaneity in the face of
the social experience.[11]

It is evident that class consciousness still figures promin-
ently in this Auchincloss account of the "social experience"
(Reese Parmelee's mother simply does not recognize the
existence of the "different world" from which his second
wife comes), and that the drama of social aspiration — that
favorite theme of novelists of manners — is still played out.
However, the lines in the social matrix are no longer so rigidly fixed, and many people seem to possess the necessary
"social mobility" to climb. As the plutocracy now mingles
freely with the aristocracy, the Derrick Hartleys and Rex
Geers replace the Trasks and Primes in positions of power,
the latter content simply to "sense intuitively which parvenu
would make the grade and which divorcée would be for-
given." The increasing fluidity of the social structure begins
to create a social vacuum. The change is crystallized, the
amalgamation completed, in Auchincloss's *A World of Profit*
(1968), wherein the Shallcross world is conquered by the Jay
Livingstons. "Old New York, new New York. What was the
difference? What was the distinction between the ratty furs
and seed pearls of the old-maid Shallcross cousins and Jay's
blue suit and ruby cufflinks?"

Though Auchincloss indicts fashionable society harshly
— perhaps a bit too harshly — still his acid description of
the social swim provides amusing as well as sober moments
for the reader, for he, like so many novelists of manners,
wields the weapon of satire most skillfully. With considerable glee, he makes his "swimmers" wiggle before our eyes.
George Emlen shows the "peculiar ungraciousness that is

only found in the best society." His mother has the most tremendous reverence "for the smallest principles of tax avoidance," though her sizable fortune could stand severe tax inroads. Some characters exhibit "the comfortable assurance of a mind that had never been opened." Others try desperately "to spread the small coverlid of their college years over the expanded surface of life." Most are either "declassé dowagers" or "pale anachronisms," gentlemen "cultivated to near decadence."

Much, very much, in their world inspires derision, the ruthless jockeying for promotion on the part of the men, the equally ruthless matchmaking on the part of the women. The strong emphasis on materialism[12] all but precludes taste or cultivation — if Lucius Hoyt has built up a perfect collection of French impressionists, he has been aware that they are "good investments." Everyone pays homage to the "real money" of the Vanderbilt type, the "brownstone Medici," and the result is a New York society that is marked by a "heavy, tawdry opulence, blinking out at one from heavily laden dinner tables where sour, sleepy-eyed magnates and their stertorous, big-busted wives overate."

Fortunately, Auchincloss has the style — an astringent and polished one — to make his barbs and his bubble-pricking effective. In the first place, his figures of speech, particularly the similes, show sparkle and wit as well as appropriateness to the context. His description of the process of handling the closing papers — checks, bonds, mortgages, assignments, affidavits, guarantees, and so on — in a legal deal captures the ritualistic and elaborate nature of the performance by likening the shuffling of the papers across the long table to the "labored solemnity of a Japanese dance." When the pampered Clarissa Dale is being badgered with trying questions for once in her life, it is as if all the "shiny faucets that continually poured hot consoling water in the bathtub of her complacency had turned suddenly into writhing, scalding hoses uncontrolled." When her equally pampered sister Mrs. Emlen is placed on the witness stand, her eyes rove around the courtroom "as if looking for the rack." Granny Parmelee has a mind "like the neat center of a garden approached by many narrow hedged paths. Once out of the center, one had to wait till she had come to the end of her particular path and turned back."

As in this latter instance, the figures grow naturally out of the world the author is describing. Michael Farish is delineated as one who lives for the minor pleasures, small events that glittered like shiny silver cups in the immediate future, children's trophies at a lawn party. The ocean is viewed as a thin long line of billows curving like a lemon peel under the bartender's knife. Court analogies frequently appear — Newport is the huge, pale, pursy sovereign, gorgeously bedizened and nervously giggling at social arbiter Mrs. Bell, its sallow, unpleasantly grinning jester — and often the imagery suggests the stiff "period piece" world being presented. The formal garden comparison mentioned above,[13] or life "as a moving belt bearing dummies in different costumes and attitudes," or dowager Mrs. Coit keeping the fabric of grandeur tightly laced around her all serve to illustrate.

Complementing the use of the upper-class "idiom" — "the rivalries of the summer colony had to be played by the gentle rules of parlor games"; ". . . to have his wedding reception in the room where he had gone to dancing class would be to fox-trot into marriage over the parquet floor of a childhood preparation" — is the reliance on terminology such as "Social Register law practice," "social position," "tiers of society," "social game." All are in keeping, all emphasize the stratified sphere that is Auchincloss's fictional domain.

The tone of urbane comedy is maintained in the novels by the well-bred allusions — from Tiepolo to W. W. Storey, from Nattier to Frederick Lonsdale (not to mention frequent references to Henry James and Edith Wharton) – and by the cleverly turned phrases that abound. Philip Hilliard, the reader is told, did not have a speculative mind. "He was first and foremost a collector of facts that fitted into the little drawers and cubbyholes in the mental chest that he had built for them." His mind was "like a street lamp at night; it lit up everything in the sector that it illuminated, but if one ventured the least bit beyond that, all was black." Mr. Minturn, the headmaster of Averhill, represented God to two generations of Averhill graduates whenever "in their atrophied religious consciousness they thought of a deity." "Lunch," for Beverly Stregelinus, "bristled attractively at the end of the morning with a refreshing vision of vichyssoise and gossip."

Such a supple and variegated prose can be found on almost every Auchincloss page. Tim Colt realizes that he should not bore Eileen Shallcross with "legal details stacked in his favor, to gain a release from her lips that had no validity even in the court of his depreciated conscience." Esther Rodman regards worry as like a pagan sacrifice: ". . . the more relatives who joined in it, the more were the gods propitiated."[14] Even her consolation has the "same note of worried superiority that Sybil had resented in the past; she was still the Cassandra who smiled sadly at the collapse of ideals that she had never sponsored." Miss Johanna Shepard's little group, "knowing how apt social climbers were to use a summer resort as a way of attacking the soft underbelly of the old guard in their home towns, always held aloof until their leader had scouted the field." The old families, like the Shallcrosses, "for all their pious pronouncements, sacrificed their old doormen to self-service elevators." But the examples need not be multiplied; Auchincloss clearly has an incisive and effectively dry style at his command.

As an interpreter of Old-New New York, Auchincloss thus reveals impeccable credentials. One may be disgusted with the shoddy values of the people in his world, their self-righteousness ("they were vocally conscious of the excellence of their own pedigree"), and fatuity, the smugness of their belief that everyone is really "all right." One may dislike the sadistic Harry Hamiltons, malicious David Fairchilds, and cold Derrick Hartleys who inhabit this world, and one may not even altogether approve of the partly rebelling heroes and heroines. Yet he is convinced the people are as the author says they are and their society as foible strewn as Auchincloss would have us believe. Moreover, the reader cannot fail to enjoy the performance, the witty and intelligent, if also cynical, dissection of the "great world."

As an authoritative student of this world — of "whatever survives as an upper class in America,"[15] Auchincloss takes his place in the American novel of manners tradition, seemingly accepting the Jamesian code that manners are "the very core of our social heritage." This acceptance notwithstanding, he shows that overinsistence upon manners, at least in their superficial manifestation, and too great subservience to social codes prevents individual self-fulfillment and should be avoided. One must not suffer too much social contamination, nor be guided to too great a degree by tribal principles and taboos and totem terrors. Few, alas, in the Auchincloss realm achieve a proper balance of social responsibility and individual moral concern.

NOTES TO CHAPTER 10

1. The first of Auchincloss's novels and short story collections appeared in 1947 (to be followed by more than fifteen others in the course of the next twenty-five years), but no critical attention was bestowed upon him until the 1960s.

2. Hugh Holman, in his book on Marquand, says: "Louis Auchincloss is certainly approaching a comparable mastery of the world of high society in New York, but so far his considerable talents and his perceptive eye have been tied to areas much narrower than Marquand's finally proved to be" (Hugh Holman, *John P. Marquand* [Minneapolis, Minn;: University of Minnesota Press, 1965], p. 36). Other critics have found him at times banal and slick, even limp, yet agree in labeling him a skillful and engaging writer, and one who is in the words of R. W. B. Lewis, "as responsible, as craftsmanlike and honorable a representative of this crucial literary species as any one can think of" (R. W. B. Lewis, "Silver Spoons and Golden Bowls," *Book Week, Chicago Sunday Sun-Times,* February 20, 1966, p. 8).

3. "If [this world] is not deep enough to be explored in great depth, Auchincloss has been exploring it to the depth and width it possesses" (Lewis,"Silver Spoons and Golden Bowls," p. 1).

4. For Auchincloss's own account of his career, see an interview recorded in a *New Yorker* "Talk of the Town" column, *The New Yorker* 36 (August 13, 1960): 23-25.

5. Like other novelists of manners, Auchincloss is fond of describing exteriers and interiors of homes and offices, art galleries and clubs. *The House of Five Talents* (1960), for example, is filled with pictures of Fifth Avenue brownstone fronts, Westchester estates, and Newport "cottages."

6. Occasionally an exotic type like the expatriate Horace Havistock — "a malevolent survival from an early Bourget novel" — may appear.

7. One notes how Auchincloss tempers his full-length portrait of a possible "king," Francis Prescott, the rector of Justin. Though refusing to "reduce" his subject in a Strachey-like manner, nevertheless, he sets forth one who "looks too much like a great man to be one."

8. The individual-at-odds-with-society thesis, cited in chap. 1 as running throughout the manners genre, appears again, the focus on the "outsider whose responses fail to meet normal expectations and fall outside the pattern as given" (Chester E. Eisinger, *Fiction of the Forties* [Chicago and London: University of Chicago Press, 1963], p. 292).

9. "One could be gay, but not too gay, and kind but not too kind. One had to care about clothes, but not too much, and the arts, but not too much, and sex, but not too much, and God, but not too much."

10. As Patrica Kane points out, in an interesting article on the legal world as presented in Auchincloss's fiction, the senior partner in the law firm — like Mr.

Knox — manages to remain ethical even while manipulating power and aiding the rich. Moral values, Miss Kane says, can and do reside within the conventions and disciplines of the law firm. (See Patricia Kane, "Lawyers at the Top: the Fiction of Louis Auchincloss," *Critque* 7 [Winter 1964-65] : 36-46.)

11. In perusing the Auchincloss novels, the reader is always mindful of the author's sensitively developed moral sense, lying behind his sometimes brittle novelist-of-manners facade. As Elizabeth Janeway says, in reviewing *Portrait in Brownstone,* "One's impression is . . . that Auchincloss has observed this world, and is simply reporting that within it one will lead a better life if one is moderate, generous, honorable and brave — if, in fact, one does one's duty" (Elizabeth Janeway, Review of *Portrait in Brownstone, The New York Times Book Review,* July 15, 1962, p. 1).

12. This provides *The House of Five Talents* with its subject, the Millinder "talent," which, in five successive generations, is certainly not hidden. As Augusta Millinder frankly says, we had "as much talent and beauty and capacity for living as most other families" but "no one of us would have stood out from the crowd without the money."

13. This is paralleled in the description of the beautifully erected structure of Mrs. Arleus Stroud's existence, "elaborate, organized, with fountains symmetrically plashing and gravel walks carefully raked."

14. The anthropological images relied upon by his predecessors are borrowed here by Auchincloss. Another illustration is the phrase, "the household gods of Fifty-Third Street," which occurs and reoccurs in *Portrait in Brownstone.*

15. Granville Hicks, Review of *Powers of Attorney* (1963), *Saturday Review* 46 (August 17, 1963): 15.

11

Recent Exemplars

*T*HE note of change in the American social scene that Auchincloss remarks on is echoed by many contemporary novelists, who seem to agree with his contention that travel between the social strata, in the modern era of social mobility, has tended to become a "clanging escalator."[1] The suburban scene, which so often provides the backdrop for recent novels of manners, is filled, in the words of John Cheever, with "disorder, moving vans, bank loans at high interest . . . arrivals and departures" (*Bullet Park*, [1969]), as the junior executives climb the business ladder in rather rapid fashion. While class lines blur, though, the interest in class and status remains, and to this interest a number of recent writers speak, offering in their work realistic notations of manners and customs.

Jean Stafford, for one, in novels like *Boston Adventure* (1944) and *The Catherine Wheel* (1952), finds people — the New England spinster — and places — Beacon Hill, the Maine summer colony — to utilize in her Proustian remembrance of the past, recalling, with a most observant eye, a racy wit, and considerable psychological penetration, the routines of the "oldest aristocracy," the "weatherproof Bostonians." Thus echoing Marquand in locale and character type, Miss Stafford echoes him as well in registering objections to the vulgar present, whose manners lack the individuality of taste of earlier times. For the protagonist of *The Catherine Wheel*, Katherine Congreve, there was *only* "past time," and so "her anecdotes were as archaic and yet as timeless as her carriage and as the ostrich-feather fan which she carried with her when she went out to dine with Hawthorne's summer gentry." In her rarefied world, she countenanced no change. To Miss Stafford's credit, be it said, she summons up so pleasing a picture of this "rarefied world" that the reader could almost wish "cousin Katherine" success in her attempt to arrest time. The author imbues *The Catherine Wheel* with a poignancy that makes subtle without sentimentalizing[2] the account of Katherine Congreve, her young nieces and nephew, and her "ancient playmates" at tea — the "twilight eucharist" — on the lawn of Congreve House, large and white and regal, ensphered by orchards and gardens and looking down from the top of a "monarchical hill."

John Cheever resorts to New England as well. In fact, in his *The Wapshot Chronicle* (1957) and *The Wapshot Scandal* (1963), he makes use of the community, Newburyport, Massachusetts, that had served Marquand's turn before him. With affectionate detail he reconstructs the "old river town of St. Botolph's," with its "factory that manufactured table silver and a few other small industries," and with its many attractive old homes, like that of Honora Wapshot. The town and its environs, from Peter Covell's place to the Pluzinski farm to the honest shabbiness of Theophilus Gates's house, are spread out before the reader, and blowing over all are the "evening winds that in New England smell of orris root and toilet soap and rented rooms, chamber pots and sorrel soup and roses and gingham and lawn." It was difficult, the author declares, "not to spread over the village the rich, dark varnish of decorum and quaintness." Certainly New York City, where "the value of permanence has never been grasped," and Washington, with "its theatrical air of impermanence," are less alluring, and even less so are the town of Talifer, the regimented site of a missile research center, and "Proxmire Manor," standard upper-middle suburbia personified. Cheever likes the stability and "character" of St. Botolph's, as he likes the nearby seaside resort of Nangasakit, even in the rain, even before the summer season has begun, as he likes, too, Leander Wapshot's "yacht," the S. S. *Topaze*, which blithely "smelled of summery refuse."

Cheever produces such local details in order to anchor the Wapshot family, most notably Honora and her brother Leander, Yankee eccentrics par excellence but of sturdy integrity at the same time, and representative of a solid tradition that is fast disappearing. Leander may never have made much money, Honora may be reduced to bickering with her cook, but they will leave a colorful example behind, as suggested by the former's legacy to his sons: "Never put whiskey into hot water bottles crossing borders of dry states or countries . . . Stand up straight. Admire the world. Relish the love of a gentle woman. Trust in the Lord."

The Cheever saga of the Wapshots is written in a vein more humorous and more zany by far than that usually found in the novel of manners. Slapstick incidents like that of the Woman's Club float careening across the countryside at the mercy of runaway horses as "Chairwoman" Wapshot yet retains her poise at the lectern, and bizarre characters like the antivivisectionist Reba Heaslop and the "foxy old dancing mistress" Justine Wapshot Molesworth Scaddon seem rather too extravagant for a mannered "manners" account. The satiric touches ("To refuse anything was a mark of character. The ladies were always hungry when they left the dinner table, but their sense of purpose was always refreshed. In their own bailiwick, of course, they ate like wolves") have a greater zestiness as well.

Cheever seems most akin to the novelist of manners in his reliance on the salient detail, as Leander's morning cold bath without soap but smelling of sea salts in the old sponges that he used, or his wife's own "arcane rites" such as arranging flowers and cleaning closets, and in the full-flavored style, especially replete with vivid descriptive adjectives and nouns, from the "bitter flower water" to the "Vuitton trunks and glittering lobbies of Grand Hotels." He is most akin to one predecessor in particular, J. P. Marquand, in his preferring the dignified past to the greedy and shabby present (all hamburger stands and used-car lots), and in his regret that the marvelously idiosyncratic Honora Wapshot will be replaced by her hardly as remarkable nieces-in-law, Melissa and Betsy.

The most recent novel to come from John Cheever, *Bullet Park,* concentrates on an "everyplace" suburban locale and on "everyman" suburban types ("all you have to do is get your clothes at Brooks, catch the train and show up in church once a week and no one will ever ask a question about your identity"). The author again supplies the right details to capture the environment — one has to be able to chat at cocktail parties about pool chemicals and tackrooms — and couches these details in appropriate language, filled with topical allusions and words like "talisman" and "tribal." His commentary on suburbia borders on travesty, however — how can one take seriously a novel whose antagonist is named Hammer and whose protagonist is named Nailles? — and thus an incipient novel of manners (Tony Nailles *might* represent, in his defense of monogamy and of paternal responsibility, the individual at odds with his society) turns into an entertaining farce.

Some of the more recent writers who also concern themselves with social frames single out rather special environments, Mary McCarthy and Gerald Warner Brace, for example, choosing, in some of their work, to reproduce the academic world. Miss McCarthy's *The Groves of Academe* (1951) anticipates O'Hara's *Elizabeth Appleton* in its focus on the small college community, and, though Miss McCarthy is chiefly occupied with her political subject, the leftist professor threatened by Joseph McCarthyism, she thoroughly exposes, in her characteristically tart way, the college scene, the "progressive community where the casserole and the cocktail and the disposable diaper reigned," along with administration-faculty clashes, poetry conferences, and the other "folkways" of this not always "congenial bivouac." Brace's university setting in *The Department* (1968) inevitably differs somewhat from Miss McCarthy's "progressive college," but the local-color trappings, the "great ferris wheel" of committees, conferences, exams, and papers, the eager young teachers of Freshman English using their classes as sounding boards for their own social gospels, the sometimes charmless students, and the often pinched quality of the professiorial social existence remain much the same. Both writers are involved, too, in similar — and staple — manners themes, the nuances of power, one-upmanship, status hopes — the old collegiate upper-class type with some combination of manner, family, money, and prowess versus the bearded-youth instructor, back from Somaliland or Alabama with strong convictions about how to save people from persecution and caring not a hoot about manner and family, though not oblivious to money and prowess — and even the "tradition bit" that still manifests itself in the "cultural matrix" that is Academia.

Another level of the academic sphere appears in John Knowles's *A Separate Peace* (1959), the milieu of the preparatory school. Knowles unfolds his young man's initiation theme against a scrupulously detailed backdrop — an old New England town of houses that are clever modernizations of Colonial manses, extensions in Victorian wood, and capacious Greek Revival temples located along streets lined with elms, the "most Republican, bankerish of trees." School customs and rituals form part of the background, for example, the traditional term tea held in the Headmaster's house (on the sun-porch conservatory containing chocolate-brown wicker furniture that shot out menacing twigs), or the chapel service, or the dungeonlike dormitory Butt Room. Intermittent descriptions of the changing seasons — the wet, self-pitying November day; the late winter of congealed snow, with the river a hard, gray-white lane of ice between gaunt trees and the sun blazing icily; the delightful summer, like a blessing, a response to all the cogitation and deadness of winter — intensify the local color as well.

Knowles manifests his craftsmanship in a number of ways: in his tight structural pattern, careful preservation of the first-person point of view, and competent style, one marked by graphic figurative language ("fear like stale air in an unopened room"), neat diction (the masters' attitude of "floating, chronic disapproval"), and natural dialogue. His rendition of the so ancient "know thyself" motif in the prep-school-on-the-eve-of-World War II atmosphere is engrossing, humorous, poignant, and authoritative.

More truly in the novel-of-manners vein, however, are two later works by Knowles, *Morning in Antibes* (1962) and *Indian Summer* (1966), tales that, as James McDonald has said,[3] show affinities with the efforts of such predecessors as James and Fitzgerald. The Riviera setting of *Morning in Antibes* recalls the latter, as does also the book's reliance on gestures, tones, dress, and decoration as signs of cultural patterns. Knowles searches, too, for the moral implications behind the patterns, having his "heroine," Liliane, reject — finally — the affluent and cultivated but also decidedly corrupt atmosphere in which Marc de la Croie and his sister Madame Courcelles flourish. It is a Jamesian replay. *Morning in Antibes's* sucessor, *Indian Summer,* advances a major theme in American fiction, the dissolving of the "American dream," and does so in terms of cultural proclivities. Cleet Kinsolving, like Jay Gatsby, encounters the world of the rich, the careless, ruthless Reardon world, that "secret confraternity, with special totems and rituals and, above all, special rights." In achieving their success, the Reardons have lost sight of the American dream, the vision of the ideal. Cleet Kinsolving — of Indian blood and therefore perhaps close to the Adamic figure — remembers what might have been. Knowles writes of this "outsider" and of the unhappy leadership of the "elite" with understanding, and with technical skill as well.

Another representative figure of the current literary scene, James Stevenson, follows the mode. His *The Summer Houses* (1963) deals with issues of class consciousness, snobbery, and hypocrisy and outlines with a nice circumstantiality the ways of the American upper strata. The summer colonists at Great Heron Island, fleeing, for a time, the New York "Executive Life" for the "Gracious Living" and "Togetherness" of their summer resort, enjoy a genial social round of croquet and cocktail parties, swims and Sunday lunches — until, that is, their blissful exclusivity is suddenly threatened by a real estate developer. In a situation dripping with irony because the "colonists," while priding themselves on their

sense of tradition and their old-money label, quickly cap-
itulate to "progress" and "new money," Stevenson articu-
lately unveils the shortcomings of this upper-class group,
their intellectual limitations, conventionality, and snobbish
and grooved responses.

Clearly establishing the setting of comfortable summer
houses at the outset, Stevenson creates a sense of the social
routine — for example, families are now reduced to one servant, a girl imported from Germany and known as a "mother's
helper." He then introduces a familiar cast of characters,
such as Eddie Benning contemplating a little extramarital dal-
liance, Monroe Huck fighting a middle-aged spread by playing
squash, the Warner Hoopes socking away the stingers, and he
attaches them to his plot line, indicating the problems
involved in maintaining the serenity of the resort. Finally, he
tells about it all in a graceful, lucid style, composed of barbed
understatement, provocative paradox, and natural images,
and thus he lightly and brightly carries on the manners
pattern.

Most explicitly in the Marquand-Auchincloss line,[4] however, is John Leggett, who, beginning his writing career in
1960 with *Wilder Stone*, has been steadily refining his talents
and producing pleasing works in the manners genre. It must
be said that *Wilder Stone* reproduces the format only intermittently, chiefly in its use of particulars about characters'
clothes (the dark suit bought at Rogers Peet), schooling,
and homes (the Stone house, a rambling, "rather elaborate,
turn-of-the-century summer cottage," its dormers and bowers
giving it an aspect of comfortable middle age), and in its
witty metaphors and similes (the placid pond of her disposition, his face a palimpsest, worry and fatigue like two
companions, "like a machine out of fuel that has been
clanging along on impetus, the conversation stopped with a
murmur and a wheeze"). The novel's sympathetic but none-

theless spineless "hero" resembles a prevalent manners type, too, just as the author's sourish tone in describing Wilder Stone's career resembles a prevalent manners attitude. Yet the book's theme, to be extracted from observation of Stone's life, does not underscore firmly enough the author's belief that the individual *can* manifest ethical conduct in confronting the follies of the present-day social order.

A crystallization of this theme, a fuller realization of background, and a more adroit use of the flashback structural pattern are to be found in Leggett's second novel, *The Gloucester Branch* (1964). The book deals with familiar topics, crises in the career and in the marriage of its protagonist, Sam Fayles, and it presents a familiar milieu, the affluent, mobile, upper-middle-class suburban world. Leggett's mildly rebelling "organization man," leading in large measure a mechanical life (getting up in the morning, Sam Fayles thinks of facing the "machinery of the day" ahead), is patterned after Lewis's Babbitt, or, more closely — and more flatteringly — after Marquand's Charles Gray.

Despite the lack of originality of the material, Leggett has produced an effective book. The account of the strains in the Fayles marriage and of Sam's business maneuverings, to secure from his brokerage firm financial backing for a textbook publishing company that is being revitalized, is believable and engrossing, as is the preserving-one's-integrity theme. With "a spirit that had had enough of retreating," Sam Fayles maintains his stand in the business matter at hand, and he stabilizes his marriage at the novel's end ("She was his very skin. Yes, a skin he could not part with — yet also his itching carapace"). It is a downbeat resolution, to be sure:

> And yet to survive was something. Just to keep from stumbling, falling. He visualized a thick rubber carpet endlessly moving

through the well-kept gardens of a life where small pleasures and sound decisions grew . . . finally, reluctantly, he embraced the reality and found it was endurable. [Pp. 247-48]

Leggett shares the Marquandian sense of fatalism ("the inevitableness of his life and, he supposed, of all men's lives"), as he does also the Marquandian settling for a qualified contentment.

The book achieves success largely through its intensely faithful reproduction of the upper-middle-class "Gloucester branch" sphere. The cast of characters includes predictable types like the "easily recognized New Englander," Archer Lyman, of disciplined vigor and well-schooled voice, and his feminine counterpart, Camilla Angel, whose dresses looked as though they had come from a mail-order house — "and this homespun look took a great deal of will and ingenuity to achieve at Bonwit Teller's." These, together with old-school publisher, Mr. Hastie, and the partners in the brokerage firm, Arthur Turnbull, Harriet Clarke, and Caleb Curtis, and Sam and Julia Fayles as well, contrast sharply with the Johnny-come-lately Martin Chalk, who doesn't share a conversation but gives one, and whose clothing is the "work of a chain clothier." If Sam Fayles and Martin Chalk are "lashed together in an intricate fellowship of interests," they will never be friends.

The Bostonian breed is posed against its city and country habitats in the novel. The reader moves from the "impressive" Partners' Room at Angel's brokerage house to the home of Julia Fayles's parents in Dedham, a Victorian pile of weathered stone and, inside, a churchly labyrinth of oak balusters and stairs, smelling of furniture polish, apples, and roast beef, and then back to the Somerset Club in town, in whose dining room "a waitress with a prioress's manner" is to be seen and the "pointed nasal precisions of good Boston voices" are to be heard. At other times, the reader glimpses Beacon Hill in a "chill scrim of fog," which lends "magical grace to the old houses . . . extra softness to their pink brick." There is a back side of Beacon Hill, to be sure, the rank and steamy Bohemia sliding into the grimy slums of the North End, but this, together with "the soiled mouth of the M.T.A. at the Tremont Street corner," can usually be ignored. One simply passes them on the way to and from his North Shore home, as does Sam Fayles commuting to his house in Follyhead. The Fayles dwelling hardly compares, albeit comfortable and even elaborate, with the Hastie house at Topsfield, complete with greenhouses and libraries, nor does it perhaps measure up, in character, to Julia's childhood summer home on Hale's Point, "a matronly, shingled hulk," suggesting the "money all around, though nothing in excess" of that exclusive summer resort. Still, it represents "gracious living."

Leggett also supplies in abundance the "lore" of that special world, the vocabulary of "shoes-off chats" and "handsy" men, the "cutesy" nicknames for the big horsy girls, the clothes (Wooster Clements's thick brogans with their eggplant glow; Sam Fayles, "dressed simply, protectively, in a dark-brown Brooks suit, white shirt, green foulard, all of which gave the illusion he was unconscious of his appearance"), the Winsor School accents that make "even the coarsest word curiously inoffensive," the possessions like Niles Cutting's elegant car filled with yachting equipment, the ritual of English biscuits served with the Hasties' tea. Occasionally, too, details about a more prosaic, more accessible environment appear, as the description of the baby-sitter's code ("which forbids brush and Brillo to her manicured fingers and leaves her own ice-cream dish and glass for the master's attention"), or of the Follyhead town meeting. One notes, however, that, at the meeting, the "Hale's Point" people are set apart from the Moynihans.

A swift-moving and resourceful style lends appeal to *The Gloucester Branch* as well. Leggett phrases briskly ("give a woman a man to order around and she went Borgia every time"). He calls the various senses into play (the "peaty vapor of greenhouses;" the range of laughs, from the bass bray of Mr. Turnbull, to the modulated arpeggio of Mrs. Clarke, to the sibilant wheezing of Mr. Curtis). He employs effective figures ("like a band of revelers leaving a party"), expressive diction (the "bladed gust of the east wind and chilling breath of the sea"), apt allusions (Thomas Eakins, Styles Bridges), and appropriate shoptalk (customers' man, account executive, company wife). Sentences like these — "The sparring was preliminary to a plunge into vicious acrimony; they had lost the brakes of yielding and humor," or "He was skewered with tensions, and infinite pockets of fatigue clustered like grapes along his spine" — indicate his stylistic ease.

What really makes the book work well, however, is the presence of a likeable protagonist. From the opening pages, one senses that Sam Fayles, however much embroiled he is in a keeping-up-with-the-Joneses world, has retained a reasonable degree of individuality (note his deliberately utilitarian office, which clashes with the "gentleman's club" atmosphere so studiously cultivated at Angel's). As his character is fleshed out — by means of a series of neatly inserted flashbacks — one sees his sensitivity and honesty, and one is caught up in his "emotional disarray" brought on by his business and marital problems, his "Pandora's box of anxieties." One is glad, finally, when the tensions are resolved, and when, though the inadequacies remain, the "small pleasures and sound decisions" grow. If still forced into the playing of a role, Sam will at the same time march for the most part "to some tune he hums to himself."

A longer and more complex work, *Who Took the Gold*

Away (1969), followed *The Gloucester Branch.* Though the purlieus remain the same, the scope has broadened, and the single protagonist has turned into a twosome, the novel being devoted to developing a contrast between two friends, Pierce Jay and Ben Moseley. As their lives are followed over a twenty-year span, a waxing-for-Ben and waning-for-Pierce pattern is established, the author thus making a provocative juxtaposition and, in this instance, adapting the manners genre into a duo-character study.

By means of a four-part structure, Leggett presents the essential background and chronology. Part I is set in New Haven in 1938, Part II in Newport in 1948, Part III in Cambridge in 1951, and Part IV off the Maine coast in 1959. The sequence is followed by an "Afterword," giving an account of the death and funeral of Pierce, which takes place a few years later, in New York City.

As the young men meet at Yale, the contrast is immediately drawn. Wealthy New Yorker Pierce Jay epitomizes the aristocrat, his arrogance combined with looks and manner, his careless manifestation of money, and his willfulness, intriguing Ben Moseley, the middle-class boy from Providence. Like a "Ford from Grosse Point, Pillsbury from Wayzata, Rockefeller from Greenwich, Biddle from Philadelphia, Armour from Lake Forest, Dillingham from Honolulu," Pierce Jay had it all. As Ben Moseley reflects,[5] "The telling marks on a man were his prep school, his dress and what he did with his leisure. Grace, detachment, not seeming to care and, above all, being with acceptable companions — these were prized." Initially, Pierce prizes them, too, and perfectly embodies what Ben thinks of as the "code": poise, style in clothes and behavior, good manners, particular indifference (at least outward) to intellectual pursuits, and, as Pierce remarks, if you're going to be a snob, you might as well go at it with guys who've been brought up to do it right.

At an early stage in their relationship, however, Ben obtains "a glimpse of vulnerableness" in Pierce Jay, and soon Pierce begins to veer from the pattern, giving up football to heel for the Yale Daily News, buckling down, for a while, to his studies. Later, he becomes the maverick on the News staff, rejects the final clubs, and goes off to World War II before completing his college career. Ben, of course, contributes to Pierce's forsaking the "model" role, mostly by blocking Pierce's aspirations to become chairman of the News board. Always admiring, always bound, Ben is also always jealous of his friend.

Part II, transpiring almost a decade later, focuses on the postwar years when the Jay-Moseley generation faces commitment to marriages and careers. Ben has made a solid marriage to a girl of good background (Nancy can wear the "silks," but she also has "starch" underneath, having learned horse sense through some teenage adversity, brought on by her family's loss of its money) and is about to receive his law-school degree. Pierce, on the other hand, has neither job nor wife — though, of course, plenty of money and plenty of girls. The waxing-waning connection becomes apparent, as one remembers, too, that Ben had made his name at Yale and had flown and received medals in the war, medals that would seem to have been reserved for Pierce. The action in Part II, a visit made by the Moseleys to the Jay summer "cottage" at Newport, illustrates Pierce's descent, his idleness, and his drinking — though Ben has not written him off, for "he can make miraculous things happen."

Three years later, in Part III, the three are gathered in Cambridge, Pierce meanwhile having acquired a wife, Lily, and seemingly having found a career, running a small electronics firm. Beneath the surface run uneasy currents, though, Pierce appearing to Ben to adopt poses, first as a political liberal, then as one in tune with Lily's "odd-ball" intellectual friends. As Ben plods along, beginning to establish himself as a successful lawyer, Pierce "operates" in Cambridge and Washington, trying to maintain a good relationship with his science professor partner and trying to win contracts for his firm. At times the old magic appears to be there, as in a celebration dinner in Washington, Pierce's "good mind steadied at last," thinks Ben, rather prematurely.

Part IV, its "story" being a cruise taken by the two couples a few years later, brings matters to a head. Pierce's business difficulties and his not-good-though-not-impossible marriage lead him, as Ben sees it, to the "blunt fact of failure." "Committed to acting out his collapse," Ben and Lily engage in adultery. With a "new awareness of Pierce's vulnerability," Ben feels that "I had reached a pinnacle in the topography of my life." As Nancy watches with "caustic whimsy," and Lily comments that nothing "is more complicated than what goes on between a couple of old Blues," the waxing and waning seem complete — "the rite, feral and inevitable, acknowledging Pierce's collapse as a man and abdication as a husband," the end, in Ben's words, of a "lovely young illusion." Lily sums up Pierce's nature at his funeral: he knew that there was a way to some heroic pattern for his life. He carried that belief like a shiny coin in his pocket. There was always some grandness beyond his grasp. But the "grandness" wasn't there, of course, nor the possibility of a "heroic pattern." Ben, knowing this ("my disgust with my times was complete"), knowing, moreover, his own potential, was able to grasp a good deal, was able to wax as Pierce waned.

Most obviously, however, his life did not fall into a "heroic pattern" either. If intelligent, sensitive, and hard-working, if also moderate and dependable, he can blunt some of these good qualities as he displays his "knack of mobility," using, for example, his "guilelessness" to such effect that it certainly becomes guile. He can harm his best friend, Pierce, out of pure jealousy, and he can turn away from his first love, Angela Rice, for fear of "being blackballed through someone you love." He will cut the corners in his law practice and even seduce his best friend's wife. Though he might blame fate ("their lack of choice") or the loose contemporary moral standards, his life is essentially of his own design, and it is not a lofty design.

The setting for this very modern version of the Damon-Pythias legend is actualized by a number of small but significant details. In creating the Ivy League ambiance, Leggett talks of clothes (cluster-striped school ties and red-soled white buck shoes), clubs (Fence was "almost exclusively church-school and stud-book"), studies (one took the gut courses like "Pots and Pans" and "Cowboys and Indians"), and recreations (the locale for these so often being the little world of the East Fifties, where the bandleaders' ears were cocked for the debutantes' wishes). Sutton Place apartments (all plum-hued French tapestries and walnut paneling), Newport summer homes (the Bledsoes' house, Greenfields, a potpourri of porches and "curiously impractical ramblings of scalloped shingle, spiked here and there with a lightning rod," was very much an exception in lacking pretension — and, as such, a retort to the neighboring châteaus and palazzi), the monstrously ugly house on Linnaean Street in Cambridge much refurbished by the Jays in order to eliminate its effluvia of bean suppers and ancient plumbing — these are the locales for those in the "aristocratic tradition."

The book's language again and again complements this tradition, in that it is poised, graceful, and "smart." The figures of speech (Angela Rice "tossing off great, girlish beach balls of conversation," Pierce Jay going about his seductions "like a probationary Comanche after scalps" or collecting information about armed service requirements "like a boy at a boat show") exhibit these qualities, as does the phrasing generally (jousting for the debutante lists, jealousy's teeter-totter, the sharky wariness of the gate-crashers at a Jay party). If Leggett basically employs an informal sentence pattern, he spices it by his apt choice of words ("I saw Jake lean into his humiliation warily").

Like so many of his predecessors, Leggett relies heavily on satire, mocking such events as the Tap Day ceremonies at Yale, where a nimbus cloaks the "knighted" who make the senior societies, scoffing at the clannishness of the "sated *jeunesse dorée*" who constitute the Jay circle, and laughing at the artificiality of Lily Jay's "intensely archeological" and intensely ingrown university circle, as also at the inefficiency of Washington "officialdom."

Indeed, Leggett recalls his predecessors in the field of manners in many, many ways. Like them he captures time and place by means of the relevant detail: the drinks of the era, as the "cuba libre," the national beverage of the late thirties; the courtship customs of the college crowd — beer and songs at Poughkeepsie or Northampton; and the lure of the impending war, one that would "cauterize men's disappointments, sluicing away the foulness they had made about them." He repeats the upper class setting of English nannies, pony carts and lunches at the Colony Club, and he echoes earlier themes — the issue of integrity, the note of determinism, the clash of class, the money-makes-a-difference question, and the past-present contrast. The "everyman" protagonist is also reintroduced and is again treated with temperate irony as he tries to cope with societal ties and the dissonances between ethical absolutes and social norms. Even the technical devices like the flashback structure return, and the emotion-charged atmosphere as well.[6]

One is tempted to conclude that "plus ça change, c'est plus le même chose," for, though American society may be undergoing change in recent times, the treatment of it has not varied to a great degree. Cheever's robust note of humor may offer a modification of the genre, and Leggett's *Who Took The Gold Away,* in its concentrated study of two characters, may provide another. In general, though, the 1960s format remains remarkably close to the central tradition.

NOTES TO CHAPTER 11

1. Louis Auchincloss, *Reflections of a Jacobite* (Boston: Houghton Mifflin Co., 1961), p. 141.

2. Her often acerbic touch helps reduce the sentiment, as in her comparison of fashionable Newport with unfashionable Hawthorne. Miss Congreve's visitors, reports Miss Stafford, scampered back as fast as they could to midday cocktails upon the humid sands of Bailey's Beach, for Hawthorne had nothing much to offer, no clubs, no proper swimming beach, no summer theater, no sailboat races, and its sprawling cottages, all gingerbread and trailing porches and purposeless stained-glass windows appeared, to the visitors, like tasteless if kindly frumps in the entourage of a famous belle.

3. See James L. McDonald, "The Novels of John Knowles," *Arizona Quarterly* 23 (Winter 1967): 335.

4. Auchincloss himself acknowledges this, a bookjacket blurb attached to Leggett's *The Gloucester Branch* quoting him to this effect.

5. Using Moseley as a first-person narrator, Leggett introduces a proper sense of informality and intimacy — as well as an admittedly slanted point of view.

6. A case in point in *Who Took the Gold Away:* the Jay-Moseley blow-up occurs on a rainy day, one of a succession, when the "funky smell from bilge" and the "curtains of rain" sweeping down the hatchway intensify the claustrophobic environment of the boat, the close quarters combining with the weather to crystallize the dissension.

12

Conclusion

*A*S, then, one compiles a "history" of the American novel of manners, it becomes manifest that a substantial number of writers were involved in fostering the tradition. Even putting aside the major practitioners, the ones who lent special value to the genre, one can produce a plethora of names over a span of 150 years.[1] Early in the nineteenth century, authors like James Fenimore Cooper, Catharine Maria Sedgwick, John Pendleton Kennedy, and John Esten Cooke chose to record communal links, to discuss man's behavior in a "ruled" social set up, and occasionally to associate manners with moral vision. They were subsequently joined by such writers as George Washington Cable, Constance Fenimore Woolson, and F. Hopkinson Smith, and just slightly later, as the nineteenth century gave way to the twentieth, a group including Arlo Bates, Robert Grant, and Anne Douglas Sedgwick followed suit, writing novels strong in the "sense of society" and often hinging upon an acceptance of or

272

rejection of "social morality," Nor was the focus lost in the "Roaring Twenties" (regard Booth Tarkington and Carl Van Vechten), and, indeed, the type flourishes in the present era, as the Cheevers, Leggetts, and Stevensons continue the practice of posing their fictional material against a particular organization — for example, the New England "kinship" strain in Cheever — and maintaining a consciousness of class standing as a social determinant. A surprising number have, in short, adopted the Jane Austen model.

Most of these "minor" exemplars represent the tradition less faithfully and less effectively, to be sure, than James, Howells, Marquand, Wharton, Glasgow, Fitzgerald, O'Hara, Cozzens, and Auchincloss. In the first place, they are less precise in their delineation of a society that is marked by distinct strata, and less exact about cultural proclivities, prejudices, niceties of deportment, social instances, and the like. Second, they often adapt the genre to other purposes — for example, the historical romance, the local-color tale, the broad farce — and in the process subvert it. Third, they exhibit aesthetic shortcomings — perhaps sprawling structures, a "busyness" of plotting, or conventional characterization; more often, a prosy style and uncertain tone. It remains for the James-to-Auchincloss coterie to present the novel of manners at its best, a seriocomic exploration of the conflicts between ethical standards and social virtues as seen, usually, through a particular individual experience.

Whether perfectly or imperfectly rendered, the novel of manners probably will not disappear from the literary scene, for it is inevitably a popular type.[2] Moreover, it affords more diversity than some have been willing to grant. It might, for one thing, function in the area of ethnic groups — as the Boston Irish, whom Edwin O'Connor took as his province — or of the "jet set" world, that seemingly uneasy amalgam of titled Europeans, Texas tycoons, and Hollywood stars. Such areas call out for fictional description.

The authors who might respond could fruitfully use the themes of their predecessors, for example, the social climb or the European expatriation, or other themes involving social relationships. The cultural jars to be found in urban-rustic contrasts, the capital versus the province, Philistia versus Bohemia, still exist in American society, as does the reality of hard cash as a strongly conditioning social factor. The previously employed themes of a more general nature, the clash of generations, the effects of time on a culture, the search for identity ("In my walk of life," says Auchincloss's Jay Livingston, "a man's got to shed his antecedents if he wants to get ahead"), still can fit into the manners format.

The genre presents some special problems in the present "fluid" era, to be sure. The characters of the current "open society" seem less susceptible to precise definition than the members of Boston's Somerset Club or Lake Forest's Onwentsia, and their backgrounds, as well. In place of old homes on old streets in old cities, the novelist must substitute any cosmopolitan city, any ski resort, any Riviera watering place. Modern society is too mobile for positive identification with a locale. The bittersweet tone of a Marquand or Wharton might need replacement, too, an unadulteratedly acid pen (such as that wielded by Alison Lurie in *The War Between the Tates*, [1974]) seeming the only appropriate weapon with which to describe the contemporary standardless as well as tasteless "beautiful people." The more extreme methods, fantasy or farce or burlesque (as seen in Stevenson's *The Summer Houses),* would probably offer the most viable approaches, for the subtely and finesse of the Jamesian school would be wasted on groups so lacking in "ceremonious intercourse," and the tragic aura lingering around an Archer or an Apley would appear inappropriate when attached to Penelope Tree or Lee Radziwill. Still, writers like John Leggett have managed to inspire an empathetic reaction on the part of the reader toward their gray-flannel-suited protagonists, and perhaps the very modern world still holds, albeit tenuously, to "social tradition" and to the Jamesian belief that manners are the essence of individuals and their civilizations.

One would not wish, of course, to proclaim decidedly major importance for the novel-of-manners form. The genre by its very nature demands a lightness of touch, and the performers within its domain more readily evince urbane than philosophical minds. Their characters generally lack tragic proportions, and the glitter-glamor world they inhabit flaunts a rather superficial air. The type, in short, produces a little more entertainment than enlightenment.

Nonetheless, it can be firmly said that "manners in the widest sense [i.e., the Jamesian sense] have not ceased to serve the novel."[3] When one takes manners to mean more than rigid chaperonage or family tennis or the view from the country-club porch, to mean, instead, a "culture's hum and buzz of implication . . . the indication of the direction of man's soul,"[4] he inevitably attaches both depth and significance to the novel-of-manners genre. Fiction that tests moral values by dramatizing relationships within fixed social groups becomes more than pleasantly comic — it becomes serious, if not tragic.

Such is the case with the best work of the cultivators of the field. Their books have talked of principle as well as of fatuity, and they have cogently revealed the role of manners in giving substance to moral vision.[5] In thus utilizing social experience to test moral action, the novelists have struck universal chords and have created productions of lasting worth.

NOTES TO CHAPTER 12

1. Among the many writers who *might* have been discussed in this survey is Howard Sturgis, whose three novels, expecially *Belchamber* (1904), neatly illustrate the genre. *Belchamber*, a book admired by Sturgis's friends, Henry James and Edith Wharton, offers an indictment of the English aristocracy, the novel assembling an unappetizing group of lords and ladies outlining their activities (mostly arranging marriages for money), and deploying them against a background of Jacobean country houses, yachting at Cowes, hunting in Scotland, racing at Goodwood. Sturgis writes very knowledgeably (though an American, he lived all his life in England) as well as wryly about coming-of-age celebrations, liaisons between young gentlemen and music hall "actresses," society weddings and charity bazaars. Whatever the "situation," he points out, ethical solidity was quite lacking.

2. Louis Auchincloss has declared that the "psychological novel, or the stream-of-consciousness novel, or the symbolic novel, has never enjoyed even a small fraction of the popularity of the novel of manners" (Louis Auchincloss, *Reflections of a Jacobite* [Boston: Houghton Mifflin Co., 1961], p. 142), and the fact that Wharton, Glasgow, Fitzgerald, and Lewis sold well in their day, and that, more recently, Marquand, O'Hara, and Cozzens, not to mention Auchincloss himself, have often lingered at the top of the best-seller lists would seem to bear him out.

3. Ihab Hassan, *Radical Innocence: Studies in the Contemporary American Novel* (Princeton, N.J.: Princeton University Press, 1961), p. 108.

4. Lionel Trilling, *The Liberal Imagination* (Garden City, N.Y.: Doubleday & Co., Inc., Anchor Books, 1950), pp. 200, 205.

5. This is seen, for example, in the recurring pattern of the superior individual's exercise of conscience and moral judgment in the face of the constricting conventional codes of his society (as Milly Theale, or Edmonia Bredalbane, or Abner Coates).

Bibliography

Novels

Auchincloss, Louis. *The Indifferent Children.* New York: Prentice Hall, 1947.
——. *Sybil.* Boston: Houghton Mifflin Co., 1952.
——. *A Law for the Lion.* Boston: Houghton Mifflin Co., 1953.
——. *The Romantic Egoists.* Boston: Houghton Mifflin Co., 1954.
——. *The Great World and Timothy Colt.* Boston: Houghton Mifflin Co., 1956.
——. *Venus in Sparta.* Boston: Houghton Mifflin Co., 1958.
——. *Pursuit of the Prodigal.* Boston: Houghton Mifflin Co., 1959.
——. *The House of Five Talents.* Boston: Houghton Mifflin Co., 1960.
——. *Portrait in Brownstone.* Boston: Houghton Mifflin Co., 1962.
——. *The Rector of Justin.* Boston: Houghton Mifflin Co., 1964.
——. *The Embezzler.* Boston: Houghton Mifflin Co., 1966.
——. *A World of Profit.* Boston: Houghton Mifflin Co., 1968.
——. *Second Chance.* Boston: Houghton Mifflin Co., 1970.
——. *I Come as a Thief.* Boston: Houghton Mifflin Co., 1972.
——. *The Partners.* Boston: Houghton Mifflin Co., 1973.

Bates, Arlo. *The Philistines.* Boston: Ticknor & Co., 1889.
——. *The Puritans.* Boston and New York: Houghton Mifflin Co., 1898.

Brace, Gerald Warner. *The Department.* New York: W. W. Norton Co., 1968.

Brackenridge, H. H. *Modern Chivalry.* Pittsburgh, Pa.: R. Patterson & Lambdin, 1792-1815.

Cable, George Washington. *The Grandissimes.* New York: Charles Scribner's Sons, 1880.

——. *Dr. Sevier.* Boston: James R. Osgood & Co., 1885.

——. *John March, Southerner.* New York: Charles Scribner's Sons, 1894.

Carney, Otis. *When the Bough Breaks.* Boston: Houghton Mifflin Co., 1957.

Cheever, John. *The Wapshot Chronicle.* New York: Harper & Row, 1957.

——. *The Wapshot Scandal.* New York: Harper & Row, 1963.

——. *Bullet Park.* New York: A. A. Knopf, 1969.

Cooke, John Esten. *Virginia Comedians.* New York: D. Appleton & Co., 1854.

——. *Fanchette.* Boston: James R. Osgood & Co., 1883.

Cooper, James Fenimore. *Precaution.* New York: A. T. Goodrich & Co., 1820.

——. *Homeward Bound.* Philadelphia: Carey, Lea & Blanchard, 1838.

——. *Home as Found.* Philadelphia: Lea & Blanchard, 1838.

——. *Autobiography of a Pocket Handkerchief.* 1843. Reprint. Chapel Hill, N.C.: G. F. Horner, 1949.

——. *Satanstoe.* New York: Burgess, Stringer & Co., 1845.

——. *The Chainbearer.* New York: Burgess, Stringer & Co., 1845.

——. *The Redskins.* New York: Burgess, Stringer & Co., 1846.

Cozzens, James Gould. *Men and Brethren.* New York: Harcourt, Brace & Co. 1936.

——. *Ask Me Tomorrow.* Harcourt, Brace & Co., 1940.

——. *The Just and the Unjust.* New York: Harcourt, Brace & Co., 1942.

——. *Guard of Honor.* New York: Harcourt, Brace & Co., 1948.

——. *By Love Possessed.* New York: Harcourt, Brace & Co., 1957.

——. *Morning, Noon and Night.* New York: Harcourt, Brace & Co., 1968.

Fitzgerald, F. Scott. *This Side of Paradise.* New York: A. L. Burt, 1920.

——. *The Great Gatsby.* New York: Charles Scribner's Sons, 1925.

——. *Tender Is the Night.* New York: Charles Scribner's Sons, 1934.

Glasgow, Ellen. *Virginia.* Garden City, N.Y.: Doubleday Page & Co., 1913.

——. *Life and Gabriella.* Garden City, N.Y.: Doubleday Page & Co., 1916.

——. *The Romantic Comedians.* Garden City, N.Y.: Doubleday Page & Co., 1926.

——. *They Stooped to Folly.* Garden City, N.Y.: Doubleday Doran & Co., 1929.

——. *The Sheltered Life.* Garden City, N.Y.: Doubleday Doran & Co., 1932.

Grant Robert. *Unleavened Bread.* New York: Charles Scribner's Sons, 1900.

——. *The Chippendales.* New York: Charles Scribner's Sons, 1909.

Howells, William Dean. *Their Wedding Journey.* Boston: James R. Osgood & Co., 1872.

——. *A Chance Acquaintance.* Boston: James R. Osgood & Co., 1873.

——. *A Foregone Conclusion.* Boston: James R. Osgood & Co., 1875.

——. *The Lady of the Aroostook.* Boston: Houghton, Osgood & Co., 1879.

——. *A Fearful Responsibility.* Boston: James R. Osgood & Co., 1881.

——. *The Rise of Silas Lapham.* Boston: Ticknor & Co., 1885.

——. *Indian Summer.* Boston: Ticknor & Co., 1886.

——. *April Hopes.* New York: Harper & Brothers, 1888.

——. *Their Silver Wedding Journey.* New York and London: Harper & Brothers, 1899.

——. *The Kentons.* New York: Harper & Brothers, 1902.

——. *The Vacation of the Kelwyns.* New York and London: Harper & Brothers, 1920.

James, Henry. *A Passionate Pilgrim and Other Tales.* Boston: James R. Osgood & Co., 1875.

——. *The American.* Boston: James R. Osgood & Co., 1877.

——. *Daisy Miller.* New York: Harper & Brothers, 1878.

——. *An International Episode.* New York: Harper & Brothers, 1878.

——. *The Europeans.* London: Macmillan & Co., 1878.

——. *The Portrait of a Lady.* London: Macmillan & Co., 1881.

——. *The Spoils of Poynton.* Boston and New York: Houghton Mifflin Co., 1897.

——. *The Wings of the Dove*. New York: Charles Scribner's Sons, 1902.

——. *The Ambassadors*. New York and London: Harper & Brothers, 1903.

——. *The Golden Bowl*. New York: Charles Scribner's Sons, 1904.

Kennedy, John Pendleton. *Swallow Barn*. Philadelphia: Carey & Lea, 1832.

Knowles, John. *A Separate Peace*. New York: Macmillan & Co., 1959.

——. *Morning in Antibes*. New York: Macmillan & Co., 1962.

——. *Indian Summer*. New York: Random House, 1966.

Leggett, John. *Wilder Stone*. New York: Harper & Row, 1960.

——. *The Gloucester Branch*. New York: Harper & Row, 1964.

——. *Who Took the Gold Away*. New York: Random House, 1969.

Lewis, Sinclair. *Main Street*. New York: Harcourt, Brace & Co., 1920.

——. *Babbitt*. New York: Harcourt, Brace & Co., 1922.

——. *Dodsworth*. New York: Harcourt, Brace & Co., 1929.

Lurie, Alison, *The War Between the Tates*. New York: Random House, 1974.

McCarthy, Mary. *The Groves of Academe*. New York: Harcourt, Brace & Co., 1951.

Marquand, John P. *The Late George Apley*. Boston: Little, Brown & Co., 1937.

——. *Wickford Point*. Boston: Little, Brown & Co., 1939.

——. *H. M. Pulham, Esq*. Boston: Little, Brown & Co., 1941.

——. *Point of No Return*. Boston: Little, Brown & Co., 1949.

——. *Women and Thomas Harrow*. Boston: Little, Brown & Co., 1958.

O'Hara, John. *Appointment in Samarra*. New York: Harcourt, Brace & Co., 1934.

——. *A Rage To Live*. New York: Random House, 1949.

——. *Ourselves To Know*. New York: Random House, 1950.

——. *From the Terrace*. New York: Random House, 1958.

——. *Elizabeth Appleton*. New York: Random House, 1963.

——. *The Lockwood Concern*. New York: Random House, 1965.

Sedgwick, Anne Douglas. *A Fountain Sealed*. Boston and New York: Houghton Mifflin Co., 1907.

——. *Tante*. New York: The Century Co., 1912.

——. *The Little French Girl*. Boston and New York: Houghton Mifflin Co., 1924.

Sedgwick, Catharine M. *Clarence.* Philadelphia: Carey & Lea, 1830.
——. *Married or Single?.* New York: Harper and Brothers, 1857.

Stafford, Jean. *Boston Adventure.* New York: Harcourt, Brace & Co., 1944.
——. *The Catherine Wheel.* New York: Harcourt, Brace & Co., 1952.

Stevenson, James. *The Summer Houses.* New York: The Macmillan Co., 1963.

Sturgis, Howard O. *Belchamber.* New York: G. P. Putnam's Sons, 1904.

Tarkington, Booth. *The Magnificent Ambersons.* Garden City, N.Y.: Doubleday Page & Co., 1918.
——. *Alice Adams.* Garden City, N.Y.: Doubleday Page & Co., 1921.
——. *Gentle Julia.* Garden City, N.Y.: Doubleday Page & Co., 1922.
——. *The Midlander.* Garden City, N.Y.: Doubleday Page & Co., 1924.
——. *The Plutocrat.* Garden City, N.Y.: Doubleday Page & Co., 1927.

Van Vechten, Carl. *The Tattooed Countess.* New York: A. A. Knopf, 1924.
——. *Firecrackers.* New York: A. A. Knopf, 1925.
——. *Parties.* New York: A. A. Knopf, 1930.

Wharton, Edith. *The House of Mirth.* New York: Charles Scribner's Sons, 1905.
——. *The Reef.* New York: D. Appleton & Co., 1912.
——. *The Custom of the Country.* New York: Charles Scribner's Sons, 1913.
——. *The Age of Innocence.* New York: D. Appleton & Co., 1920.
——. *Old New York.* New York: D. Appleton & Co., 1924.
——. *The Mother's Recompense.* New York: D. Appleton & Co., 1925.
——. *Twilight Sleep.* New York: D. Appleton & Co., 1927.
——. *Hudson River Bracketed.* New York: D. Appleton & Co., 1929.
——. *The Gods Arrive.* New York: D. Appleton & Co., 1932.
——. *The Buccaneers.* New York: D. Appleton & Co., 1938.

General

Auchincloss, Louis. *Pioneers and Caretakers: A Study of Nine American Women Novelists.* Minneapolis, Minn.: University of Minnesota Press, 1965.
——. *Reflections of a Jacobite.* Boston: Houghton Mifflin, 1961.

Balakian, Nona, and Simmons, Charles, ed., *The Creative Present: Notes on Contemporary Fiction*. Garden City, N.Y.: Doubleday, 1963.

Baumbach, Jonathan. "The Economy of Love: The Novels of Bernard Malamud." *Kenyon Review* 25 (Summer 1963): 438-57.

Bradbury, Malcolm. *Possibilities: Essays on the State of the Novel*. London, Oxford, New York: Oxford University Press, 1973.

Chase, Richard. *The American Novel and Its Tradition*. Garden City, N.Y.: Doubleday Anchor Book, 1957.

Eisinger, Chester E. *Fiction of the Forties*. Chicago and London: University of Chicago Press, 1963.

Fergusson, Francis. "Three Novels." *Perspectives, USA* 6 (Winter 1954): 30-44.

Frohock, W. M. *Strangers To This Ground*. Dallas, Tex.: Southern Methodist University Press, 1961.

Gaines, Francis P. *The Southern Plantation*. New York: Columbia University Press, 1924.

Guttmann, Allen, *The Conservative Tradition in America*. New York: Oxford University Press, 1967.

Hassan, Ihab. *Radical Innocence: Studies in the Contemporary American Novel*. Princeton, N.J.: Princeton University Press, 1961.

Hierth, Harrison E. "The Class Novel." *The CEA Critic* 27, no. 3 (December 1964): 1,3,4.

Howe, Irving. *A World More Attractive (A View of Modern Literature and Politics)*. New York: Horizon Press, 1963.

Kaul, A. N. *The American Vision*. New Haven and London: Yale University Press, 1963.

Kronenberger, Louis. *The Thread of Laughter*. New York: Alfred A. Knopf, 1952.

Lewis, R. W. B. *Trials of the Word: Essays in American Literature*. New Haven and London: Yale University Press, 1965.

Loggins, Vernon. *I Hear America*. New York: Thomas Y. Crowell Co., 1937.

Millgate, Michael. *American Social Fiction: James to Cozzens*. New York: Barnes & Noble, Inc., 1974.

Mizener, Arthur. "The Novel of Manners in America." *Kenyon Review* 12 (Winter 1950): 1-19.

Persons, Stow. *The Decline of American Gentility.* New York and London: Columbia University Press, 1973.

Rubin, Louis, and Moore, John R. *The Idea of an American Novel.* New York: Thomas Y. Crowell Co., 1961.

Trilling, Lionel. *The Liberal Imagination.* Garden City, N.Y.: Doubleday Anchor Book, 1950.

Tuttleton, James W. *The Novel of Manners in America.* Chapel Hill, N.C.: University of North Carolina Press, 1972.

Wagenknecht, Edward. *Cavalcade of the American Novel.* New York: Henry Holt & Co., 1952.

Wright, Nathalia. *American Novelists in Italy.* Philadelphia: University of Pennsylvania Press, 1965.

Cooper

Ringe, Donald A. *James Fenimore Cooper.* New York: Twayne Publishers, Inc., 1962.

Ross, Morton Lee. *"The Rhetoric of Manners: The Art of James Fenimore Cooper's Social Criticism."* Ph.D. dissertation, State University of Iowa, 1964.

Kennedy

Ridgely, J. W. *John Pendleton Kennedy.* New York: Twayne Publishers, Inc., 1966.

Sedgwick

Foster, Edward H. *Catharine Maria Sedgwick.* New York: Twayne Publishers, Inc., 1974.

James

Bowden, Edwin T. *The Themes of Henry James.* New Haven, Conn.: Yale University Press, 1956.

Cargill, Oscar. *The Novels of Henry James.* New York: The Macmillan Co., 1961.

Crews, Frederick C. *The Tragedy of Manners, Moral Drama in the Later Novels of Henry James.* New Haven, Conn.: Yale University Press, 1957.

Edel, Leon. *Henry James.* Minneapolis, Minn.: University of Minnesota Press, 1960.

Edel, Leon, ed. *Henry James: A Collection of Critical Essays.* Englewood Cliffs, N.J.: Prentice-Hall, Inc., 1963.

Hoffman, Charles G. *The Short Novels of Henry James.* New York: Bookman Associates, 1957.

Holland, Laurence B. *The Expense of Vision: Essays on the Craft of Henry James.* Princeton, N.J.: Princeton University Press, 1964.

James, Henry. *The Question of Our Speech. The Lesson of Balzac. Two Lectures.* Boston and New York: Houghton Mifflin, 1905.

Krook, Dorothea. *The Ordeal of Consciousness in Henry James.* Cambridge: At the University Press, 1962.

Lubbock, Percy, selec. and ed. *The Letters of Henry James.* London: Macmillan & Co., Ltd., 1920.

McElderry, Bruce R., Jr. *Henry James.* New York: Twayne Publishers, Inc., 1965.

Morris, Wright. *The Territory Ahead.* New York: Harcourt, Brace & Co., 1958.

Poirier, Richard. *The Comic Sense of Henry James.* New York: Oxford University Press, 1960.

Sayre, Robert F. *The Examined Self: Benjamin Franklin, Henry Adams, Henry James.* Princeton, N.J.: Princeton University Press, 1964.

Ward, J. A. *The Search for Form (Studies in the Structure of James' Fiction).* Chapel Hill, N.C.: University of North Carolina Press, 1967.

Wegelin, Christof. *The Image of Europe in Henry James.* Dallas, Tex.: Southern Methodist University Press, 1958.

——. "The Rise of the International Novel." *PMLA* 77 (June 1962): 305-10.

Wright, Walter F. *The Madness of Art: A Study of Henry James.* Lincoln, Neb.: University of Nebraska Press, 1962.

Howells

Baxter, Annette K. "Caste and Class: Howells' Boston and Wharton's New York." *Midwest Quarterly* 4 (Summer 1963): 353-61.

Bennett, George N. *William Dean Howells, The Development of a*

Novelist. Norman, Okla.: University of Oklahoma Press, 1959.

Brooks, Van Wyck. *Howells: His Life and World.* New York: E. P. Dutton & Co.. 1959.

Cady, Edwin. *The Realist at War. The Mature Years 1885-1920 of William Dean Howells.* Syracuse, N.Y.: Syracuse University Press, 1958.

——. *The Road to Realism. The Early Years 1837-1885 of William Dean Howells.* Syracuse, N.Y.: Syracuse University Press, 1965.

Carrington, George C., Jr. *The Immense Complex Drama: The World and Art of the Howells Novel.* Columbus, Ohio: Ohio State University Press 1966.

Carter, Everett. *Howells and the Age of Realism.* Philadelphia and New York: J. B. Lippincott Co., 1954.

Fryckstedt, Olov W. *In Quest of America (A Study of Howells' Early Development as a Novelist).* Upsala, Sweden, 1958.

Gibson, William M. *William Dean Howells.* Minneapolis, Minn.: University of Minnesota Press, 1967.

Gifford, Henry. "W. D. Howells: His Moral Conservatism." *Kenyon Review* 20 (Winter 1958): 124-33.

Hough, Robert L. *The Quiet Rebel: William Dean Howells as Social Commentator.* Lincoln, Neb.: University of Nebraska Press, 1959.

Kazin, Alfred. "Howells the Bostonian." *Clio* 3 (February 1974): 219-34.

Kirk, Clara M., and Kirk, Rudolf. *William Dean Howells.* New York: Twayne Publishers, Inc., 1962.

McMurray, William. *The Literary Realism of William Dean Howells.* Carbondale and Edwardsville, Ill.: Southern Illinois University Press, 1967.

Vanderbilt, Kermit. *The Achievement of William Dean Howells.* Princeton, N.J.: Princeton University Press, 1968.

Woodress, James L., Jr. *Howells and Italy.* Durham, N.C.: Duke University Press, 1952.

Grant

Hamblen, Abigail A. "Judge Grant and the Forgotten Chippendales." *The University Review* 53 (Spring 1967): 293-99.

Tarkington

Fennimore, Keith J. *Booth Tarkington.* New York: Twayne Publishers, Inc., 1974.

Woodress, James. *Booth Tarkington: Gentleman from Indiana.* Philadelphia and New York: J. B. Lippincott Co., 1954.

Wharton

Auchincloss, Louis. *Edith Wharton.* Minneapolis, Minn.: University of Minnesota Press, 1961.

——. "Edith Wharton and her New Yorks." *Partisan Review* 18 (July-August 1951): 411-19.

Beach, Joseph Warren. *The Twentieth Century Novel.* New York and London: The Century Co., 1932.

Bell, Millicent. *Edith Wharton & Henry James.* New York: George Braziller, 1965.

Gleason, James. "Edith Wharton and the Architecture of Life-Style." Talk before the Midwest Modern Language Association, Milwaukee, Wis., October 1970.

Herrick, Robert. "Mrs. Wharton's World." *New Republic* 2 (February 13, 1915): 40-42.

Hoffman, Frederick J. "Points of Moral Reference: A Comparative English Study of Edith Wharton and F. Scott Fitzgerald." In *English Institute Essays.* New York: Columbia University Press, 1950. Pp. 147-76.

Hopkins, Viola. "The Ordering Style of *The Age of Innocence.*" *American Literature* 30 (November 1958): 345-57.

Howe, Irving, ed. *Edith Wharton, A Collection of Critical Essays.* Englewood Cliffs, N.J.: Prentice-Hall, Inc., 1962.

Kazin, Alfred. *On Native Grounds.* New York: Reynal & Hitchcock, 1942.

Lovett, Robert Morss. *Edith Wharton.* New York: Robert H. McBride & Co., 1925.

Lubbock, Percy. *Portrait of Edith Wharton.* London: Jonathan Cape, 1947.

Lyde, Marilyn J. *Edith Wharton: Convention and Morality in the Work of a Novelist.* Norman, Okla.: University of Oklahoma Press, 1959.

Moseley, Edwin M. *"The Age of Innocence;* Edith Wharton's Weak Faust." *College English* 21 (December 1959): 156-60.

Nevius, Blake. *Edith Wharton: A Study of Her Fiction.* Berkeley and Los Angeles, Calif.: University of California Press, 1953.

Rideout, Walter. *"The House of Mirth."* Included in *Twelve Original Essays on Great American Novels,* edited by Charles Shapiro. Detroit, Mich.: Wayne State University Press, 1958.

Trilling, Diana. *"The House of Mirth* Revisited." *The American Scholar* 32 (Winter 1962-63): 113-28.

Tuttleton, James W. "Edith Wharton: The Archeological Motive." *Yale Review* 61 (Summer 1972): 562-74.

—— "Edith Wharton and the Novel of Manners." Ph.D. dissertation, University of North Carolina, 1963.

Wegelin, Christof. "Edith Wharton and the Twilight of the International Novel." *The Southern Review* 5 (Spring 1969): 398-418.

Wharton, Edith. *A Backward Glance.* New York and London: D. Appleton-Century Co., 1934.

—— *A Motor-Flight Through France.* New York: Charles Scribner's Sons, 1925.

—— *The Writing of Fiction.* New York: Charles Scribner's Sons, 1925.

Wilson, Edmund. *Classics and Commercials.* London: W. H. Allen, 1951.

Glasgow

Auchincloss, Louis. *Ellen Glasgow.* Minneapolis, Minn.: University of Minnesota Press, 1964.

Brickell, Herschel. "Miss Glasgow and Mr. Marquand." *Virginia Quarterly Review* 17 (Summer 1941): 405-17.

Glasgow, Ellen. *A Certain Measure: An Interpretation of Prose Fiction.* New York: Harcourt, Brace & Co., 1938.

—— *The Woman Within.* New York: Harcourt, Brace & Co., 1954.

Hoffman, Frederick J. *The Modern Novel in America, 1900-1950.* Chicago: Henry Regnery Co., 1951.

McDowell, Frederick P. W. *Ellen Glasgow and the Ironic Art of Fiction.* Madison, Wis.: University of Wisconsin Press, 1960.

Monroe, N. Elizabeth. "Ellen Glasgow." Included in *Fifty Years of the American Novel,* edited by Harold O. Gardiner. New York and London: Charles Scribner's Sons, 1952.

Rouse, Blair. *Ellen Glasgow.* New York: Twayne Publishers, Inc., 1962.

——,ed. *Letters of Ellen Glasgow.* New York: Harcourt, Brace & Co., 1958.

Santas, Joan F. *Ellen Glasgow's American Dream.* Charlottesville,Va.: University Press of Virginia, 1965.

Wilson, James S. "Ellen Glasgow: 1941." *Virginia Quarterly Review* 17 (Spring 1941): 317-20.

Marquand

Beach, Joseph Warren. *American Fiction, 1920-1940.* New York: The Macmillan Co., 1942.

Benedict, Stewart H. "The Pattern of Determinism in J. P. Marquand's Novels." *Ball State Teachers College Forum* 2 (Winter 1961-62): 60-64.

Carpenter, Frederick I. *American Literature and the Dream.* New York: Philosophical Library, 1955.

Cochran, Robert W. "In Search of Perspective: A Study of the Serious Novels of J. P. Marquand." Ph.D. dissertation, University of Michigan, 1957.

Glick, Nathan. "Marquand's Vanishing Aristocracy." *Commentary* 9 (May 1950): 435-41.

Gross, John. *John P. Marquand.* New York: Twayne Publishers, Inc., 1963.

Gurko, Leo. "The High-Level Formula of J. P. Marquand." *The American Scholar* 21 (Autumn 1952): 443-53.

Haigh, Robert F. "The Dilemma of John P. Marquand." *Michigan Alumnus Quarterly Review* 59 (Autumn 1952): 19-24.

Hicks, Granville. "Marquand of Newburyport." *Harper's Magazine* 200 (April 1950): 101-8.

Holman, C. Hugh. *John P. Marquand.* Minneapolis, Minn.: University of Minnesota Press, 1965.

Kazin, Alfred. "J. P. Marquand and the American Failure." *The Atlantic* 202 (November 1958): 152-56.

Marquand, John P. "Apley, Wickford Point and Pulham, My Early Struggles." *The Atlantic* 198 (September 1956): 71-74.

Oppenheimer, Franz M. "The Novels of John P. Marquand." *The Antioch Review* 18 (Spring 1958): 41-61.

Smith, William James. "J. P. Marquand, Esq." *Commonweal* 69 (November 7, 1958): 148-50.

Lewis

Dooley, D. J. *The Art of Sinclair Lewis.* Lincoln, Neb.: University of Nebraska Press, 1967.

Grebstein, Sheldon N. *Sinclair Lewis.* New York: Twayne Publishers, Inc., 1962.

Schorer, Mark. *Sinclair Lewis.* Minneapolis, Minn.: University of Minnesota Press, 1963.

Fitzgerald

Cross, K. G. W. *Scott Fitzgerald.* Edinburgh and London: Oliver & Boyd, Ltd., 1964.

Eble, Kenneth. *F. Scott Fitzgerald.* New York: Twayne Publishers, Inc., 1963.

Goldhurst, William. *F. Scott Fitzgerald and His Contemporaries.* Cleveland and New York: The World Publishing Co., 1963.

Miller, James E., Jr. *The Fictional Technique of Scott Fitzgerald.* The Hague, Netherlands: Martinus Nijhoff, 1957.

Mizener, Arthur, ed. *F. Scott Fitzgerald: A Collection of Critical Essays.* Englewood Cliffs, N.J.: Prentice-Hall, Inc., 1963.

Perosa, Sergio. *The Art of F. Scott Fitzgerald.* Ann Arbor, Mich.: University of Michigan Press, 1965.

Shain, Charles E. *F. Scott Fitzgerald.* Minneapolis, Minn.: University of Minnesota Press, 1961.

Cozzens

Bracher, Frederick. *The Novels of James Gould Cozzens.* New York: Harcourt, Brace & Co., 1959.

Hicks, Granville. *James Gould Cozzens.* Minneapolis, Minn.: University of Minnesota Press, 1966.

Long, Richard A. "The Image of Man in James Gould Cozzens." *College Language Association Journal* 10 (June 1967): 299-307.

Maxwell, D. E. S. *Cozzens.* Edinburgh and London: Oliver & Boyd, Ltd., 1964.

Mooney, Harry J., Jr. *James Gould Cozzens: Novelist of Intellect.* Pittsburgh, Pa.: University of Pittsburgh Press, 1963.

Scholes, Robert E. "The Commitment of James Gould Cozzens." *Arizona Quarterly* 16 (Summer 1960): 129-44.

Ward, John W. "James Gould Cozzens and the Condition of Modern Man." *The American Scholar* 27 (Winter 1957-58): 92-99.

O'Hara

Bier, Jesse. "O'Hara's *Appointment in Samarra:* His First and Only Real Novel." *College English* 25 (November 1963): 135-41.

Bruccoli, Matthew J. *"Appointment in Samarra."* Included in *Tough Guy Writers of the Thirties,* edited by David Madden. Carbondale and Edwardsville, Ill.: Southern Illinois University Press, 1968.

Carson, E. Russell. *The Fiction of John O'Hara.* Pittsburgh, Pa.: University of Pittsburgh Press, 1961.

Grebstein, Sheldon N. *John O'Hara.* New York: Twayne Publishers, Inc., 1966.

McCormick, Bernard. "A John O'Hara Geography." *Journal of Modern Literature* 1, no. 2 (1970-71): 151-68.

O'Hara, John. *Sweet and Sour.* New York: Random House, 1953.

Walcutt, Charles C. *John O'Hara.* Minneapolis, Minn.: University of Minnesota Press, 1969.

Auchincloss

Boroff, David. Review of *The House of Five Talents. The Saturday Review* 43 (September 10, 1960): 25.

Hicks, Granville. Review of *Portrait in Brownstone. The Saturday Review* 45 (July 14, 1962): 21, 33.

——. Review of *Powers of Attorney. The Saturday Review* 46 (August 17, 1963): 15-16.

Janeway, Elizabeth. Review of *Portrait in Brownstone. The New York Times Book Review,* July 15, 1962, pp. 1, 29.

Kane, Patricia. "Lawyers at the Top: The Fiction of Louis Auchincloss." *Critique* 7 (Winter 1964-65): 36-46.

Lewis, R. W. B. "Silver Spoons and Golden Bowls." *Book Week, Chicago Sun-Times,* February 20, 1966, pp. i, 8.

Milne, Gordon. "Auchincloss and the Novel of Manners." *The University of Kansas City Review* 29 (March 1963): 177-85.

Rolo, Charles. Review of *Venus in Sparta. The Atlantic* 202 (December 1958): 93-94.

———. "Talk of the Town." *The New Yorker* 36 (August 13, 1960): 23-25.

Knowles

McDonald, James L. "The Novels of John Knowles." *Arizona Quarterly* 23 (Winter 1967): 335-42.

Index

293